**CLIMBING
THE SEVEN
SUMMITS**

CLIMBING THE SEVEN SUMMITS

A COMPREHENSIVE GUIDE TO THE CONTINENTS' HIGHEST PEAKS

MIKE HAMILL

FOREWORD BY PHIL ERSHLER

THE MOUNTAINEERS BOOKS

Topping out on
the fixed lines
below Camp 2 on
Vinson Massif

For my family; especially my sister, Kelley, with whom I shared
many climbing and cycling adventures in our youth.

THE MOUNTAINEERS BOOKS
is the nonprofit publishing arm of The Mountaineers, an organization founded in 1906 and
dedicated to the exploration, preservation, and enjoyment of outdoor and wilderness areas.

1001 SW Klickitat Way, Suite 201, Seattle, WA 98134

Distributed in the United Kingdom by Cordee, www.cordee.co.uk
Manufactured in China

Copy Editor: Kris Fulsaas
Design and Layout: Heidi Smets, heidismets.com
Cartographer: Pease Press Cartography
All photos by author unless credited otherwise
Cover photograph: *Descending from Denali Pass above high camp; Mount Foraker in background.* (Photo by Mike Hamill)

Library of Congress Cataloging-in-Publication Data
Hamill, Mike.
Climbing the seven summits : a comprehensive guide to the continents' highest peaks / by Mike Hamill. — 1st ed.
  p. cm.
Includes bibliographical references and index.
ISBN 978-1-59485-648-8 (pbk. : alk. paper) — ISBN 978-1-59485-649-5 (ebook : alk. paper)
1. Mountaineering. 2. Mountains. 3. Continents. I. Title.
GV200.H36 2012
796.522—dc23
                2011043486

ISBN (paperback): 978-1-59485-648-8
ISBN (e-book): 978-1-59485-649-5

CONTENTS

FOREWORD

Early in my guiding career, I had the good fortune to become involved with two unique individuals who had not only the imagination to dream but the strength, tenacity—and resources—to do what was necessary to convert their dreams into reality. Frank Wells reached the top of six of the Seven Summits, and in 1985 Dick Bass became the first person to climb all of the Seven Summits: the highest peak on each of the world's seven continents. Records are made to be broken, but a first is forever; Dick will always be known as the first man to climb the Seven Summits.

I followed in their footsteps and, in 1989, also completed the Seven Summits. My wife, Susan, even talked me into doing them a second time, with her. We walked those final few feet up the Southeast Ridge of Mount Everest in May 2002 and became the first couple to complete the Seven Summits together. It also appears that, with that summitting of Everest, I became the first person crazy enough to complete the Seven Summits twice.

Dick and Frank led the way, and now many more have followed. This is the true and lasting legacy of their accomplishment: they lit a fire under many of us to get out, challenge ourselves, and explore our mountain world.

Frankly, climbing the Seven Summits is not the most difficult of mountaineering accomplishments. It is, however, a great excuse to go out and see the world. Each summit is unique: the climb itself, the country in which it's located, and the cultures encountered on the journey. Whether they climb one or all Seven Summits, countless experienced and not so experienced mountaineers owe Dick and Frank a sincere thank you for helping show the way.

Mike Hamill's new guidebook, *Climbing the Seven Summits*, will further inspire climbers and help keep the dream alive. Few people would have been capable of writing this book. As an owner of International Mountain Guides, I've worked with Mike for more than a decade. Mike is not only an accomplished climber in his own right but also an accomplished guide. And there's a huge difference. As a guide, Mike knows the ins and outs, the fine points, and all the tricks. He knows what works and what doesn't. He's seen it all. As my wife, Susan, always says when speaking to corporate audiences, "Expert resources can shave years off your learning curve." I guess that's what we all want in a guidebook—*inspiration* and *information*.

Mike has "lapped" the original Seven Summits four times now. He has taken fifteen years' worth of collective information and wisdom about the Seven Summits and put it in a very usable form. Maps, photos, route descriptions, equipment lists, fun facts, and guides' tips are all included. And I wouldn't be surprised if Mike would say that putting all he's learned about the Seven Summits in this book was harder than the actual climbing itself.

Of greatest interest to an old guide like me are the contributions Mike has solicited from many well-known climbers who have unique perspectives and stories regarding the different peaks that make up the Seven Summits. Think about it: any of these summits is really just a big pile of rock, snow, and ice—albeit very attractive ones. They don't really come to life, however, until you add that personal element, the people with whom you share any of these experiences.

Reading *Climbing the Seven Summits* is a great first step and valuable tool as you begin your quest to climb any or all of the Seven Summits. The information herein serves as a strong foundation. Glean as much as possible from Mike's real-life research and then train, learn, and acquire the experience and judgment you need to go out and create your own Seven Summits memories.

—*Phil Ershler*

Everest climbers acclimatize on Lobuche while clouds blanket the Khumbu Valley below.

PREFACE

There is surprisingly little literature available on the Seven Summits. There are a number of books on the individual mountains but, aside from *Seven Summits*, the classic account of pioneers Dick Bass and Frank Wells, there are few about the Seven Summits as a whole. Yet interest in climbing the Seven Summits has skyrocketed in recent years, due to an increase in the popularity of climbing and the ease of international travel. I set out to capture this excitement in one book and help climbers achieve their goal of climbing the Seven Summits.

This book provides the foundation to safely climb the Seven Summits. It can be used for each climb separately or for the Seven Summits as a cumulative goal. The chapters in Part II are organized so readers can easily compare and contrast the climbs. I have included relevant information, photos, maps, and charts to make this guide as easy to use as possible. In addition, I have included anecdotes from climbers, guides, and climbing professionals to create an informative and engaging guide. A guidebook on the Seven Summits would be incomplete without these colorful stories that bring the mountains to life.

This reference is also practical. It's light and sturdy enough to toss in a pack. What good is a Seven Summits reference that you can't bring with you on the climbs? And since it covers all of the Seven Summits, you can use it as a single volume reference for all the mountains.

This guide can be used by novices attempting their first expedition as well as experienced climbers and guides who are new to these peaks. It details climb preparations, route information, and effective climbing techniques, among other topics, to take the less experienced from the beginning to the end of the climb. Experienced climbers will find useful knowledge specific to the climbs, from route descriptions to discussions on climbing techniques and guide tips.

This guide is intended for international climbers, regardless of gender. Climbing the Seven Summits is an international pursuit. Chapter 2 covers specific considerations for both American and international climbers on topics such as ordering gear and international travel restrictions for some nationalities. To acknowledge the increasing number of female climbers, chapter 2 also features discussions and advice from women who are outdoor professionals.

While I present some anecdotes to engage the reader, this book is primarily a climbing guide. Other books share wonderful stories about the Seven Summits and I have listed them in Resources in the back of the book. One of the greatest aspects of mountaineering is the breadth and quality of its literature. Reading more about the fascinating climbing histories of the Seven Summits will give you a better appreciation for each climb.

This book does not cover all of the possible climbing routes, since the majority of climbers stick to one or a few of them. I have, however, listed other resources for more information on alternative routes.

Most importantly, I wish to promote safe climbing and environmental responsibility on the Seven Summits. This guide educates readers on potential hazards and safety concerns, both objective and subjective, and discusses environmental responsibility and waste management. I have witnessed people unnecessarily putting themselves and others in harm's way on these mountains and engaging in practices that degrade the environment. My hope is that this book will help reduce these occurrences and promote safety and environmental stewardship on the Seven Summits.

My intent is to cover everything necessary to successfully ascend one or all of the Seven Summits. From initial preparations before the climb to ascending the last few feet to the summit, this guide will help you to achieve your Seven Summits goal.

ACKNOWLEDGMENTS

Creating this guidebook has been a group effort. Without the input and perspectives of other Seven Summits experts this guide wouldn't have been possible. Guides, climbers, and professionals from around the world have been incredibly generous with their time and knowledge in helping pull this project together. To them I owe a great deal of gratitude. These generous people include first and foremost the contributing authors: Phil Ershler, Eric Simonson, Caitlin Palmer, Jane Lee, Scott Parazynski, Vern Tejas, Conrad Anker, Jeff Strite, Damien Gildea, Willie Benegas, Luanne Freer, Melissa Arnot, and Rex Pemberton. Just as important are the staff and freelancers at The Mountaineers Books: Kate Rogers, Mary Metz, Kris Fulsaas, Heidi Smets, and Lynn Greisz, among the many others, who supported the project, gave the book life, and tirelessly refined the manuscript. I also want to thank my family for their unending support of this project and my unorthodox choice of profession. Jane Lee helped greatly with the initial stages of brainstorming and editing, helping me turn a vision into what became the final product. I have been extremely fortunate to work for International Mountain Guides and Alaska Mountaineering School on the original Seven Summits allowing me to compile the information within this book. I appreciate the efforts of Vern Tejas and Damien Gildea who spent many hours reading through the manuscript text to get it ready. Greg Vernovage offered his expertise and support throughout many expeditions on the mountains of the original Seven Summits. Jason Edwards, Eric Simonson, Eric Remza, and Jeff Strite, were particularly helpful in providing information for the chapter on Carstensz Pyramid. Others who contributed greatly to this guide and whom I would like to thank for their information and expertise are Colby Coombs, Eric Remza, Wayne Morris, Igor Tsaruk, and Craig John. I'd like to thank those who provided their photos for this book including Jane Lee, Jeff Strite, Eric Remza, Stefen Chow, Greg Vernovage, Craig John, and Wayne Morris. I'd also like to thank the guides, Sherpa, and climbers with whom I've had the privilege of sharing the mountains with over the last decade. Two behind-the-scenes VIPs who help make these trips possible, and to whom I owe thanks, are Tammy Gorman and Pirjo DeHart.

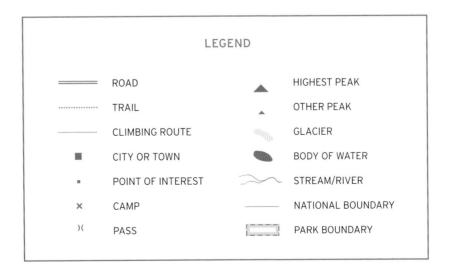

LEGEND

═══	ROAD	▲▲	HIGHEST PEAK
··········	TRAIL	▲	OTHER PEAK
··········	CLIMBING ROUTE		GLACIER
▥	CITY OR TOWN		BODY OF WATER
▪	POINT OF INTEREST	∼∼∼	STREAM/RIVER
×	CAMP	────	NATIONAL BOUNDARY
)(	PASS	▭	PARK BOUNDARY

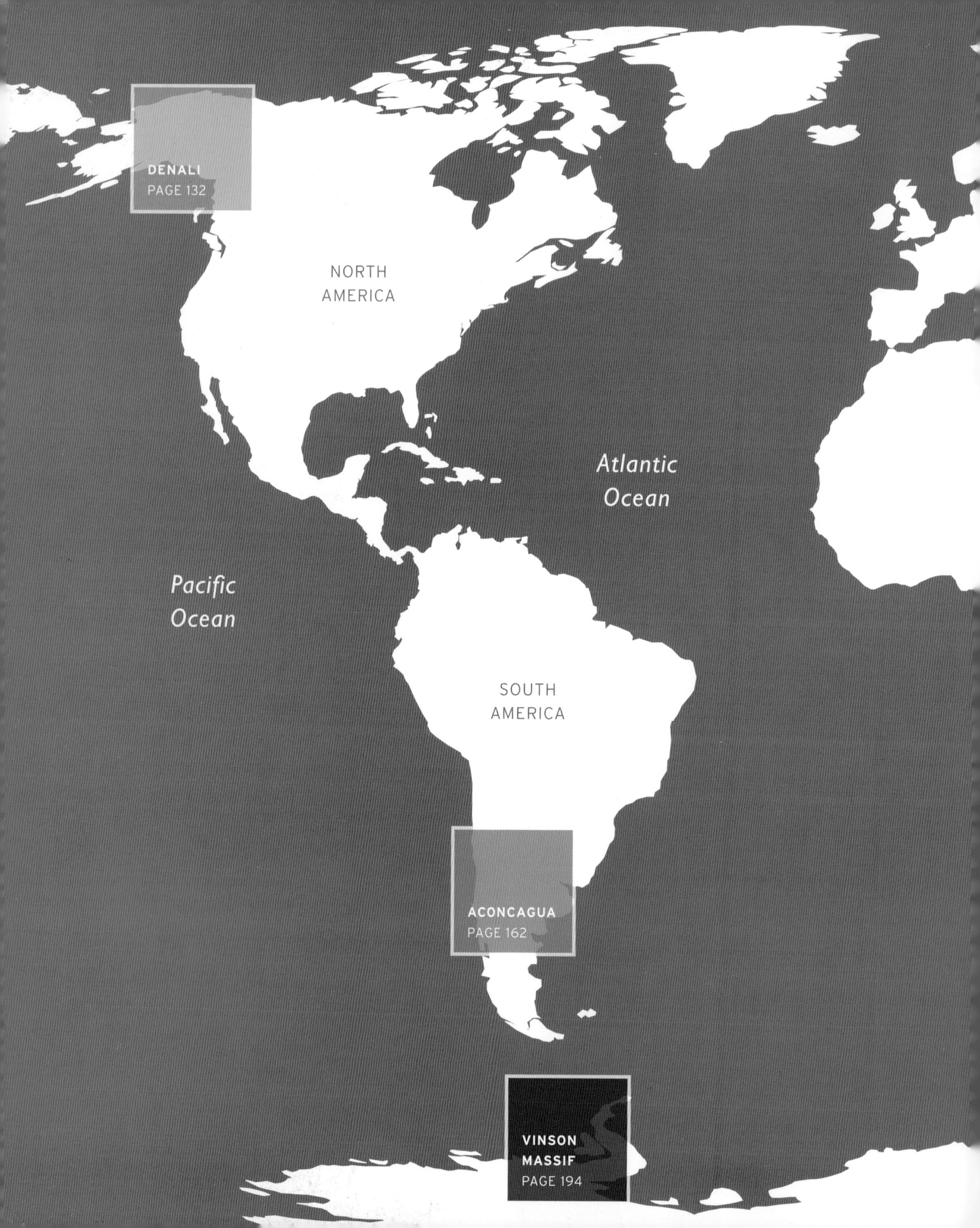

DENALI
PAGE 132

NORTH
AMERICA

*Atlantic
Ocean*

*Pacific
Ocean*

SOUTH
AMERICA

ACONCAGUA
PAGE 162

**VINSON
MASSIF**
PAGE 194

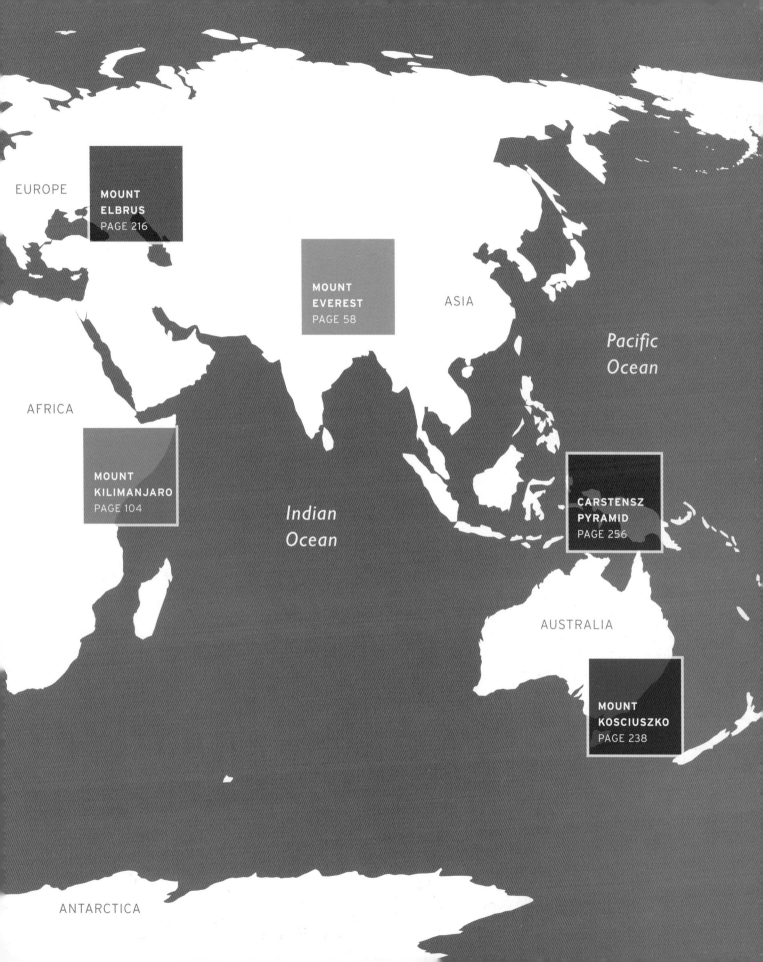

EUROPE

MOUNT ELBRUS
PAGE 216

MOUNT EVEREST
PAGE 58

ASIA

Pacific Ocean

AFRICA

MOUNT KILIMANJARO
PAGE 104

Indian Ocean

CARSTENSZ PYRAMID
PAGE 256

AUSTRALIA

MOUNT KOSCIUSZKO
PAGE 238

ANTARCTICA

Climbing out of the
Khumbu Icefall on
Mount Everest en
route to Camp 1

PART I
PREPARING FOR THE SEVEN SUMMITS

INTRODUCTION

THEIR GOAL WAS TO CLIMB THE HIGHEST
MOUNTAIN ON EACH OF THE SEVEN CONTINENTS.
IT WAS AN IMPOSING LIST: ACONCAGUA IN SOUTH
AMERICA, EVEREST IN ASIA, McKINLEY IN NORTH
AMERICA, KILIMANJARO IN AFRICA, ELBRUS IN
EUROPE, VINSON IN ANTARCTICA, KOSCIUSZKO
IN AUSTRALIA . . . NO ONE HAD EVER SCALED
ALL SEVEN SUMMITS. TO DO SO WOULD BE AN
ACCOMPLISHMENT COVETED BY THE WORLD'S
BEST MOUNTAINEERS.

— RICK RIDGEWAY, FROM *THE SEVEN SUMMITS*, BY DICK BASS, RICK RIDGEWAY,
AND FRANK WELLS (1988)

No one has had as great an impact on the idea of the Seven Summits as the men who coined the term and were the first to complete all the climbs. Dick Bass, Frank Wells, and Pat Morrow first introduced the idea and in doing so captivated the imagination of many. They turned a dream into reality by overcoming obstacles and showed the rest of us that climbing the Seven Summits could be done when Bass became the first to climb them all in 1985. Americans Bass and Wells, Canadian Morrow, and Italian Reinhold Messner were pioneers in every sense of the word in popularizing the concept of the Seven Summits.

THE SEVEN SUMMITS DEFINED

These are the highest summits on the earth's seven continents, listed in order of the largest continental landmass:

- Asia: Mount Everest
  (29,035 ft, 8850 m)

- Africa: Mount Kilimanjaro
  (19,340 ft, 5895 m)

- North America: Denali
  (20,320 ft, 6194 m)

- South America: Aconcagua
  (22,841 ft, 6962 m)

- Antarctica: Vinson Massif
  (16,050 ft, 4892 m)

- Europe: Mount Elbrus
  (18,510 ft, 5642 m)

- Australia: Mount Kosciuszko
  (7310 ft, 2228 m)

Some people define "continent" differently, leading to an alternative "seventh summit":

- Australasia: Carstensz Pyramid
  (16,023 ft, 4884 m)

Why has climbing the highest peak on each continent become a popular goal for experienced and novice climbers alike? In the last decade and a half of leading thousands of clients and climbing with many professionals on the Seven Summits, I have come to realize there are a variety of reasons for climbing the Seven Summits. These range from simply wanting to travel to each of the seven continents to fulfilling a lifetime climbing goal, to pursuing work as a guide and setting speed records. No matter why people climb the Seven Summits, they all have at least one goal in common: adventure.

My own pursuit of adventure, pure and simple, is part of what has compelled me to guide expeditions on the Seven Summits. Beyond fueling my own desire for adventure, I take satisfaction in helping others experience these awe-inspiring landscapes and attain their climbing goals. I've had the pleasure of climbing in some of the most rugged places on Earth with some of the most intriguing people on the planet. Professors, pipe-fitters, astronauts, renowned climbers, and tattoo artists are just a few of the unique individuals I've shared these mountains with. While sharing my knowledge of the climbs, I have in turn learned more from the people I climbed with—their lives, vocations, avocations, and triumphs.

Climbing the Seven Summits has been an education for me. I've learned more about countries and cultures than I could have through formal education. Conversing with local people and listening to their perspectives tells you a lot about their culture and your own. Growing up, I dreamed of traveling to exotic, remote, and rugged landscapes, with Antarctica on the top of the list. To be able to climb the tallest peak on each of the seven continents has been the icing on the cake. From viewing penguins in southern Chile to trekking with Chagga tribesmen in Tanzania, to drinking cognac with South Ossetians in southern Russia, climbing the Seven Summits has inspired me to learn about the world and the people we share it with.

In the few decades since Bass, Wells, and Morrow pioneered the idea of the Seven Summits, it has grown from just a dream to an entire industry. In the early 1980s, there were few climbers on any of the Seven Summits, but now thousands scale at least one each year. In 1985, the logistics and costs of such an endeavor were mind-boggling, and climbing on any of the Seven Summits was still in its relative infancy. Climbing gear was heavier, bulkier, and unacceptable by today's standards. Organizing the expeditions in the '80s was a full-time job, and paying for the logistics was more suited for wealthy businessmen like Bass and Wells. There wasn't a commercial guiding industry like we have today, and the climbing techniques used on the Seven Summits were quite different. Bass, Wells, and Morrow deserve a lot of credit for piecing together such a complex puzzle and surmounting these obstacles.

There is no arguing that climbing the Seven Summits has changed considerably since the '80s. The challenges that Bass, Wells, and Morrow overcame are different from what we face today. Nowhere is this truer than on Vinson Massif in Antarctica. Little was known about Vinson when Bass and Wells went there in the early '80s—and even less was known during its first ascent in 1966. Today, Antarctic Logistics and Expeditions (ALE), a company with operations in Antarctica that routinely ferries climbers on flights to and from the continent, takes care of most of these logistics for a fee.

Climbing Mount Everest has also changed significantly. People have followed Everest climbing closely since the early days of Britons George Mallory and Andrew Irvine in the 1920s, to the first ascent by New Zealander Sir Edmund Hillary and Tenzing Norgay Sherpa in 1953, and especially during the tragic climbing year 1996 when many perished on the mountain. Today, Everest is the best known of the Seven Summits, receives much press, and holds a unique place in our collective imagination. It took Dick Bass three attempts to summit Everest. In those days, only one team per year was granted a permit to climb the mountain. Today, there may be forty expeditions or more on the mountain each year. When Mallory first explored Everest from the north side in 1921, it took him more than a month just to reach base camp. Today, climbers can drive there in two days from Katmandu.

In 2011 alone, several people completed the Seven Summits, and thousands scaled at least one of them. In 1990 New Zealanders Rob Hall and Gary Ball were the first to complete the Seven Summits in less than a year, finishing just hours under seven months. Recently an American climber, Vernon Tejas, climbed them all in just 134 days! A fifteen-year-old American named Jordan Romero became the youngest person to complete the Seven Summits in 2011. Several people have now skied all of the Seven Summits.

Progress in logistics, climbing techniques, safety, and environmental responsibility on the Seven Summits is due in large part to the leaders who spent their careers scaling these great peaks. Each one has helped drive the industry forward and create a better, safer climbing experience on these mountains. Phil Ershler, a leading US guide and Himalayan climber, was an integral part of the Wells-Bass team in the early days. Beyond his expertise on peaks including Everest, K2, and Kanchenjunga, he was a pioneering guide on Aconcagua and Denali, which are part of his yearly routine. He now has more than seventy ascents of the individual peaks of the Seven Summits under his belt.

Eric Simonson, also a veteran on many Denali, Kilimanjaro, Vinson, and Aconcagua expeditions, was one of the first to offer commercial expeditions to Mount

A NOTE ABOUT SAFETY

Safety is an important concern in all outdoor activities. No guidebook can alert you to every hazard or anticipate the limitations of every reader. Therefore, the descriptions of roads, trails, routes, and natural features in this book are not representations that a particular place or excursion will be safe for your party. When you follow any of the routes described in this book, you assume responsibility for your own safety. Under normal conditions, such excursions require the usual attention to traffic, road and trail conditions, weather, terrain, the capabilities of your party, and other factors. Keeping informed on current conditions and exercising common sense are the keys to a safe, enjoyable outing.

Political conditions may add to the risks of travel in ways that this book cannot predict. When you travel, you assume this risk, and should keep informed of political developments that may make safe travel difficult or impossible.

—*The Mountaineers Books*

Karma Rita Sherpa
enjoying a rest day
on Everest

Everest. The infrastructure that he, along with others including Russell Brice, Rob Hall, and Todd Burleson, put in place in the late '80s and '90s shaped the climbing industry we see today.

Others, too, have played an integral role in the development of climbing at least one of the Seven Summits. Brian Okonek, Colby Coombs, Ray "the Pirate" Genet, Vernon Tejas, Rodrigo Mujica, Willie and Damien Benegas, Dave Hahn, Giles Kershaw, Jim Williams, and Igor Tsaruk are just a few of these leaders. Brian Okonek, Colby Coombs, and Caitlin Palmer, working with Alaska-Denali Guiding (now Alaska Mountaineering School), have helped implement standards for guiding and operation within Denali National Park and Preserve. Their cumulative knowledge was finally put in print with Colby's comprehensive guide on Denali's West Buttress Route and his Alaska Range climbing guide with Mike Wood (see Resources). Okonek recently retired from guiding on Denali, but for decades he employed a methodical approach to leadership, safety, guide development, and environmental stewardship that influenced many and set the standard for Denali protocol.

Rodrigo Mujica has done as much as anyone to develop climbing and guiding on Aconcagua, his backyard peak. A Chilean, Mujica was one of the first to pioneer the

Vacas Valley approach and make guiding Aconcagua commonplace.

The late Giles Kershaw, although he probably wouldn't have described himself as a great climber, was a pioneer on Vinson Massif, spearheading exploration on the Antarctic continent by air. Giles also championed an effort that eventually became Adventure Network International (ANI), the first commercial logistics company for Vinson expeditions.

These are just a few of the intrepid souls who have made pursuing the Seven Summits an attainable goal for the rest of us and who have implemented safety and environmental measures that help ensure climbing can continue on these peaks well into the future.

No matter how experienced climbers are in the mountains, they never know what the next expedition will bring. Weather, climbing companions, and climbing conditions are just a few of the variables that change from trip to trip, making each experience unique and exciting. Even the most benign of the Seven Summits can turn into a life-and-death struggle in the wrong conditions. This visceral desire for adventure compels us to seek out the unknown. We challenge ourselves to feel alive and, ultimately, get to know ourselves and others on a much deeper level than we could otherwise.

HOW TO USE THIS BOOK

Chapter 1, General Considerations for the Seven Summits, covers definitions of the Seven Summits, suggested climbing progressions, skills and fitness levels, the difficulty ratings I use in this book, expedition climbing styles, how to decide whether to hire a guide service or climb independently, and risks and rescues. Chapter 2, Expedition Planning for the Seven Summits, begins with general travel tips including international flights and travel insurance, covers medical concerns such as immunizations and altitude sickness, touches on gear, offers a preparation timeline and efficient climbing techniques at altitude, and concludes with environmental concerns to keep the mountains clean for those who climb after us.

Part II, Climbing the Seven Summits, covers each of the peaks in a separate chapter. These chapters begin with an information summary including difficulty ratings, an overview that covers natural history (including fast facts about the peak), cultural and political background, climbing history (with a capsule timeline), and climbing challenges. The planning section covers guided versus independent trips, climbing seasons and weather, documents required, cost estimates, conditioning suggestions, and immunization and communication concerns. The "Getting There and Getting Around" section begins with the city most climbers fly to in order to reach the mountain, then gives details on domestic flights and ground transportation from the city to the start of the approach. Some approaches allow climbers to fly to base camp; others require a multiday trek. Gateway settlements—whether near base camp or the start of a trek—are described, as are other activities such as skiing, surfing, and safaris.

Finally, each summit's chapter has a comprehensive section on climbing the peak, including a list of the common routes, acclimatization suggestions, and information on water, sanitation, and garbage—followed by a detailed sample climbing itinerary in chart form, accompanied by a narrative description of the climb, and trekking approach, if applicable. Each summit chapter concludes with gear lists broken down for traveling, trekking, and climbing, including both personal and group gear and a summit checklist.

Accompanying all this information in each summit chapter are three or more visual aids. The first is a continent map showing its highest summit, which is a detail of the global map showing all of the Seven Summits. The second is an approach map that shows

For the most up-to-date information on the Seven Summits, please visit www.climbingthesevensummits.com.

Climbing the
Lhotse Face on
Mount Everest

how to get to base camp or the start of the trek from either a gateway settlement or the city where international travelers arrive. The third is a bird's-eye view of the route from base camp to the summit, including the trekking approach if there is one, or a photo of the peak with the route overlaid on it, sometimes in segments, from base camp to the summit. Together, these illustrations of the climb augment the text descriptions.

In the appendices you'll find information on the Seven Summits, including a discussion of the controversy regarding Mount Kosciuszko versus Carstensz Pyramid (which is why this book on the Seven Summits actually includes eight climbs!) and a list of the climbers who have completed the Seven Summits as of the date of

publication. Following these is a Resources section broken down by summit.

People will continue to scale the Seven Summits, and records will continue to be surpassed. In the last few years several people younger than twenty and a handful of climbers older than sixty have climbed all the Seven Summits. Guides and videographers now summit Mount Everest on a yearly basis, and several guides, including myself, now climb most if not all of the Seven Summits each year for work. I eagerly await more amazing feats, and I hope that climbers keep themselves and others safe while not abusing these fragile landscapes. I look forward to climbing with you on the Seven Summits.

Morning light on
Pumori as seen from
the Western Cwm on
Mount Everest

CHAPTER 1

GENERAL CONSIDERATIONS FOR THE SEVEN SUMMITS

AND I GUESS THAT'S THE ANSWER. WE WANTED TO
SEE IT ALL, AND WE KNEW NO BETTER WAY THAN
FROM THE TOPS OF THE TALLEST MOUNTAINS ON
EACH OF THE SEVEN CONTINENTS.

— DICK BASS, FROM *THE SEVEN SUMMITS*, BY DICK BASS, RICK RIDGEWAY,
AND FRANK WELLS (1988)

Climbing the Seven Summits is a huge commitment that requires lots of dedication, training, time, and money. It requires making climbing a priority and, often, putting it above other financial, time, or familial commitments. Even if climbers dedicate themselves fully to the goal of the Seven Summits and climb full-time, it will still mean a commitment of at least a year, more often several years or even decades. This chapter covers a few things you should consider before diving into climbing the Seven Summits.

Aconcagua's
summit route

DEFINING THE SEVEN SUMMITS

While reading further in this book, you will undoubtedly notice that there are indeed eight mountains covered rather than seven, which will seem strange for a book titled *Climbing the Seven Summits*. Here is some background on the Seven Summits project that will clarify upfront why this is.

The idea of the Seven Summits was conceived mostly independently by several people at roughly the same time: the mid-1980s. Although Americans Dick Bass and Frank Wells, Canadian Pat Morrow, and Italian Reinhold Messner were probably not the first to think of the concept, they were some of the first to complete the

feat and popularize it, making them influential players in the history of the Seven Summits. Most notably, Bass and Morrow were competing against each other to complete the journey first. Bass ended up doing so first with a summit of Mount Kosciuszko on mainland Australia as part of his circuit. Morrow, in his well-publicized journey to climb the Seven Summits, decided to climb a more challenging peak called Puncak Jaya, or Carstensz Pyramid, as part of his Seven Summits and finished not long after Bass. Morrow had decided that Carstensz laid claim to the highest point on the Australian continent by using a different definition that included the continental shelf and Irian Jaya, in

SEVEN SUMMITS FAST FACTS

- More then 350 people have finished all the Seven Summits, including either Mount Kosciuszko or Carstensz Pyramid, as of 2011.
- 30 percent of those have climbed both Kosciuszko and Carstensz.
- More than 50 women have finished all the Seven Summits, including either Kosciuszko or Carstensz.
- More than 100 Americans, the most climbers from one country, have climbed the Seven Summits.

Indonesia 60-plus miles (more than 96 km) off the north coast of Australia.

Overwhelmingly the climbing community accepted Bass's version of the Seven Summits when he completed his climbs, but a divide was created when Morrow chose another peak. This divide was broadened when Messner, the most influential climber of his day, decided to complete his Seven Summits circuit by including Carstensz Pyramid as well, while other influential climbers went with Kosciuszko. To this day, climbers have differing opinions about which peak is the true Seventh Summit and climb the peak that best suits their definition—or climb them both to "cover their bases." Because there are two main versions of the Seven Summits, I include both peaks in this guide to allow readers to decide which peak they will include.

Please see "Debunking Carstensz as the Seventh Summit" in the back of the book for my analysis of this controversy and arguments.

CLIMBING PROGRESSIONS

First, where should you start? It's probably obvious that you should start with smaller, shorter expeditions, then work your way up to bigger, more committing climbs.

Climbers have different opinions about which peak is more serious and which should be tackled first. I list two sample climbing progressions below to help you decide in which order to attempt the mountains. These are not the only order in which to climb them, obviously, but these examples should give you a better idea of how others approach this question.

It's important to have an overview of the climbs before considering climbing any of the Seven Summits. This will give you an idea of whether you're up to the task and whether you'll enjoy it.

Below are two common progressions climbers employ in climbing the Seven Summits. These progressions will differ for different climbers. These two progressions present a couple of approaches to climbing the Seven Summits. Neither one is more "correct" than the other. You must consider technical and physical difficulty, as well as altitude, commitment, seriousness, and cost. It's important to think through the progression before committing to a climb.

PROGRESSION 1

Enroll in a comprehensive alpine climbing course.
Train by climbing Mount Rainier in Washington State, Grand Teton in Wyoming, Mont Blanc in France, Mount Fuji in Japan, Cayambe in Ecuador, or comparable peaks. Then,

1. Climb Mount Kilimanjaro in Africa.
2. Climb Mount Elbrus in Europe.
3. Climb Aconcagua in South America.
4. Climb Carstensz Pyramid in Indonesia.
5. Climb Vinson Massif in Antarctica.
6. Climb Denali in North America.
7. Make one last training climb, of Cho Oyu, from Tibet.
8. Climb Mount Everest in Asia.
9. Climb Mount Kosciuszko in Australia—the easiest and the icing on the cake! Bring friends and family with you for the climb to celebrate.

PROGRESSION 2

Enroll in a comprehensive alpine climbing course.
Train by climbing Mount Rainier, Grand Teton, Mont Blanc, Mount Fuji, Cayambe, or comparable peaks. Then,

1. Climb Mount Kosciuszko in Australia.
2. Climb Mount Elbrus in Europe.
3. Climb Mount Kilimanjaro in Africa.
4. Climb Carstensz Pyramid in Indonesia.
5. Climb Denali in North America.
6. Climb Aconcagua in South America.
7. Climb Vinson Massif in Antarctica.
8. Make one last training climb of Ama Dablam in Nepal.
9. Climb Mount Everest in Asia, finishing with the tallest peak on Earth!

I recommend Mounts Elbrus, Kilimanjaro, and Kosciuszko as good places to begin. These trips will give climbers an indication of how they will do on the more serious climbs and at higher altitudes. The financial and time burdens of these three trips are smaller than Mount Everest or Vinson Massif.

PRIOR EXPERIENCE AND TECHNICAL SKILLS

It's important for your safety and success and that of those around you that you gain the requisite experience before joining a climbing expedition. All climbers attempting to scale the Seven Summits must have a solid background in alpine-, ice-, and rock-climbing techniques and must be very physically fit. Climbers who jump into an attempt of the Seven Summits without any prior experience set themselves up for failure.

In this section, I identify some of the climbing skills you need to be proficient in to climb some or all of the Seven Summits. In each chapter in Part II, I discuss prerequisites for each specific climb. Here are the skills you should be comfortable with:

- Roped glacier travel
- Rigging for glacier travel with a sled
- Cramponing
- Ice ax techniques
- Self-arrest and team arrest
- Crevasse rescue
- Fixed-line ascension: using a harness, ascender (jumar), ascender carabiner, primary safety (lobster claw), secondary safety (lobster claw)—for descending or traversing while passing other climbers or anchors
- Rappeling
- Snow, ice, and rock anchors
- Running belays
- Altitude illness awareness
- Camp setup
- GPS use and routefinding
- Rest step
- Pacing
- Packing a pack
- Layering clothing

If you are unfamiliar with these terms, please enroll in a climbing course led by a reputable guide service and/or refer to *Mountaineering: The Freedom of the Hills* by The Mountaineers, *Alpine Climbing* by Kathy Cosley and Mark Houston, and *Glacier Travel and Crevasse Rescue* by Andy Selters.

FITNESS

Climbing the Seven Summits is difficult even for extremely fit individuals. Having top-notch fitness is critical to being successful in achieving your goal. Some of the climbs are easier than others or require different types of fitness (rock climbing, carrying heavy loads, etc.), and I address this in each chapter in Part II. In general, climbers should prepare for all the climbs as I have outlined below. It's important to remember that the best way to get fit for climbing is to climb! There's no substitute for getting out there and climbing, and the more you

A Masai elder near
Mount Kilimanjaro

A NOTE ABOUT THE SAMPLE CLIMBING ITINERARIES

The schedules provided in the sample climbing itineraries for each mountain are only guidelines and may need to be customized to meet each individual climber's needs due to different fitness levels and acclimatization rates. They represent conservative schedules that are used by respected guide services; they should allow climbers to acclimatize safely. It is dangerous to rush the acclimatization process! Also, weather and sickness almost always alter climbing itineraries, making it difficult to stay on a set schedule. Adapt your schedule as needed and climb smart.

climb, the more prepared you will be for an expedition.

Climbers need to be able to carry heavy loads for six to ten hours per day for multiple days in a row. Summit day on most of the Seven Summits consists of 3000–5000 feet (1000–2000 m) of elevation gain over ten to twenty hours of climbing. The more effective way to train is to hike or climb mimicking the type of climbing you will encounter on an individual mountain. Day hikes and multiday hikes of long distances at least once a week for five to ten hours at a stretch are best.

Beyond this, cardio training at a higher heart rate is important. Climbers should train five or six days per week. It helps to work with a trainer who can help map out a specific training regimen. Cardio-fitness workouts should consist of at least forty-five minutes of strenuous continual exercise with a heart rate between 110 and 150. I recommend stair climbing, bike riding, and running hills for cardio work for the bulk of your training.

Strength training for the upper and lower body several times a week helps too, but do higher repetitions for endurance. High-altitude mountaineering is more about endurance than about short, quick bursts of power.

Begin conditioning as early as possible, and continue to ramp up until two weeks before the trip begins, then taper off in order to "peak" your fitness level. Rest several days before leaving, because travel and jet lag can take a toll on the body.

Most importantly, don't get hurt just before the climb! A sprained ankle or broken arm can ruin the trip.

DIFFICULTY RATINGS

In this book, I've created a difficulty rating system to give climbers an idea of what to expect from a climb and to quickly compare different climbs. This is my own system; it is not based upon other more widely known systems that you might be familiar with.

I break the difficulty rating down into two parts. *Technical difficulty* relates to how technical the climb is in terms of steepness, technical climbing, and exposure. *Physical difficulty* refers to how strenuous a climb is in terms of load carrying, harshness of the environment, total altitude gained, length of trip, and summit altitude.

Each difficulty rating is based on a scale of 1 to 5 that pertains only to this book and the Seven Summits. At least one of the Seven Summits will score a 5 for each category, making this a simple way to compare the Seven Summits to each other but not to other mountains.

TECHNICAL DIFFICULTY

Grade 1: Technically easy. Climbing does not include a rope and harness. Most of the climb consists of walking on low-angle slopes.

Grade 2: Technically easy to moderate. The climb consists mainly of walking on slopes of 25 degrees or less with few slightly steeper pitches. A rope and harness may be used for protection against a fall on a slope or a crevasse fall.

Grade 3: Technically moderate. Climbing consists of both low-angle and moderate slopes up to 50 degrees for short periods. A rope and harness are needed, as is the use of protection against potentially serious falls. Fixed ropes may provide aid on steeper sections.

Grade 4: Technically difficult climbing. Climbing consists mainly of roped travel either as a rope team to avoid falls or on fixed lines. Slope angle often rises above 45 degrees and may approach vertical. Using protection is mandatory for most groups.

Grade 5: Extreme technical difficulty. Climbing is consistently steep and technical while exposed to hazards. Most of the terrain is steep or near vertical, and skilled rope climbing ability is requisite.

PHYSICAL DIFFICULTY

Grade 1: Physically easy. Climbers must have experience walking for extended periods of time with a small pack.

Grade 2: Physically easy to moderate. Climbers must be able to hike for hours at a time for several days in a row carrying moderate loads. Most climbing is done at low to moderate altitudes.

Grade 3: Physically moderate. Climbers must be able to carry heavy loads for multiple hours over multiple days through harsh weather conditions. Often the climbing is at moderate to high altitude.

Grade 4: Physically difficult. Climbers must be able to carry heavy loads in harsh conditions for weeks at a time at moderate altitude or to carry moderate loads at high

A MEDICAL EMERGENCY IS ALWAYS A SERIOUS SITUATION

Early in the summer of 2001, I was guiding a climb on Mount Rainier when I noticed a dull pain in my abdomen. As I continued to ascend the Muir Snowfield, the pain intensified until, by the time I reached Camp Muir at 10,000 feet (3048 m), I was barely ambulatory. Not knowing what the pain was, I assumed it was bad food or bad gas. Soon, I was shivering with chills and unable to walk without assistance. My fellow guides, suspecting appendicitis, decided they would get me off the mountain. I was promptly sledded down to Paradise by several guides and rangers, rushed to a hospital in an ambulance, and taken in to surgery within the hour. The guides had been correct; my appendix was removed and I was on a monthlong road to recovery.

Being a guide, I feel in control and comfortable in the alpine environment and hadn't considered that I might be the one needing rescue. This experience taught me a great lesson: never underestimate the mountain and always be prepared. Even if you are prepared, things can still go wrong that are out of your control. I had help from many well-trained climbers and guides during my rescue who risked their safety to ensure mine. Even the smallest of rescues is a big ordeal. If I had been climbing with a smaller group or on a more remote part of the mountain, what would the outcome have been? I was scheduled to begin a Denali expedition a few days after this incident and feel lucky to have avoided a potentially much more serious situation.

Within five weeks of surgery, I was back on Rainier guiding programs, sans appendix, and looking forward to many more days in the mountains. However, I will never forget the helplessness I felt and will always prepare for the worst while hoping for the best. I have since been able to repay the favor to others in need of rescue.

A cooktent at Camp 2 (11,200 ft) on Denali

altitude. The climbing is arduous and is compounded by the difficulty of climbing at altitude.

Grade 5: Physically extreme. Climbers must be in peak physical condition for endurance and strength. Climbing consists of carrying very heavy loads (often divided between a pack and a sled) or carrying moderate loads at extreme altitude.

EXPEDITION CLIMBING STYLES

In this book, several different types of climbing strategies are employed. The type depends on many variables, including altitude, amount of pack weight, length of climb, and hazards. Below are a few types of climbing styles and a brief description of why each one is used.

Climb high, sleep low. Climbers talk a great deal about this style of climbing; it is used a lot, and for good reason. This is used on moderate- to high-altitude climbs to aid in acclimatization. In climbing high during the day, climbers force their bodies to respond to the altitude by acclimatizing (for more information on the acclimatization process, please refer to "Medical Concerns" in chapter 2). They then return to a lower altitude to sleep, minimizing the risk of potential altitude illnesses by "tricking" their bodies into responding to a higher altitude and resting more soundly.

High-altitude rotations. This type of climbing is used

GUIDE TIP

Because guiding is a service industry, tipping is expected. Many climbers ask what an appropriate tip is. What several guide services recommend on their websites and what I have experienced to be typical is 10 to 15 percent of the price of the trip. This varies greatly, as it should, depending on the quality of the guide and the service provided.

only at very extreme altitudes such as on Mount Everest. Climbers ascend the mountain to successively higher altitudes, descending to base camp to rest and recover before going to the summit. These up-and-down cycles are called rotations. At extreme altitudes such as those of the higher camps on Mount Everest, it's impossible for your body to fully recover. Rotations allow climbers to acclimatize at very high altitudes while still resting down low.

Double-carry (caching loads). Caching loads is typically used in conjunction with climbing high and sleeping low. On mountains such as Denali and Vinson Massif, the amount of gear prohibits moving it all to higher camps in one push, so several trips must be made. Double-carrying is also a good way to slow down the pace of the climb and allow the body more time to acclimatize.

Alpine-style climbing. Alpine style means ascending a peak quickly in one push, moving fast with minimal gear. Those attempting this climbing style must already be acclimatized for the summit altitude. Expert climbers use this technique on extreme-altitude Himalayan climbs to minimize exposure to objective hazards. This style, however, increases the risk of getting altitude illness, getting caught out without the proper gear, or getting injured due to fatigue. For novices, this style of climbing is only used on climbs such as Carstensz Pyramid, Mount Kosciuszko, and Mount Elbrus because they can be climbed in a day and their summits are not at extreme altitudes.

Solo climbing. Solo climbing refers to climbing independently of others or a team, and the term usually refers to climbing done on technical terrain. There is often strength and safety in numbers, making solo climbing a more dangerous proposition. Solo climbers have less support if things go wrong, and the burden of carrying all the weight is literally on the individual. Climbers may choose to climb solo for the sense of freedom, lack of climbing partners, and ability to make decisions independently. Solo climbing can be especially dangerous on Denali and Vinson Massif where roped travel is appropriate to minimize crevasse hazard.

GUIDED TRIP VERSUS INDEPENDENT CLIMB

Most people climb the Seven Summits as part of an independent team or a guided group. In either case, being part of a team entails responsibility for being helpful, positive, and social; considering the benefits of being part of a whole; and sharing close quarters with new people. Some people dive into climbing the Seven Summits without fully understanding what it will entail. Are you willing to be part of a team?

Should you climb independently or climb with a guide service? Some people enjoy the challenge of organizing an expedition from start to finish, while others just want to show up and have all the logistics taken care of by guide services or outfitters. Climbing independently requires a higher level of preparedness and risk, as well as a larger climbing resumé and a better understanding of the mountains. Climbing independently means being self-sufficient. Independent climbers must be prepared to handle rescue situations on their own and not unnecessarily put others' lives at risk. Too often independent climbers get lost or in trouble, or shadow guided climbs.

Hiring a guide service purchases not only logistical arrangements but also climbing expertise and mountain experience. Mountain guides climb these mountains for a living and know the safest and most efficient ways to improve your chance of success. Guide services have done a lot over the years to facilitate climbing, improve safety, promote environmental stewardship, and improve the success rate of other climbers by sharing their expertise.

This expertise comes at a price, however. Choosing whether to go with a guided team will partially depend on your budget. Keep in mind there is a range of price points for guide services, but generally you get what you pay for.

It's important to educate yourself extensively about guide services before choosing one and entrusting your life to it. Some operators can offer a lower price by cutting corners on infrastructure. This may be fine if everything goes smoothly, but if there is an emergency, each team needs to be able to react. Choosing a guide service for some of the mountains may be one of the most important decisions of your life!

RISK AND RESCUES

Climbing is an inherently risky endeavor. Are you willing to put yourself in harm's way or take risks to achieve your goals? Make sure you feel comfortable with the amount of risk involved in climbing the Seven Summits before spending time and money on an expedition.

Part of what attracts people to climbing the Seven Summits is the inherent risk . . . and reward. Adventure means pushing beyond your comfort zone, and that includes some risk. Each climber needs to determine what level of risk is acceptable for him- or herself. There are things such as rockfall, avalanches, weather, and lightning that we as climbers can't control. We call these objective hazards, and I address them in each chapter in Part II.

Climbing involves taking calculated risks but shouldn't include being reckless. It's important to do everything possible to prevent rescues from being necessary. Yet every year several rescues are performed on each of the mountains in this book. Any rescue in a remote area is a big deal, putting the lives of rescuers at risk. If a rescue does become necessary, individual teams must be prepared to handle the rescue independently. Clients on guided trips should keep their "brains turned on" and consider what they'd do if a guide should become injured. But remember that climbing can be quite safe if it is approached properly and responsibly.

Emergency locator beacons (spot devices) are used by some climbers, but I find radios and satellite phones to be more effective for rescues. These devices are now commonly used for updating friends and families via texting or Facebook updates with short preprogrammed messages.

THERE IS A NOTABLE DIFFERENCE BETWEEN A GAMBLE AND A CALCULATED RISK. IN A CALCULATED RISK YOU CONSIDER ALL THE ODDS, JUSTIFY THE RISK, AND THEN MAKE AN INTELLIGENT DECISION BASED ON CONSERVATIVE JUDGMENT. A GAMBLE IS SOMETHING OVER WHICH YOU HAVE NO CONTROL AND THE OUTCOME IS JUST A ROLL OF THE DICE.

— DARYL R. MILLER, CLIMBING RANGER, DENALI NATIONAL PARK AND PRESERVE

Motorcycle Hill
above Camp 2
on Denali

A climber uses the "night schedule" to avoid the heat of the day while ascending the lower Kahiltna Glacier on Denali.

CHAPTER 2

EXPEDITION PLANNING FOR THE SEVEN SUMMITS

FOR SOME IT IS AN EXCUSE TO TRAVEL AROUND THE WORLD; OTHERS MAY HAVE CLIMBED SEVERAL OF THE MOUNTAINS ALREADY, THEN SIMPLY DECIDE TO FINISH THEM OFF FOR FUN; A FEW MAY NEVER HAVE CLIMBED BEFORE, BECOME CAPTIVATED BY THE SEVEN SUMMITS, AND THEN SELL THEIR CLIMBING BOOTS AFTER COMPLETING THEM. FOR EVERYONE IT'S A HUGE CHALLENGE WHICH DEMANDS DETERMINATION, COMMITMENT, FITNESS, AND RISK. WHATEVER THE MOTIVATION, THE REWARD IS GREAT.

—STEVE BELL, *SEVEN SUMMITS: THE QUEST TO REACH THE HIGHEST POINT ON EVERY CONTINENT* (2000)

I always tell my clients that half the battle is just getting out the front door. Preparing for any expedition, let alone one to the tallest mountains on Earth, is a huge endeavor, one that must be approached with diligence and attention to detail. Even when you are climbing with a guide service or logistics provider, there is still a lot to prepare. It's important to make sure that all the logistical aspects of the trip are in place before embarking on the trip and that all personal items have been attended to. It's often small details—not having the proper eyewear, issues with the oxygen system, family issues at home, getting sick from poorly prepared food—that prevent climbers from being successful on mountains such as Mount Everest.

Do what you can to minimize variables and improve your chances of success. Have you done your research? Have you trained hard enough and appropriately? Have you taken care of everything at home that needs to be done through the date you'll return? Do you have the right gear? The preparation and planning that go into a climb are just as important as physical fitness or climbing ability. You'll never make it to summit day if everything else isn't in place. This chapter outlines what you need to do before an expedition.

GENERAL TRAVEL TIPS

Below are a few important general travel tips to keep in mind whenever you are going on an expedition:

- Leave expensive items at home.
- Use a safe travel wallet—one that can be hidden underneath clothes either around your neck or waist.
- Photocopy your passport—always keep a spare in another location in case the original gets lost.
- Check visa requirements well before the date of departure and obtain a visa as necessary.
- Keep a pen handy for filling out embarkation forms, etc.
- Wear modest clothing.
- Bring one set of nice clothes—for celebrating the climb at nice restaurants.
- Bring a day pack for a carry-on that can double as a light hiking pack.

- Two big, rugged, waterproof duffels with locks are indispensable! You can travel with these and throw them on a yak or a smelly mule if you need to. Use locks approved by the Transportation Security Administration (TSA) if you are traveling from or through the United States.
- Bring plenty of cash in small bills—you'll probably want to purchase incidentals and bring back souvenirs for your family and friends. Small bills are good for small purchases and tipping. Credit cards are not accepted everywhere, and automated teller machines (ATMs) can be hard to find.
- Know the exchange rate before you go—this gives you a good idea whether people are trying to rip you off or not.
- Bring an altimeter watch with an alarm.
- Travel in groups—it's always safer to explore with others than alone.

Note that in this guidebook, all monetary amounts are given in US dollars unless noted otherwise.

INTERNATIONAL CLIMBERS

Climbing the Seven Summits is increasingly an international pursuit. Originally, these mountains were dominated by North Americans and Europeans, but today many Asians, South Americans, Africans, and Australians are climbing the Seven Summits.

SEVEN SUMMITS RECORDS

American Jordan Romero, at fifteen, is the youngest to finish the Seven Summits, bumping Briton George Atkinson from the title he held for less than a year. Jordan finished on December 24, 2011 with Mount Vinson. It took him six years to complete them all. He summitted Everest when he was thirteen!

The oldest person to climb the Seven Summits is Ramón Blanco from Spain, at almost seventy-four years of age.

The most Seven Summits ascents have been completed by American Vernon Tejas: nine.

The fastest to complete the Seven Summits is Tejas, in 134 days. He has also completed two full ascents of the Seven Summits in 355 days.

Kiwis (New Zealanders) Rob Hall and Gary Ball were the first to climb the Seven Summits in under a year.

In October 2006, American Kit Deslauriers became the first person to ski parts of all Seven Summits.

Swedes Olaf Sundstrom and Martin Letzer became the first to ski down as much as possible of each of the Seven Summits (including all of Everest and part of Carstensz Pyramid).

International climbers may have different considerations which I address throughout this book.

Visa fees and regulations vary widely from country to country. It's important to check the regulations of your country well in advance of the trip date to avoid complications.

Climbers from countries with smaller economies might not be able to exchange their local currency in some of the Seven Summit countries. It's smart to change money before traveling or to buy American currency or euros. American dollars are easy to change and are accepted in many locations without converting them to the local currency first.

Buying and ordering technical climbing gear is difficult in most African, South American, and some Asian countries. It may be necessary to order from the United States or Europe, and expensive tariffs might be put on these products if they are allowed in at all. Purchase climbing-specific items well in advance to avoid any import issues. If you are climbing with a guide service, it may be possible to send items to their business to bring on the trip for you. One of my clients from South Africa ordered gear from the United States that cost a small fortune to get delivered, took a very long time, and was ultimately almost rejected by customs officials!

FEMALE CLIMBERS

The increase in numbers of women climbing the Seven Summits over the last few decades has been astounding. The Seven Summits were overwhelmingly dominated by men twenty years ago, but now a significant percentage of climbers are women. I have guided several trips on which women outnumbered men and have seen more all-women's expeditions in recent years.

The mountain environment can be especially challenging for women. Privacy can be tough to come by for anyone on an expedition but especially for women and especially in inclement weather. It's important that women have a firm grasp of what life will be like on the mountain before going. It might be necessary to share a tent with a man if there is an odd number of women.

Teammates can help the women in the team feel more comfortable. Having a private designated spot for a toilet is a good idea. Putting women on the end of the climbing rope and having male climbers look the other way when nature calls can help significantly. Several urination devices on the market, such as the Lady J and the Stand by Your Man, can make things easier. It's important to get used to using these devices before the expedition. Some women limit their fluid intake to decrease the frequency of urination. This is the worst thing to do because it can lead to serious problems

Denali's
summit ridge

such as dehydration (see "Medical Concerns," below) or urinary tract infections. Proper hygiene is very important to mitigate the incidence of urinary tract infections, as well.

If a female member of the team feels uncomfortable about a situation, it's very important that she discuss it with the team leaders and other teammates. If teams communicate effectively about this and other issues, there are rarely problems.

Having more than one woman on a climbing team can usually make these concerns easier to deal with. Talking to women with climbing experience or to guide services can give you invaluable information as to what mountain life is like. If you don't feel comfortable that you will be able to maintain your level of modesty on the expedition, then consider an all-female team—or perhaps this isn't the right environment for you.

A FEMALE PERSPECTIVE ON BIG-MOUNTAIN EXPEDITIONS

There is no doubt that females are a minority in the subculture of big-mountain climbing. Even so, I find that people who are drawn to climbing have more similarities than differences. All high-altitude climbers have a love of big mountains and share the common goals of climbing with strength to the top and back again, challenging themselves, and having a good time while they're at it.

The majority of climbers are fair-minded, and regardless of your sex, if you can climb steadily, carry your portion of the weight, share a laugh, and appreciate your surroundings, you will be a well-respected member of your climbing team. Climbing, like all sports, is performance based, and if you can climb as well as or better than your teammates, you'll fit right in.

I have climbed high-altitude mountains with all-female groups and with combined male-female teams, and on many expeditions I have been the only woman. By far, my preference is an expedition with both women and men. From my experience, together they balance the expedition behavior or attitude of the team as a whole, and that fine detail can make or break the success of an expedition. Climbing big mountains requires a team, and its success relies on each team member's strengths and the collective positive attitude.

Your fitness level is within your control; acclimatization is not. Certain people acclimatize better than others for a variety of physiological reasons, though a person's sex does not appear to be a determining factor. My best advice to everyone who wants to climb to high altitude is to train seriously and become comfortable living and traveling in the mountains. I find that the best way to do this is through experience—spend as much time in the mountains as possible.

Here are some practical considerations that a female climber faces on a big-mountain expedition:

Menstrual cycle: You may have your period, skip your period, or get your period at an unexpected time. Expect the unexpected, and don't worry about it; just figure out your system for keeping clean and organized before you depart on your climb. I carry a designated stuff sack with all my needed supplies: tampons, pads, toilet paper, individually wrapped wet wipes, and small plastic bags for garbage. This stuff sack comes with me each time I go to the toilet area, and while I'm climbing it is always easily accessible in my pack, so I am always prepared.

Birth control: Some common birth-control methods such as Depo-Provera and the pill may also increase your risk of hazardous blood clots and therefore are not recommended by most doctors who are familiar with high-altitude medicine. Ask a doctor which, if any, method is right for you during your high-altitude expedition. Don't start or stop any medications immediately before your climb. I suggest allowing your body several months to adjust to any changes that you decide to make.

Privacy: There is very little privacy for anyone on a big-mountain expedition. You share your tent and travel in close groups constantly, so when you need privacy for a bodily function, just ask for it; your teammates will be happy to look the other way.

Urination: Some women use a pee funnel for additional privacy and convenience during an expedition. These devices can be very helpful in windy and cold situations, but they require practice. Some women find it a challenge to completely empty their bladder when using a funnel. I use a funnel for stormy days, though my preference is always the traditional squat. Urination at night can also turn into an annoying task; use a designated wide-mouth water bottle with or without a funnel, or get up and go outside; whatever you do, don't hold it. Take the time to find the methods that work best for you.

While on an expedition, it is more important than you think to be at ease going to the bathroom in a variety of situations and environments. If you're comfortable with it, you will eat and hydrate well and stay healthy and strong. If you have sustained problems with elimination, you will most likely eat and drink less and, at a minimum, will suffer from lack of energy and become dehydrated. This can be extremely dangerous in the mountains; if this happens to you, your expedition might not be successful.

Infections: While on long backcountry expeditions, yeast infections and urinary tract infections can be common for women. Take precautions against these by staying clean and dry. Talk with your doctor about which medications you should bring to address these infections if they arise.

On a couple of rare occasions, I have witnessed some deep concern from male climbers prior to climbing big mountains with women. Let's face it: some guys have never been around a self-sufficient woman who can carry a sixty-five-pound pack, coil a rope, and set up a tent. Once on the expedition, the concerned guys will soon realize that the gals are contributing the same or more work to make the expedition a success. If you are a woman facing this predicament, have patience and give them some time to learn what you are capable of and to see your contributions. Also, it may help to let them pick up your heavy pack on occasion. The few men that I know of who questioned climbing with women before their climb returned holding their female teammates in high regard.

CAITLIN PALMER
CO-OWNER OF ALASKA MOUNTAINEERING SCHOOL AND
A LEAD GUIDE ON DENALI AND ACONCAGUA

FLIGHTS

Climbers should book air tickets well in advance, especially when traveling to Africa, Asia, and Antarctica. Since the climbing dates on most expeditions are not fixed due to weather or other delays, it's important to have flexible tickets and to work with a travel agent who understands the nature of climbing.

TRAVEL INSURANCE

Anyone climbing the Seven Summits should purchase travel insurance. Insurance adds an additional cost but assures you that any trip interruptions will be covered. The more expensive the expedition, the more important it is for a climber to opt for travel insurance. Antarctica Logistics and Expeditions (ALE), the flight service provider on Vinson Massif, requires travel insurance.

Travel insurance typically covers trip interruptions, cancellations, lost baggage, and trip delays. Most companies offer a variety of services to choose from. Make sure you read the fine print to understand what is covered and what isn't.

Newer to the market are rescue insurance policies such as Global Rescue. These offer medical and political evacuation, mountain rescue, and body repatriation in the case of a climbing death. This type of service is very different from more traditional travel insurance. Rescue insurance is becoming more popular, especially for those traveling to areas of political unrest.

MEDICAL CONCERNS

Medical issues while climbing in remote areas can be exacerbated by the increased time needed to reach medical care, difficulty of rescue, and sanitation in the backcountry. A relatively insignificant injury on Vinson Massif can become life threatening if not treated correctly, whereas the same injury in a modern city might not be an issue at all because of immediate access to medical treatment. This means you need to educate yourself before going into the backcountry and take even minor injuries and illnesses very seriously.

Medical concerns you are most likely to deal with on the Seven Summits are high-altitude illnesses, infections, cold injuries, and burns. In this section I discuss altitude illnesses briefly, but this is by no means comprehensive and doesn't cover other important medical issues. To learn more, you should take, at a minimum, a backcountry first-aid and cardiopulmonary resuscitation course and read about acute mountain sickness and related issues.

Each climber should carry a first-aid kit and repair kit. I have listed some suggested items later in this section. These are only basic lists, and you most likely should supplement them. Adventure Medical Kits offers a great variety of kits that can be customized.

IMMUNIZATIONS

Travelers should have the proper immunizations when traveling to a new country. Generally the list of immunizations is the same wherever you travel, but there are some specific considerations for individual countries. Most people from developed countries will have had most of these already but may need a booster. Consult your immunization record and discuss this with a doctor,

local travel clinic, or the Centers for Disease Control and Prevention (CDC) well before the expedition date. Some immunization courses take several months. I discuss these specific concerns in each chapter in Part II but present a general list here as well:

- Diphtheria-tetanus (DPT)
- Polio
- Measles, mumps, and rubella (MMR)
- Meningitis
- Hepatitis A and B
- Cholera and typhoid
- Rabies
- Malaria—this disease can be an issue in some places including Africa. Consider taking a malaria chemoprophylaxis.

Organizing mule loads at Los Penitentes for Aconcagua

THE BEST TREATMENT FOR ANY
TYPE OF ALTITUDE ILLNESS IS
RAPID DESCENT TO A LOWER
ALTITUDE. NORMALLY, ANYONE WITH
ALTITUDE ILLNESS WHO STARTS
DOWN EARLY AFTER ONSET WILL
RECOVER RAPIDLY AND COMPLETELY
... DELAY MOVING TO A HIGHER
ALTITUDE WITH SYMPTOMS OF AMS.

*— DENALI NATIONAL PARK AND PRESERVE
MOUNTAINEERING HANDBOOK*

COMMON BACKCOUNTRY ISSUES

Hydration: One of the best things climbers can do to perform well and be healthy on an expedition is to stay hydrated. Dehydrated climbers are more susceptible to medical problems, and lingering issues will be magnified. It's difficult to drink enough water in the mountains because of the amount of physical effort required and the dry, cold air at altitude. Water is lost throughout the day through sweating, urinating, and breathing. To make up for this, it might be necessary to drink four to six quarts (liters) of water per day. Electrolyte replacement drinks are great because they make water more palatable and increase performance by maintaining electrolyte balance in your body.

Water purification: Boiling, commercial water-purifying tablets, and filters are effective ways to make water safe for drinking, which is necessary on most mountains. Tablets and filters can save valuable fuel. Iodine purification works well and filters can do a good job, too.

Nutrition: It's also difficult to get enough calories to make up for what the body burns through while climbing and trying to stay warm. Most people come back from an expedition skinnier even if they try to gorge on as many calories as possible. Lightweight dehydrated foods can be unpalatable, making it even harder to get the needed calories. As with hydration, the body cannot perform without calories. Maintaining weight on a climb, especially a long expedition such as Mount Everest, may require eating even when you aren't hungry. Many climbers lose their appetite at moderate to extreme altitudes.

Sanitation: The food that you do eat needs to be clean. It's very common for climbers to get sick from unsanitary mountain food in places where they can't completely control the quality of food. It's important to use hand sanitizer to kill germs and to keep people healthy. Make sure everyone in the team uses sanitizer before meals and after visiting the loo.

Sun exposure: Sunburn and snowblindness can quickly end an expedition. It is best to take preventive measures so these don't become an issue. The nature of climbing is to be outside for long periods of time, often in the sun, and sometimes on glaciers that reflect the sun's powerful rays. On climbs such as Denali and Vinson Massif, the temperature can swing as much as 100 degrees Fahrenheit (38°C) throughout the course of the day, depending on if the sun is out or not. Take precautions for sun protection: On hot, sunny days, cover all exposed skin, lather up with sunscreen with a high sun protection factor (SPF), and reapply it frequently. Wear the darkest glacier glasses possible, with good side protection, to avoid snowblindness. Good hydration can help prevent sunburn; a bottle of aloe gel is always welcome after it occurs.

Cold injuries: On the Seven Summits, cold injuries are quite common, although they are usually a result of apathy. Most frostbite and hypothermia can be prevented by listening to your body and adapting to changing conditions as needed. If you start shivering, take the time to stop and put on another layer of clothing. If your toes lose feeling, stop to warm them up before frostbite sets in. No mountain is worth losing a digit for. Many guides have been climbing in the coldest environments on Earth for a long time and have never gotten frostbite because

A climber's first view of Mount Everest during the trek through the Khumbu Valley

they are diligent. A sign of a good climber is someone who has all fingers and toes, not someone who has lost them. If frostbite occurs, it's important not to let the tissue refreeze after the affected area has been warmed up.

HIGH-ALTITUDE MEDICINE

Part of the allure of the Seven Summits is the challenge of climbing at high altitude. The altitudes of the respective peaks range from moderate to extreme, leading to a variety of potential problems. High-altitude medicine is a relatively new discipline that studies the causes of, effects of, and solutions to altitude illness. Each year that professionals study cases of altitude illness, we learn a bit more about what the factors are.

Acute mountain sickness (AMS) is a general term applied to altitude sickness. Susceptibility to AMS varies from climber to climber and, currently, cannot be reliably predicted. This means that you won't know how you'll perform at increasingly high altitudes until you go there. AMS is common on the Seven Summits. By climbing smart, you can greatly reduce the incidence of altitude-related issues and improve safety and success.

Mild AMS presents as headache, fatigue, loss of appetite, and shortness of breath. Climbers with more severe conditions such as high-altitude pulmonary edema (HAPE) or high-altitude cerebral edema (HACE) can experience edema, or swelling, throughout the body, caused by increased arterial pressure. Cerebral edema and pulmonary edema, if allowed to progress, can be very serious conditions, whereas peripheral edema (swelling in the hands, face, or elsewhere) is usually benign but may indicate susceptibility to HACE or HAPE.

Many of the serious injuries and deaths on the Seven Summits are a result of altitude illnesses. Knowing what the signs and symptoms of these are can keep your team safe. If a climber feels ill, reevaluate the climbing schedule. Don't push beyond the limits of anyone on your team and risk a serious rescue scenario.

HIMALAYAN RESCUE ASSOCIATION AND EVEREST ER

The Himalayan Rescue Association is a voluntary nonprofit organization formed in 1973 to reduce casualties in the Nepal Himalaya. It serves the increasing numbers of Nepalese and foreigners who trek into the remote wilderness. One of the most important tasks of the HRA is to prevent deaths from altitude illness. For nearly forty years, the HRA has staffed a small aid post in the Khumbu village of Pheriche at an altitude of 14,343 feet (4372 m) and in Manang at 11,545 feet (3519 m). The clinics are staffed during the spring and fall trekking seasons by volunteer doctors from all over the world.

In 1976 there were 14,000 trekkers to Nepal; by 1986 there were 49,000. During that time, deaths among trekkers due to acute mountain sickness remained at one per year (a fourfold decrease in incidence, due largely to preventive education and medical care provided in the region by the HRA). The trekking industry continues to grow, drawing less-experienced trekkers (sometimes with inexperienced leaders), and as a result, the absolute number of those with serious altitude illness is on the rise.

The Everest base camp medical clinic, Everest ER, was founded in 2003 as a response to the growing need for expert and altitude-experienced medical care even farther up the mountains at Everest base camp, and its mission, in line with HRA, is compelling. Volunteer physicians put their personal comfort and careers on hold to serve in order not only to save lives but also to generate funds that subsidize free or low-cost health care for the Sherpa people. Everest ER provides medical care and other assistance to the Nepali people, educates the public about prevention of altitude illness, and conducts medical research to improve care of medical problems occurring at extreme altitudes. The Everest ER has treated nearly 3000 patients in its first nine years and will celebrate its ten-year anniversary in spring 2012. An exciting new extension of the mission will involve the creation of a Sherpa-run technical rescue team on Everest, which began with technical rescue training delivered at the yearly Khumbu Climbing School in Phortse, Nepal.

The Everest ER is subsidized by a US-based nonprofit, HRA-USA (visit www.EverestER.org for more information). For more information about the Himalayan Rescue Association, visit www.himalayanrescue.org. Both sites offer lay and health-care information about mountain and altitude medicine and prevention strategies.

LUANNE FREER
FOUNDER AND DIRECTOR,
EVEREST BASE CAMP ER CLINIC

A snow sculpture at Union Glacier camp, Antarctica

FIRST-AID KITS

Each climber should carry a first-aid kit, which I've broken down into a medical and repair kit and a drug kit, when climbing. Below I list some of the basic items you should have in your kits. Add to and customize the lists to meet your individual needs.

MEDICAL AND REPAIR KIT

- Extra sunglasses
- Light emergency bivouac sack
- Adhesive bandages
- Molefoam
- Thermometer
- Medical tape
- Skin closure strips
- Gauze pads and other assorted bandages
- Nail clippers
- Scissors
- Multitool (with pliers)
- Zip ties
- Small quantity of baling wire
- Duct tape

DRUG KIT

- Acetaminophen for headaches and pain
- Acetazolamide (Diamox) for acute mountain sickness and acclimatization
- Aloe gel or moisturizer for sunburn treatment and dry skin
- Antibiotic ointment for wounds care

- Antibiotics (Azithromycin, Ciproflaxin) for respiratory infections, digestive tract infection, etc.
- Dexamethazone for cerebral edema
- Diphenhydramine for allergies, sleeping
- Ibuprofen for pain, headache, swelling, frostbite
- Immodium for diarrhea
- Lip balm with sunscreen for lip moisturizer and protection
- Nifedipine for pulmonary edema
- Throat lozenges
- Zinc for sunscreen and sunburns

1. GPS, compass, and map
2. Sun protection—sunscreen, sun hat, dark sunglasses, lip balm with SPF
3. Extra warm gear
4. Headlamp and extra batteries
5. First-aid kit
6. Lighter or matches
7. Repair kit, including pocketknife
8. Food
9. Water
10. Raingear (top and bottom)

GEAR

The old adage "ounces turn into pounds" is applicable to all climbs and certainly the Seven Summits. What this means is, leave the kitchen sink at home! Bringing unnecessary items will add weight quickly, decreasing your chance of success. Find a balance between being prepared and bringing too much. Some climbers might be able to carry extra gear, but why do it? Make the trip easier and more enjoyable by not bringing excess. "Light is right."

Gear has become very lightweight, but this often comes at a price. Choose the gear that is right for your budget. If you can comfortably afford the ultralight titanium or carbon fiber gizmo, then consider going for that option. If you can't, it's not the end of the world and doesn't mean you won't be able to climb the Seven Summits. Your pack, assuming you packed wisely, will still be a lot lighter than that of climbers thirty years ago.

Climbing is an inherently gear-intensive sport requiring a certain amount of investment to climb safely. Often you can save a lot of money by doing your homework and looking around for discounts. If climbing with a guide service, use the knowledge and expertise of the guide staff to steer you in the right direction. Guide companies will be happy to help you buy the right gear before the trip rather than having you suffer on the trip.

Below is a list of gear that all climbers should bring on every climb; bring an appropriate-size pack to put it in. For gear specific to each of the Seven Summits, see the gear lists at the end of each chapter in Part II.

A NOTE ABOUT THE GLOBAL POSITIONING SYSTEM (GPS)

Global Positioning System devices are a necessary piece of safety equipment whether you're climbing independently or with a guide. A GPS device uses satellites to determine your altitude and position on the ground. Although a map and compass are great to have and effective to use, GPS devices have largely supplanted them. Make sure you learn how to use your device and practice with it before venturing into the mountains. Even those climbing with a guide service should be proficient in using a GPS and bring one along. Climbers need to be prepared for the possibility that something could happen to the guide.

If you're climbing with a guide service, they may provide GPS coordinates to you. I provide the summit waypoints in the individual chapters in Part II. Plug all the relevant waypoints into your GPS unit before you begin an expedition. The waypoints you get from your guide service should be accurate but be sure you confirm and mark your own waypoints while on the climb; changes in climbing routes or glacial movement may mean changes in GPS coordinates, too.

COMMUNICATION EQUIPMENT

Communications are an important aspect of any expedition's safety and effectiveness. Communication equipment provides contact with outfitters, other teams, rescuers, and weather services, as well as among team

Before or after your Aconcagua climb, enjoy a traditional Argentinean meal in Mendoza. (Photo by Jane Lee)

members. A communications system provides an invaluable lifeline in case of an emergency. No party should be without at least one type of communication device; most guided parties will carry several.

The two most common communication devices are VHF (very high frequency) or UHF (ultra high frequency) radios and satellite phones. Most guided groups bring VHF or UHF radios for communication within the team and with other teams on the mountain and a satellite phone for communication domestically with the guide service headquarters or internationally with home. Places such as Mounts Kilimanjaro and Elbrus have good cell phone coverage, but Vinson Massif and Denali do not.

VHF and UHF radios: Some VHF radios come with a UHF component: dual band radios. This allows teams to talk over stronger VHF frequencies and pick up weather stations while still being able to talk to talk-about users (see below). Climbers formerly used VHF exclusively but now have shifted more to UHF, especially on Denali. On Aconcagua and Vinson Massif, rescue officials still primarily use VHF, however. Use radios that can use AA batteries—and carry extra batteries with you because you won't always be able to recharge them.

Prayers cover the rocks on the trek through the Khumbu Valley.

Talk-abouts: These are small, simple, cheap handheld UHF radios. They're lightweight, reliable, and effective. The Rangers Service on Denali now gives their daily weather forecasts on a UHF frequency. Most are five watts, which is sufficient to communicate 10–15 miles (16–24 km) in a direct line of sight. This distance reduces dramatically when there are obstructions in the way.

Satellite phones: These are great to communicate with the outside world. New models are light, easy to use, and reliable (depending on the network) due to geosynchronous technology. Older networks are increasingly unreliable. Do your homework to choose a network that works well in the regions of the world you plan to use it in. Most countries require that you declare satellite phones at customs. There may or may not be a fee associated with registering your phone.

Cell phones: Cell phones work on Aconcagua and Mounts Kilimanjaro, Elbrus, Kosciuszko, and Everest in places. Almost all analog cell towers have been replaced by digital systems. A new cell tower that covers Mount Everest base camp on the south side was erected in 2010. Cell phones are a cheap and effective way to communicate with others on and off the mountain. Consider buying a phone with an interchangeable subscriber identity module (SIM) card slot to use wherever you travel.

Short-wave radios: Another device I find useful is a short-wave radio. Even some of the most remote parts of the globe offer radio stations such as the British Broadcasting Company and Voice of America, as well as many others not in English.

A NOTE ABOUT SUPPLEMENTAL OXYGEN

Everest is the only one of the Seven Summits on which climbers use supplemental oxygen. Using supplemental oxygen properly is a skill in itself and requires its own gear such as oxygen tanks, masks, and regulators. All of this equipment takes practice to learn how to use properly. Make sure to run through the setup and usage techniques several times at base camp and throughout the climb before committing to its use on summit day. Supplemental oxygen can be an important safety tool on Mount Everest if used properly.

PREPARATION TIMELINE

Before you start booking tickets take some time to research the climbs, do some serious thinking, and decide if climbing the Seven Summits is something you really want to pursue and are mentally, physically, and financially prepared to do. If it is, decide where you want to start and, for each climb, work your way through the following checklists.

MORE THAN TWO MONTHS BEFORE THE CLIMB

- Have funding for the expedition in place.
- Adhere to a training regimen, taking care not to injure yourself.
- Buy insurance for the climb.
- Have a medical check-up and immunizations (take your immunization card with you).
- Have a dental check-up.
- Organize permits for the climb and get a travel visa for the host country.
- Organize an independent team or sign on with a guided trip.
- Obtain a passport or get more pages if yours is almost full (must be valid for at least six months after date of travel).
- Obtain technical training (take climbing courses and climb mountains to prepare for the rigors of climbing the Seven Summits).

TWO MONTHS BEFORE THE CLIMB

- Have all gear bought and in order.
- Use all of your gear to make sure it works properly, fits well, and is in good working order.
- Pack, unpack, and test several times to make sure you know your gear and how it works.
- Buy food for an independent expedition (not necessary if joining a guided expedition).

A Himalayan snow cock searches for food near the trail to Everest base camp.

THE WEEK BEFORE DEPARTURE

- Finish all preparations for the climb.
- Finish emails and work obligations; touch base with friends and family before taking off.
- Print out a copy of your flight itinerary and double check that the flight has not changed.
- Buy snack food for the trip.
- Stop training (don't take a chance of hurting yourself; rest your body before the flight, jet lag, and climb).
- Print out all climb-related documents that you might need for the trip (contacts, forms, guide service information, etc.).

WHEN YOU ARRIVE IN THE HOST COUNTRY OR REGION

- Obtain climbing permits and check in with climb officials or contacts.

- Double check that all logistics and arrangements for the climb are in order and haven't changed.
- Meet up with your team.
- Buy last-minute items or fresh food for the climb.

ON THE CLIMB

- Think ahead to later in the trip and set yourself up for success.
- Take care of yourself to save as much energy and strength for later (rest, eat, and hydrate).
- Contact your travel agent to update your return flight when you know the end date.

HIGH-ALTITUDE CLIMBING TECHNIQUES AND SKILLS

Becoming proficient at mountaineering is a progression. As in all sports, climbers must work up to higher and more difficult climbs by starting small and learning the requisite skills the correct way and building their climbing resumé. The goal for climbing the Seven Summits should be as much about becoming a proficient climber as it is about summiting the mountains.

Climbing the Seven Summits doesn't require climbers to be able to climb 5.13b (Yosemite Decimal System) or huge frozen waterfalls, but there are skills climbers need to feel comfortable with to climb safely. These are mostly general mountaineering techniques such as cramponing and ice ax work but also include specialty techniques such as crevasse rescue, fixed-line ascension, and high-altitude efficiency techniques.

ACCLIMATIZATION

The rarefied air of high-altitude peaks makes climbing more difficult and forces us to slow down. Air density at 18,000 feet (5486 m) is half of what it is at sea level, and at 29,035 feet (8850 m) it's only about a third! This is extremely hard on the body, and you must work to counteract the thin air's effect on the body by acclimatizing, being more efficient, staying hydrated, and sometimes using supplemental oxygen—the latter only on Mount Everest when climbing the Seven Summits.

Acclimatizing slowly and effectively is the best thing climbers can do to climb well at altitude. This acclimatization period gives your body time to adapt by producing extra red blood cells to carry more oxygen, among other physiological changes. Climbers wouldn't survive long on the summit of Mount Everest without this acclimatization period. In each chapter in part II, I describe steps for acclimatizing on that peak, and I build these steps into the sample climbing itinerary as well.

EFFICIENCY TECHNIQUES

In addition to acclimatizing, there are techniques you can use to make work at high altitude easier. Experienced climbers use efficiency techniques at high altitude to accomplish more while expending less energy. Without them, I personally wouldn't have made it to the top of all

Seven Summits. Master these techniques, and they will help you achieve your climbing goals.

REST STEP

The "rest step" is now a term in almost every high-altitude mountaineer's vocabulary. The rest step is a simple efficiency technique that allows you to take a micro-rest on your skeletal structure with every step. This saves your muscles and allows climbers to cover more distance easier.

The rest step works like this: Take a step up the hill and stop. You will naturally shift your weight on to your back (downhill) leg. If you lock your downhill knee, the weight will be on your skeletal structure and not on flexed muscles. This is essentially it. Take a small rest with each step uphill on a locked back leg.

Here are a few more ideas that will help you master the rest step:

1. Take small steps—big steps will put you out of balance.
2. If on snow, scuff the soles of your boots into the snow—this creates a flat platform that will give you purchase and prevent slipping.
3. Stand up straight—a balanced position will force you to keep your weight over your back leg in a rest position. It will also keep your lungs open, allowing you to climb stronger.
4. Maintain your cadence—the rest step should not affect your pace. You can incorporate rest steps into even a fast walk by shortening the rests.
5. Make sure to rest on the back leg—the most common mistake I see is a climber trying to rest on the front (uphill) leg. This is more difficult.

PRESSURE BREATHING

Climbing at high altitudes is difficult because, due to the rarefied air, you don't assimilate as much oxygen as you do at sea level. The simple act of breathing more forces more oxygen into your system. When you breathe more, and more forcefully, your body assimilates more

A crowded camp
on Aconcagua

oxygen, raising your body's oxygen saturation. Put a Pulse-Oximeter on your finger and hyperventilate. Your oxygen saturation will begin to climb by as much as 10 percentage points almost immediately. This shows the importance of breathing more frequently and forcefully.

What's most important in this technique is to focus on breathing forcefully as often as possible. The increased oxygenation will make you feel better and climb stronger. Don't wait until you start to feel bad. Train yourself to use this technique anytime you're working hard at altitude to keep yourself out of oxygen debt so it becomes automatic.

PACING

Maintaining a slow, steady pace is one of the best things you can do to save energy. Most climbers climb way too fast and fail to find an efficient rhythm. The goal is to get into camp having used as little energy as possible, with reserves for the next day's effort.

This is a classic case of the tortoise and the hare. If climbers run from one camp to the next, they will have stressed their body much more than climbers who maintain a slow, steady pace. I constantly see people going too hard and struggling to keep up later in the expedition because of fatigue. Whatever type of climbing you're doing, whether it's ascending a fixed line, climbing a vertical pitch of rock, or just slogging up a snowfield, try to climb in the most efficient manner.

LAYERING CLOTHING

Proper layering is also an efficiency technique. Getting hot and sweating is inefficient and forces your body to work harder than it needs to. Also, getting too cold forces the body to work harder to stay warm, burning calories unnecessarily. Take the time to adjust your clothing layers so you can climb efficiently. See the gear lists at the end of each chapter in Part II.

ENVIRONMENTAL CONCERNS AND WASTE

One of the largest responsibilities we have as climbers is to protect and preserve the natural environment. It is important for us to be respectful of the mountain environment and keep it clean so that others will have the same experience we had.

On some of the Seven Summits, regulations are in place that mandate environmental stewardship, but we need to perpetuate this ethic even where there are no regulations. All trash, including human waste, must be carried off all of the mountains. This is especially true in Antarctica, where there is very little snowfall. Anything that gets left on the continent is visible for many years to come, including human waste and trash. On Denali, human waste can be dumped into crevasses, although some teams pack it out.

Climbers
acclimatizing on
Lobuche before
beginning their
Everest attempts

PART II
CLIMBING THE SEVEN SUMMITS

SEVEN SUMMITS COMPARISON CHART

	Mount Everest	Mount Kilimanjaro	Denali	Aconcagua
Continent	Asia	Africa	North America	South America
Altitude	29,035ft (8850 m)	19,340 ft (5895 m)	20,320 ft (6194 m)	22,841 ft (6962 m)
Difficulty Ratings	Technical: 4 Physical: 5	Technical: 1-2 Physical: 2-3	Technical: 3 Physical: 5	Technical: 2 Physical: 3-4
First Ascent	1953, Nepali Tenzing Norgay Sherpa and New Zealander Sir Edmund Hillary via South Col	German Hans Meyer	1913, Americans Hudson Stuck, Harry Karstens, Walter Harper, and Robert Tatum	Swiss Mattias Zurbriggen
GPS Coordinates	N 27 59.28677 E86 55.51464	S 03 04.585 E 37 21.240	N 63 06.9256 W 151 01.5472	S 32 39.13 W 70 00.45
Route Names	South Ridge Route; Northeast Ridge Route	Machame Route; Marangu (Coca-Cola) Route	West Buttress Route	Normal Route via Horcones Valley; False Polish Route via Vacas Valley
Altitude Gain (Base Camp to Summit)	South Ridge 11,560 ft (3523 m), plus 8980 ft (2737 m) on trekking approach (total 20,540 ft, 6260 m) Northeast Ridge 11,445 ft (3489 m)	Machame Route 13,403 ft (4085 m) Marangu Route 13,109 ft (3995 m)	12,717 ft (3877 m)	Normal Route 8832 ft (2692 m), plus 4659 ft (1420 m) on trekking approach (total 13,500, 4100 m) False Polish Route 9163 ft (2792 m), plus 6050 ft (1845 m) on trekking approach (total 15,200 ft, 4637 m)
Load Weight	30-70 lbs (14-32 kg)	10-30 lbs (6-14 kg)	60-100 lbs (27-45 kg)	40-70 lbs (18-32 kg)
Climbing Season	April-June 1 (premonsoon) September-October (postmonsoon)	January-mid-March June-mid-October	Early May-mid-July	December-February
Climbing Style	High-altitude rotations; climb high, sleep low; double-carry loads	Slow acclimatization, camp to camp	Climb high, sleep low; double-carry loads	Climb high, sleep low; double-carry loads
Ascents per year	500	25,000-30,000	1200	4000
Country and Protected Status	South Ridge: Nepal (54,363 sq mi, 140,800 sq km) *Sagarmatha National Park* Northeast Ridge: China (3,705,386 sq mi, 9,596,960 sq km)	Tanzania (364,899 sq mi, 945,090 sq km) *Kilimanjaro National Park*	United States of America (3,618,765 sq mi, 9,372,610 sq km) *Denali National Park and Preserve*	Argentina (1,068,296 sq mi, 2,766,890 sq km) *Aconcagua Provincial Park*
Capital	South Ridge: Katmandu; Northeast Ridge: Beijing	Dodoma	Washington, DC	Buenos Aires
Language	South Ridge: Nepali and Sherpa Northeast Ridge: Mandarin Chinese, Tibetan	Swahili and English	English	Spanish
Currency	South Ridge: Nepalese rupee Northeast Ridge: Chinese yuan	Tanzanian shilling	US dollar	Argentinean peso
Exchange Rate	South Ridge: $1US=70 rupees Northeast Ridge: $1US=7 yuan	$1US=1505 Tanzanian shillings	NA	$1US=3-5 Argentinean pesos
Local Time Compared to Greenwich Mean Time)	South Ridge: GMT +5.5 hrs Northeast Ridge: GMT +8 hrs	GMT +3 hrs	Alaska: GMT -9 hrs (-8 hrs during daylight savings time); USA: GMT -5-11 hrs	GMT -3 hrs
Country Telephone Code	South Ridge: +977 Northeast Ridge: +86	Tanzania: +255 Kenya: +254	+1	+54
Power Supply	South Ridge: 230V Northeast Ridge: 220V	220V	110V	220V

Vinson Massif	Mount Elbrus	Mount Kosciuszko	Carstensz Pyramid
Antarctica	Europe	Australia	Australasia
16,050 ft (4892 m)	18,510 ft (5642 m)	7310 ft (2228 m)	16,024 ft (4884 m)
Technical: 3 Physical: 3	Technical: 2 Physical: 2-3	Technical: 1 Physical: 2	Technical: 5 Physical: 3
1966, Americans Barry Corbet, John Evans, William Long, and Pete Schoening, led by Nicholas Clinch	1874, English A. W. Moore, F. Gardiner, F. Crauford Grove, and H. Walker, guided by Swiss Peter Knubel	Date unknown, Monaro Aboriginals	1962, New Zealander Philip Temple, German Heinrich Harrer, Austrian Russell Kippax, Dutch Albert Huizenga
S 78 31.088 W 85 37.585	N 43 21.129 E 42 26.010	S 36 27.250 E 148 16.196	S 4 04.733 E 137 09.572
Normal Route	Normal Route	via Charlotte's Pass; via Thredbo Ski Resort	Normal Route (North Face)
9160 ft (2792 m)	5715 ft (1742 m) from barrel huts	via Charlotte's Pass 1273 ft (388 m) from trailhead via Thredbo Ski Resort 991 ft (302 m) from top of chairlift	3124 ft (952 m)
55-70 lbs (25-32 kg)	20-40 lbs (9-18 kg)	8-25 lbs (4-11 kg)	20-40 lbs (9-18 kg)
November-January	June-August	December-February best March-April, October-November OK	Year-round
Climb high, sleep low; double-carry loads	Climb high, sleep low (acclimatize, then day climb alpine style)	Day hike alpine style	Acclimatize, then day climb alpine style
150	3000	1000+	Several hundred (varies)
Antarctica (5,405,400 sq mi, 14,000,000 sq km)	Russia (6,592,800 sq mi, 17,075,400 sq km)	Australia (2,967,893 sq mi, 7,686,850 sq km) *Kosciuszko National Park*	Indonesia (741,096 sq mi, 1,919,440 sq km)
NA	Moscow	Canberra	Jakarta
Antarctica: NA Chile: Spanish	Russian	English	Bahasa, Indonesian, and tribal languages
Antarctica: NA Chile: Chilean peso	Russian ruble	Australian dollar	Indonesian rupiah
Antarctica: NA Chile: $1US=500 Chilean pesos	$1US=31 rubles	$1US=$1.15 Australian dollars	$1US=9100 Indonesian rupiahs
Antarctica: GMT + 12 hrs Chile: GMT -4 hrs	GMT +3-12 hrs	GMT +10 hrs	GMT +7-9 hrs
Antarctica: +672 Chile: +56	+7	+61	+62
Antarctica: NA Chile: 220V	220V	230V	formerly 127V, mostly converted to 230V

MOUNT EVEREST

ALTITUDE
29,035 feet (8850 m)

DIFFICULTY RATINGS
Technical: 4
Physical: 5

SUMMIT GPS WAYPOINTS
N 27 59.28677
E 86 55.51464

ELEVATION GAIN
(base camp to summit)
South Ridge Route:
11,560 feet (3523 m), plus 8980 feet
(2737 m) on trekking approach
(total 20,540 feet, 6260 m)
Northeast Ridge Route:
11,445 feet (3489 m)

DISTANCE
(base camp to summit)
South Ridge Route: 12.5 miles (20 km),
plus 50 miles (80 km) on trekking
approach (total 62.5 miles, 100 km)
Northeast Ridge Route: 22.75 miles
(36.5 km)

TIME
(door-to-door)
South Ridge Route: 57 days
Northeast Ridge Route: 58 days

SEASON
April 1–June 1
September–October

One of many ladder
crossings in the
Khumbu Icefall

CHAPTER 3

MOUNT EVEREST

ASIA'S HIGHEST SUMMIT

I'VE ALWAYS HATED THE DANGER PART OF CLIMBING, AND IT'S GREAT TO COME DOWN AGAIN BECAUSE IT'S SAFE ... BUT THERE IS SOMETHING ABOUT BUILDING UP A COMRADESHIP—THAT I STILL BELIEVE IS THE GREATEST OF ALL FEATS—AND SHARING IN THE DANGERS WITH YOUR COMPANY OF PEERS. IT'S THE INTENSE EFFORT, THE GIVING OF EVERYTHING YOU'VE GOT. IT'S REALLY A VERY PLEASANT SENSATION.

—SIR EDMUND HILLARY QUOTED IN "SIR EDMUND HILLARY, A PIONEERING CONQUERER OF EVEREST, DIES AT 88," *NEW YORK TIMES* (JANUARY 10, 2008)

Mount Everest is one of the most iconic symbols in the world. Whether you are a climber or not, you will undoubtedly have heard of Mount Everest and the climbing lore and reputation that goes with it. Mount Everest has pervaded popular culture, and the recent climbing boom has made Everest a household name. Mount Everest is certainly the most well known of the Seven Summits and the crowning achievement of the quest to climb them all.

Goraks feel at home in the high mountain air.

Mount Everest lies on the border between China and Nepal, which marks the crest of the Himalayan mountain chain that stretches from Pakistan in the west some 1800 miles (3000 km) east to Bhutan and China. The world's largest mountain chain, it is still growing. The word Himalaya comes from the Sanskrit words *him*, meaning "snow," and *alaya*, meaning "abode." Other names for the mountain include Chomolungma (Tibetan) and Sagarmatha (Sanskrit).

The Nepalese part of the Himalayan chain includes eight of the fourteen 26,000-foot (8000 m) peaks. Mount Everest isn't alone in dominating this great chain of mountains. Lhotse, Cho Oyu, Makalu, and Kangchenjunga, the world's fourth-, sixth-, fifth-, and third-tallest mountains, all lie within the immediate vicinity.

Nepal first opened Everest to climbing in 1949 and protected its portion of the mountain in Sagarmatha National Park in 1976. Now, tens of thousands of trekkers and climbers come from all over the globe each year to witness its natural beauty, with the most popular destination being Mount Everest base camp. During the high season (pre- and postmonsoon), a hundred trekkers or more may visit the camp each day. This industry does a lot to support the people of Nepal and create opportunities within the country. The Khumbu Valley has become one of the richest regions of Nepal due to the trekking and climbing industries.

THE DEMOCRATIZATION OF EVEREST

We've all had that moment: when we first looked at a picture of Mount Everest and realized that we could identify some of the features. Right there: it's the Great Couloir, the West Ridge, the Khumbu Icefall! And in that instant, we change from being just a spectator to being a participant in the Mount Everest experience.

I had that revelation as a ten-year-old boy growing up in Tacoma, Washington, when my father took me to see a slide show by the 1963 American Everest climbers. That evening, I learned about the mountain and decided that I wanted to climb it.

However, back in those days, there was just no way for a "normal" person to do it. You had to be well connected and get invited to join a team, and many of those teams were selected by national committees or powerful people who could make or break your climbing dreams. Heaven forbid if you were not a member of the "in" crowd, or if you had rubbed someone the wrong way!

In the 1980s and '90s, though, things began to change. First, the pool of experienced climbers was increasing, and all over the world climbers were starting to travel and gain more high-altitude experience. Second, the media started taking great notice of mountaineering, highlighted by Dick Bass and Frank Wells's Seven Summits quest, Jim Whittaker's Peace Climb, the 1996 Everest disasters, and the subsequent blockbuster status of Jon Krakauer's *Into Thin Air*. Third, the advent of satellite communications and Internet access in the '90s made it possible for climbers to tell their own stories directly from the mountain, without having to rely on traditional media. Fourth, in 1993 both China and Nepal began liberalizing their longtime one-expedition-at-a-time policies, which meant more climbers could now go each season to Mount Everest. Finally, starting in the early '90s, the first commercial teams began organizing expeditions to climb Everest.

The result of all of these changes has been exponential growth in the interest for all-things-Everest, a trend with no end in sight. For every climber from a western country who has become jaded to the latest exploits on Mount Everest, there are countless more from the developing world just coming under the spell of Chomolungma or Sagarmatha for the first time. After personally making ten expeditions to Everest and organizing another ten more, I can say that it is a truly international mountain these days.

When I led the 1999 expedition to search for the remains of George Mallory and Andrew Irvine, the famous British climbers lost on Everest in 1924, I always thought that climbers would be interested in our story. After we actually found Mallory's body, however, I was totally amazed to see how the story appealed to a much wider audience. Everest is the world's largest stage, and each year a new group of actors show up to perform. Some do well; others do poorly. Regardless, you always know that it will be a great show!

ERIC SIMONSON

CO-OWNER OF INTERNATIONAL MOUNTAIN GUIDES, SEVEN SUMMITER, AND LEADER OF THE MALLORY AND IRVINE RESEARCH EXPEDITIONS

NATURAL HISTORY

The Himalayas are a very young mountain range that has grown at an impressive rate of 2.4 inches (6.1 cm) a year. The enormous height of the Himalayas is due to the fast collision rate between the Indian Plate sliding underneath the larger Eurasian Plate, forcing ocean sediments and rock into the air. The Tibetan Plateau, which was once the ocean floor, now averages a height of 14,763 feet

(4500 m). Mount Everest is mostly composed of limestone, shale, and marble overlaying leuco granites.

This subduction and resulting uprising created two markedly different ecosystems on either side of the Himalayas. The Mount Everest region encompasses a variety of niche ecosystems that have adapted over millions of years to this rugged landscape. Mount Everest separates the harsh seminomadic life on the rolling high Tibetan Plateau to the north from the more sedentary agricultural life of the steep, mountainous gorges to the south. The Chinese side is an austere, windswept landscape where relatively few plants and animals can survive. The Nepal side begins rocky and barren abutting the Himalayas but quickly drops away into lush, fertile valleys. The diversity of plant and animal life grows denser farther south.

The main resources on the Tibetan Plateau are *tsampa* (barley), yaks, goats, and salt. The Tibetans have historically used salt to trade with Nepalis over the border for commodities such as sugar, a trade that continues today. *Tsampa*, a hearty crop that survives in the rugged Tibetan landscape, has been the staple Tibetan food for centuries. Locals mix plain barley with either water or milk and sugar in a bowl several times a day for meals.

Most of the flora in Tibet consists of low-lying plants that have adapted to survive the long winters, cold temperatures, and persistent wind. Some of the more than 6000 species of vascular plants include rhododendrons, gentian, and 120 species of *Primula*. Trees survive only in the lower and wetter reaches of Tibet. Tibetan eagles, marmots, Himalayan mouse hares, foxes, ravens, wild asses, ibexes, snow leopards, yaks, and Tibetan antelopes are some of the hearty animals that live on the plateau.

Many plants have taken up residence on the southern slopes of Mount Everest. The most obvious to tourists visiting the region in the late spring are the forests of flowering rhododendrons, making for picturesque trekking. They can grow 30–50 feet (9–15 m) tall. Evergreen forests populate the drier hillsides. These forests are interspersed with alpine shrub and meadows. Beautiful terrace work produces crops—rice, barley, millet, and lentils—that the Sherpas rely upon.

One notable animal is the rarely seen snow leopard. Other unusual creatures include the cliff-dwelling blue sheep, high-altitude goraks, yaks, goats, Himalayan snow cocks, and musk deer.

CULTURAL AND POLITICAL BACKGROUND

Buddhism is the prevalent religion in the Khumbu Valley, although the majority of Nepalese, including most people in Katmandu, are Hindus. Hinduism and Buddhism share a long history, and are closely connected philosophies and religions.

The political history of the Tibetan region of China has been turbulent. Tibet has been under Chinese rule for more than a half century. The Chinese presence in Tibet has steadily grown over the years since the takeover. Today, there are almost as many Han Chinese from eastern China in Tibet as there are native Tibetans. Since this is such a volatile and sensitive area of China, you will notice a lot of Chinese military presence when you travel there.

The Nepalese side has arguably been less stable in recent years. Maoist rebels throughout Nepal began their campaign for power and change more than a decade ago and recently became part of the parliamentary government. In 2008 the country did away with the monarchy

---

MOUNT EVEREST FAST FACTS

- Mount Everest is the tallest mountain on Earth.
- Mount Everest lies on the border of China and Nepal in the heart of the Himalayan mountain chain.
- Sherpas inhabit the Khumbu Valley, which lies on the south side of Mount Everest, and have played a crucial role in the success of almost all Everest expeditions.

Yaks are an important part of Tibetan life.

and ousted King Gyanendra. Gyanendra had become king after the murder of his brother, King Birendra, and his wife, Queen Aiswarya, by their son over a marriage dispute. Their son, Dipendra, committed suicide after the attack but while in a coma was crowned king and held that title for several days before he died.

The Maoist rebels gained influence in the countryside first and then later in the major cities. Despite all this, Katmandu is considered a relatively safe city. There are occasional strikes and roadblocks to gain publicity for certain causes, but they are rarely violent and protesters go out of their way to not target tourists who contribute to the Nepali economy. The strikes can shut down the city, however, and are not necessarily announced ahead of time, causing delays for climbers.

CLIMBING HISTORY

In 1856, when Andrew Waugh, British Surveyor General of India, released his calculations concluding that Mount Everest was the highest mountain in the world at 29,002 feet (8840 m), the world began to take interest. The first serious expedition to the mountain was by the British in 1921 and included George Mallory. The team wasn't equipped to make a summit attempt. It took Mallory and his compatriots a month just to reach the base of the mountain. After a tragic attempt in 1922, Mallory returned to the north side with another British team in 1924. On a last-ditch attempt to reach the summit after another member of the team, Edward Norton, had returned from more than 28,000 feet (8500 m), George Mallory and Andrew (Sandy) Irvine went for the top. This pair of talented climbers made it high on the mountain and eventually disappeared. Mallory's body was later found by the Mallory and Irvine Research Expedition led by Eric Simonson, at almost 27,000 feet (8200 m), in 1999. It is not known conclusively whether Mallory and Irvine made the summit or not.

International expeditions continued to flock to the mountain to challenge the slopes in search of fame and glory. Finally, in 1953, a British-funded international expedition led by Sir John Hunt ventured to the south

MOUNT EVEREST TIMELINE

1921 Charles Howard-Bury, a Brit, leads the first Mount Everest expedition.

1924 Briton Edward Norton climbs to within 820 feet (250 m) of the summit.

1924 Four days after Norton's climb, Britons George Mallory and Sandy Irvine disappear high on the mountain and may have summited.

1953 First ascent of Mount Everest; Sir John Hunt leads a British and Commonwealth expedition that puts two climbers on the summit, Sir Edmund Hillary and Tenzing Norgay Sherpa.

1963 Jim Whittaker becomes first American to summit. Teammates Tom Hornbein and Willi Unsoeld make the first traverse of Mount Everest climbing the West Ridge/Hornbein Couloir and descending the South Ridge.

1975 British climber Chris Bonington leads the successful British Southwest Face expedition ("The Hard Way").

1978 Italian Reinhold Messner and Austrian Peter Habeler make the first ascent without supplemental oxygen.

1980 Messner makes the first solo ascent.

1983 First ascent of the Kangshung Face made by a large American team.

1986 Swiss climbers Jean Troillet and Erhard Loretan climb the Hornbein Couloir in forty-two hours roundtrip.

2011 Apa Sherpa summits Everest for the twenty-first time.

side of the mountain and was successful in reaching the top. This large, well-funded effort put a New Zealander and a Nepali Sherpa on top just as time was running out in the season. Sir Edmund Hillary and Tenzing Norgay Sherpa climbed from the Balcony camp to the summit on May 29, becoming the first humans to undeniably stand on top of the world. This conquest captured the attention of the world and made Hillary and Tenzing two instant international sensations.

In the decades following Hillary and Tenzing's success, many other notable ascents were made of Mount Everest. Two Americans, Willi Unsoeld and Tom Hornbein, made the first traverse of the mountain in 1963 by scaling the west shoulder and traversing in to a steep, committing couloir on the north face, now known as the Hornbein Couloir, and descending the South Ridge Route. In 1975 a British team led by Sir Christopher Bonington completed the Southwest Face Route on their second attempt. In 1978 Italian Reinhold Messner and Austrian Peter Habeler completed the first

FAST FACT

Buddhists believe that when the wind blows prayer flags, the prayers written on them are sent off. This is why prayer flags are often placed at high points such as passes and summits where the wind is the strongest.

ascent of the mountain without supplemental oxygen. This groundbreaking ascent advanced the boundaries of high-altitude mountaineering and proved that Everest could be climbed without a large team or the use of supplemental oxygen. The speed record for the Northeast Ridge was set by Austrian Christian Stangl in 2007 in a time of sixteen hours and forty-two minutes, and the fastest ascent for the Southeast Ridge was set in 2003 by Lapka Geln Sherpa in ten hours, fifty-six minutes, forty-six seconds. By 2011 Apa Sherpa (Nepal) had climbed the mountain a record twenty-one times.

TOUCHING THE NIGHT SKY

There are few experiences in the known universe akin to exiting the safety and warmth of the International Space Station's airlock and gracefully floating out into the pitch-black vacuum of space. After many months of intense training and great anticipation, not to mention the exhilaration of rocketing off of the planet in a space shuttle, you arrive at what is a defining moment in your life. You and your space-walking partner are alone in the void of space, reliant upon each other to accomplish a series of very difficult tasks and safely return in six-plus hours. You have crewmates inside the station and shuttle, and flight controllers with watchful eyes and helpful direction communicating from Mission Control Houston, but the ultimate responsibility for making a "round trip" outside falls upon you and your space-walking buddy. I've made seven such trips, which we call EVAs—short for Extravehicular Activity—and memories from each are forever etched in my mind. The butterflies—the commitment—are especially intense those first few minutes out the hatch, tempered only once we get to work in this rarified world....

I guess I've always been driven to visit high, lofty places, and not just confined to aircraft and spacecraft. I began climbing in earnest in my teens, and after many hard-won summits, it was only natural to test myself on the world's highest peak. I had the good fortune of spending a couple of seasons on Everest with Mike Hamill, climbing in parallel with him and his guided clients, and sharing the base camp support of the International Mountain Guides team. I remember having some great conversations with him in various camps along the way to the top of the world, including finding similarities between Himalayan mountaineering and EVA. Believe it or not, a summit day on Everest is a very close cousin to space walking, allowing me to touch the night sky....

I vividly recall the evening of May 20, 2009, poised to go into my wind-battered tent at 26,000-foot (7925 m) Camp IV. I'd been lying low since arrival at camp around 9:30 AM, sucking down one and a half quarts (liters) a minute of supplemental oxygen, a few quarts of water, and an occasional ramen, thinking about the night ahead. Much like the pre-EVA jitters I'd experienced in the past, I wondered how my next twenty-four hours would unfold. Would I successfully summit? Success could only be measured as a complete round trip, so I wondered about the stability of the weather, the route, my health, my teammates (especially my friend and sidekick, Danuru Sherpa, from Phortse), and other elements beyond my control.

Bundled in a thick down suit, wearing a backpack containing my oxygen and emergency gear, I trundled out the vestibule of my tent at 8:00 PM that windblown night with just the illumination of my headlamp and a sliver of the moon. For all intents and purposes, I was exiting into the vacuum of space, since the air was almost as thin as "upstairs" outside the International Space Station. My thick mitts provided limited tactility, not dissimilar to my space-walking gloves, and I carefully hooked up to the fixed lines above the South Col, much as I'd done in space, hooking up a safety tether to prevent myself from "falling off" my spacecraft—which would be a very bad day. My dream had been to arrive on the summit of Everest in time to see a sunrise, complete with the full curvature of Earth. I'd seen many orbital sunrises in space—we see sixteen every day while traveling at 17,500 miles per hour (28,000 kph) around the planet—but they happen almost in a blur. As my good fortune would have it, I arrived on the summit at 4:00 AM, with the sunrise just beginning to peek up at 4:05 AM. I was treated to the equivalent of an orbital sunrise from the top of the world, savoring the full spectrum of light as it rose behind the earth's limn during my descent of the summit ridge, exhausted but elated. It remains the most magnificent sunrise of my life.

SCOTT PARAZYNSKI,
DOCTOR, NASA ASTRONAUT, AND CLIMBER

CLIMBING CHALLENGES

Attempting to climb Mount Everest is a huge physical, financial, emotional, and time commitment that should not be taken lightly. It requires several months of climbing while on the expedition, not to mention countless hours of training and preparation prior to beginning the expedition, putting life at home on hold, an immense amount of organization, and a lot of money. Climbing the mountain requires putting yourself at risk in a harsh and uncompromising environment, trying to live where humans can't survive, asking your body to push harder than it has ever pushed before, and having the mental toughness and persistence to continue climbing until the summit has been attained.

In short, climbing Mount Everest is the hardest thing you will ever do and it will push you to your limit. Every year, climbers die trying to summit Mount Everest, and many more leave the mountain disappointed simply because of sickness or their body's predisposition to not survive in this rarefied, extreme environment. Mount Everest is not a walkup, and everyone who climbs the mountain climbs it under their own power.

One needs to be diligent throughout the entire Everest process to be successful. It's as important to have the right equipment, be familiar with it, and have trained properly before the trip as it is to perform while on the mountain. Once on the mountain, the biggest challenges a climber faces are staying healthy, being physically capable of the daily rigors of the mountain, avoiding human and objective hazards, and staying mentally committed to the expedition and the summit. The challenges are many, and a certain amount of luck with the weather and equipment always seems to play a part in being successful on Mount Everest as well.

Massive blocks of
ice in the "Popcorn"
section of the
Khumbu Icefall

SOUTH SIDE

Most of the route on the south side of Mount Everest lies in a valley between the west shoulder and Nuptse, making it exposed to avalanches and rockfall. The larger avalanches originate from the west shoulder, while Nuptse usually produces only small, isolated rockfalls at irregular intervals. Once out of base camp, climbers are immediately exposed. In the Khumbu Icefall, there's potential for ice blocks to shift and collapse, as well as avalanches from the west shoulder of Everest. It's prudent to move through the icefall quickly to minimize exposure to these hazards. Crevasse falls and falls from ladders are also a risk. Practice your technical skills and walking horizontally across ladders so you are competent when it comes time to do it for real in the icefall.

Always stay clipped in to the fixed lines on the Lhotse Face. Beware of falling ice, rocks, and gear from other climbers while on the face. A climbing helmet makes a lot of sense here. There is potential for rockfall above the South Col en route to the Balcony. Wear a helmet, and watch your footing so as not to kick rocks down on others below. There is a persistent wind at the Balcony before daybreak, making cold injuries common.

Above the Balcony, the greatest risks are oxygen- and exhaustion-related due to pushing too far, leaking oxygen tanks, or frozen masks. Climbers must check their

Yak herders help transport gear on Everest's north side.

masks regularly on the climb for ice buildup on the valves. Being diligent about watching your oxygen level and flow rate can mitigate potential problems. If you are running low on oxygen, it might be necessary to turn the flow rate down or to turn around to avoid running out.

Fixed lines that you will use on summit day can become frayed and damaged. It's prudent to always check the condition of the ropes you are climbing on. Bring 100 feet (30 m) of 8-mm rope to replace bad rope if you need to.

NORTH SIDE

The Northeast Ridge Route is less exposed to avalanches and rockfall than the Khumbu Icefall and Western Cwm. However, there is avalanche potential along the entire route, and Sherpas and Westerners have been swept away and killed on this route. There is nothing comparable to the Icefall, and ladders are rarely needed to cross crevasses. The biggest hazard on the Northeast Ridge is the amount of time spent in the death zone—above 26,000 feet (8000 m)—on summit day.

Much of the danger on the lower part of the route is altitude related. If climbers are aware of their body, conservative in their climbing schedule, and experienced in dealing with altitude illness, there should be few problems. Sickness from food and water can be a problem anytime you travel in Tibet. Take all possible precautions to keep your food safe for cooking, and use hand sanitizer religiously.

Above Advanced Base Camp, the climbing becomes steeper, creating concern for ice- and rockfall. Also, climbers may drop things such as oxygen bottles, water bottles, and sleeping bags, which cascade down the fall line onto other climbers. Be aware and make sure you do not accidentally drop things on others.

Summit day consists of exposed climbing on slabby rocks. If the lines are well fixed, there's not much risk of a serious fall on the long traverses or steep rock steps. Using an ascender is prudent on the longer steep pitches, such as the first, second, and third steps. Check your oxygen mask before the climb and every fifteen minutes during the climb to make sure it's not icing up. Check your flow rate and oxygen levels frequently to make sure the oxygen system is working properly.

Evaluate the ropes on the ascent to make sure they're in good condition. Later in the summit period, ropes can become frayed and may need to be replaced.

KHUMBU CLIMBING CENTER

Climbing Everest, due to its very nature of extreme altitude and severe temperatures, is a dangerous and difficult task. A tremendous amount of food and equipment are required to overcome these challenges. The logistical pyramid of supplies necessary to realize an ascent of Everest is staggering. Climbers have been relying on indigenous people since the earliest expeditions to achieve their Himalayan dreams. The tasks of portering equipment, staffing camps, carrying loads, cooking meals, and guiding are essential to success in Himalayan climbing. On Everest it is the Sherpa, a tribe of people living at the foot of the mountain, who have made this work part of their heritage.

The ascent of Everest in 1953 by Edmund Hillary and Tenzing Norgay is a fine reflection of the skill and ability of Sherpa. Tenzing Norgay was an essential part of the first ascent and solidified the stature of Sherpa in Himalayan climbing. Climbing became a business for these people. The income allowed for a higher standard of living and significantly bettered their education opportunities.

The reputation for strength and reliability that the Sherpa have earned has come at a cost, however. It's a dangerous business. Sherpa, by group or nationality, have suffered the greatest fatality rate among climbers in the Himalaya. Whether as a result of repeated exposure to dangerous conditions or a lack of technical expertise, Sherpa are at greater risk than visiting climbers.

In 2002 my wife, Jenni, and I visited the Khumbu on a trek to Everest. During the early-season trek, we brought along ice gear and rock shoes to get a little climbing in after a day on the trail. Our staff joined in, and by the end of the trip were suggesting outcrops and ice flows where we could practice. Hiking downvalley past Phortse in late April, we looked over to the north side of Humble to see remnants of frozen water ice. When we asked if these form up in the winter, Rinji, who was by now an eager climbing partner, grinned ear to ear.

Climbers who climb for the joy of it and the happiness it brings are more aware and, hence, safer. If you are motivated through avocation, you progress to be a stronger climber. Realizing the passion for recreational climbing our Sherpa friends had and discovering the accessibility of winter water ice, we saw an opportunity to increase the technical climbing knowledge of Sherpa. In January 2004, with the assistance of PaNuru Sherpa and the village of Phortse, six of us shared the joy of water ice climbing with thirty-six Sherpa students. By teaching climbing at the same level of a university outdoor recreation class, we hoped to increase the students' technical skills and, in the process, teach them to become safer climbers.

Over the years, the classes grew to sixty, then eighty, to as many as one hundred students a year, and the program evolved into the Khumbu Climbing Center. Our mission is to increase the safety margin of Nepali climbers and high-altitude workers by encouraging responsible climbing practices in a supportive and community-based program. The curriculum, designed for the needs of a working mountain guide, includes rope work (knots, care, and storage); belay, rappel, and hauling systems; gear inspection and maintenance; mountain topography; first aid; avalanche awareness; and rescue preparedness. English is the common language on Everest expeditions, and to help with communication, English classes are held each morning. The courses last ten days and focus on leadership skills and teamwork. At the end of the course, the students have improved their skills and learned how to integrate into expeditions.

Initially the English, first-aid, earth sciences, and avalanche classes were held in makeshift classrooms: teahouses and the forest. In 2007 the village of Phortse donated land to the Khumbu Climbing Center so we could construct a building to house the program. In collaboration with the Montana State University School of Architecture and local builders, the team designed and built a solar-powered, energy-efficient, earthquake-resistant building. The building now serves as a community center and a hub for guides, and it provides the Khumbu Climbing Center a degree of permanence that instills confidence. You can visit us at www.alexlowe.org.

The interaction of western guides and climbers with their Nepali counterparts has increased the safety margin of mountain workers—which benefits their local communities and, in the big picture, makes Himalayan climbing safer. As the director of the program, I find that the greatest satisfaction comes from helping my Nepali friends transition from vocational to avocational climbers. When one climbs because it is a source of happiness, one is more aware of one's teammates and the environment. At the end of the day, for Nepali and visitors alike, this is the right direction to be heading.

CONRAD ANKER
FOUNDER AND DIRECTOR, KHUMBU CLIMBING CENTER

PLANNING AN EXPEDITION

Planning an Everest expedition is a huge endeavor whether you are climbing independently or with a guide service. I recommend beginning the process as early as possible—several years before the expedition date—to give yourself time to make sure everything is in order before you leave for the mountain and to be fully prepared mentally. The most successful climbers are those most committed to the climb. There is a lot to do to be prepared to be away from home for several months, so the more time you allow yourself, the better.

Training: A strong history of physical fitness, paired with specific intense training of at least several months, is required to be successful on Mount Everest. It's important to be on a climbing-specific training program for a climb of Mount Everest. See "Conditioning" later in this section.

Gear: Having the right gear for the climb and knowing how to use it is essential. Climbers should be very used to their climbing gear before attempting Mount Everest, which means using it on other preparatory climbs beforehand. These climbs may include other Seven Summits such as Denali and Vinson Massif.

Logistics: Logistics and logistics providers are very important. There are no operating standards for logistics companies and guide services in Nepal, so do your homework. Sign on with a logistics company or guide service a year or more before the climb date.

Flights, visas, passports: Flights and visas should be obtained several months or more prior to the expedition date. Check to see if your country of origin has specific requirements for either Nepal or China, depending on whether you plan to climb the south or the north side of the mountain.

Work: Arrangements to take several months off from work often must be made years in advance. Some

The legendary Sherpa of the Khumbu Valley carry impressive loads.

climbers have flexibility in their work schedules, work for themselves, or simply quit their jobs in order to attempt Mount Everest. Is your work situation secure? Are you eligible for paid or unpaid leave?

Bills, will, legal documents: Alert billing companies of your climb several months in advance, or make other arrangements for payment while you're gone. Have a will in place before leaving. Get all other paperwork in place well before the climb.

Family arrangements: Not only is it difficult for climbers and their families to be apart for such a long time, but the inherent danger of the climb can make for a tense situation. As many climbers leave the mountain each year for family reasons—deaths, family pressure, homesickness—as leave for illness or inability to climb. This is a very important aspect of the preparation process.

Make sure your family members are comfortable with your climb before taking any of these other steps.

Finances: Some climbers have enough disposable income to be able to afford a Mount Everest expedition on a whim, but most do not. To afford an expedition costing $30,000 to $100,000 takes some financial planning and saving. Most climbers put money aside for the climb for several years before embarking on the expedition.

LOCAL OUTFITTERS

Most expeditions work with local outfitters for logistics on Mount Everest for either south- or north-side expeditions. These outfitters are really the key to making the whole process run smoothly. Discuss the permit process with your outfitter well in advance of the start date of your expedition, and everything should run smoothly.

Climbers
traversing Everest's
summit ridge

Outfitters also organize and supply climbing Sherpas, food, gear, and oxygen for the climb. They are invaluable and usually quite inexpensive to work with. It would be nearly impossible to organize a Mount Everest expedition without them.

For north-side climbs, all teams must work with either the Chinese Mountaineering Association (CMA) or the Tibetan Mountaineering Association (TMA). These organizations can also supply climbing permits for north-side climbs. If you're climbing the north-side route, either CMA or TMA will supply the liaison officer.

CLIMBING SEASONS AND WEATHER

Climbing on Mount Everest is done in the pre- and post-monsoon seasons, with the vast majority in the premonsoon (April and May). Premonsoon weather is drier but can be very windy, while the postmonsoon season is very snowy, with an increased risk of avalanches. The premonsoon climbing season of the spring, the most popular time to climb the mountain, is bordered by the waning winter season. Winter in the Himalayas is, obviously, quite chilly! Because of this, teams shouldn't plan to start their expeditions at the end of March unless they are trying for a winter ascent. Most climbers look to arrive at base camp around the first week in April. The Tibetan Plateau, site of the north-side route, is a frigid, desolate, and inhospitable place in the winter, and teams should limit exposure to these conditions as much as possible by starting in late March, without pushing into the monsoons. Time spent in base camp in May is actually quite pleasant, with temperatures reaching 70 degrees Fahrenheit (21°C) on sunny days. The monsoons generally arrive by mid-June, so climbers should plan to be off the mountain and back in Katmandu by then.

The monsoons usually last until the end of August, if not the first week in September. It is drier on the Tibetan (north) side of the range, so the monsoons are never too aggressive there, although you can get periods of heavy rain. The Nepal side is very wet during the monsoons, with periods of heavy rain most days. Expeditions doing an autumn climb start the trip to base camp during the last week of August, arriving in base camp the first week of September. As winter approaches, the temperatures drop, and by the first week of October, there can be extremely cold temperatures on the upper reaches of the mountain. Most teams plan to be off the mountain by the middle of October. Any later than this, and the risk of getting frostbite on a summit bid becomes quite high even for very experienced mountaineers.

Mount Everest is affected by several major weather systems from around the region. Monsoons begin to form in the Bay of Bengal in late May and envelop the mountain by mid-June. The monsoon season delivers lots of precipitation and some winds, dissipating by the end of August. The monsoons soak Katmandu with rain and supply Mount Everest with the bulk of the snow it accumulates over the course of the year. Major storms from the Bay of Bengal can affect the mountain outside of monsoon season as well.

Another major influence on Mount Everest weather is the jet stream. The sheer size of Mount Everest and other mountains in the region jutting over 26,000 feet (8000 m) into the air makes them susceptible to these high winds. The jet stream can scour the mountain with winds of 100-plus miles per hour (160 kph), making it impossible to climb. The jet stream can delay climbing sometimes by weeks. The pattern is that the jet stream passes over Mount Everest at some point in both the pre- and postmonsoon seasons.

Cumulus clouds build late in the day due to thermal activity rising up the massive Himalayan walls. These heavy clouds form most afternoons and cause precipitation on the mountain but are usually benign.

Patience concerning weather is a large part of what being successful climbing on Mount Everest is all about!

DOCUMENTS

All teams climbing from Nepal need to obtain a climbing permit, which can be a frustrating process, and have a liaison officer. Just keep in mind that Nepal's Ministry of Tourism, where you obtain the permits for the south-side route, is trying to do its best job for you and that things move a little slower in this part of the world. The ministry will also allocate a liaison officer to you. The climbing permit, which should be secured at least a month before the climb date, is good for seventy-five days. Visas for Nepal can be purchased upon arrival in Katmandu for $100 and Mount Everest climbing permits are roughly $10,000 per climber.

Teams climbing from China must work with either the CMA or the TMA to obtain climbing permits and for logistical support while in China for an all-inclusive price. These mountaineering associations organize transportation, hotels, food, and climbing porters for expeditions climbing from the north. TMA and CMA work with teams of individuals as well as those with guide services. All climbing permits for China should be secured at least a month before the climb date. All teams climbing in China need to obtain Chinese visas. Climbing permits for the Chinese side of Mount Everest are somewhat less expensive than in Nepal but are packaged together with logistics (hotels, food, transport, etc.) by CMA and TMA.

Contact information for the Nepal Ministry of Tourism and the CMA is listed in Resources at the back of this book.

Due to the volatile nature of the Tibetan region of China, it is sometimes closed to foreigners without prior warning. Climbers should expect that the region could end up being closed at any point, especially in the spring. In this case, expeditions may be canceled, and permits to climb and travel visas may not be granted. This closure pertains mainly to flights in and out of Lhasa, Tibet, but can also affect vehicle traffic via the "Friendship Bridge" between Nepal and Tibet.

COSTS

Nepalese currency is the rupee; the exchange rate is about 70 rupees to $1US. Chinese currency is the yuan; the exchange rate is about 7 yuan to $1US.

- Permits: $10,000
- Guide service: $20,000–$100,000
- Visas: $100
- Domestic flight to Lukla, Nepal (round trip): $280
- International flight to Lhasa, Tibet (from Katmandu, Nepal): $300
- Lodging: $500–$1000
- Food: $500–$2000
- Yaks and porters: $500
- Oxygen: $2000–$10,000

CONDITIONING

It goes without saying that you should be in the shape of your life to climb Mount Everest! This is an incredibly demanding climb, even for the strongest high-altitude guides in the world. This mountain cannot be underestimated; it is a very serious and potentially dangerous undertaking. You should consult with your guide service and/or other professional fitness instructors to create a specific plan for the climb. Beyond spending several months at high altitude where your body continually gets weaker, you must be prepared for long, strenuous days at extreme altitude carrying loads of 30–70 pounds (14–32 kg). Summit day can last twelve to eighteen hours with little to eat or drink and maximum output for nearly the entire time. It is common to burn well over 10,000 calories on summit day. If your body cannot meet these demands, getting to the summit will be out of reach.

Day hikes and multiday hikes of long distances at least once a week for ten-plus hours at a stretch are the best way to train for a Mount Everest climb. Beyond this, cardio training at a higher heart rate is important. A routine of five or six days of training per week is necessary. Begin conditioning as early as possible, and continue to ramp up until two weeks before the trip begins, then taper off in order to "peak" your fitness level. Rest several days before leaving for Mount Everest because travel and jet lag can take a toll on the body. Most importantly, don't hurt yourself prior to the climb! A sprained ankle or broken arm can end your trip, and with the time, money, and emotional investment you will have made, this could be disastrous if you haven't bought insurance.

IMMUNIZATIONS

Consult your doctor, local travel clinic, or the Centers for Disease Control and Prevention (CDC) for updated information on immunizations for Nepal and China. Recommended immunizations include diphtheria-tetanus (DPT); polio; measles, mumps, and rubella (MMR); meningitis; hepatitis A and B; cholera and typhoid; and rabies.

Malaria shouldn't be a problem in Katmandu or on the climb. If you plan to travel to lower-elevation areas in Nepal before or after the climb, you should consider malaria chemoprophylaxis.

COMMUNICATIONS

Communications on Mount Everest are very important due to the severity of the climb and difficulty of rescue. Most teams communicate on the mountain with VHF radios on a set frequency and coordinate frequencies with other teams prior to beginning the climb. It's helpful to know other teams' frequencies in case of emergency. Satellite phones serve as the main form of communication with those off the mountain. There is now cell phone service at both north- and south-side base camps.

GETTING THERE AND GETTING AROUND

Most Everest climbers fly into Nepal via Katmandu's Tribhuvan Airport and then take local transport or a taxi into town. Some climbers choose to fly to Beijing, China, before continuing on to Lhasa, Tibet, or Katmandu. Katmandu (4593 ft, 1400 m) is synonymous with Himalayan climbing, and it offers an amazing cultural experience. It's chaotic and certainly not the cleanest city, but it has a lot of character and is an easy place to organize a climbing expedition. Katmandu's proximity to Everest and Lhasa, a wealth of climbing and trekking outfitters, and ease of securing climbing permits and visas make it an obvious transit point. It's easy to organize transport to Everest's north side or to book a flight to Lhasa from Katmandu.

Thamel, the chaotic tourist center of Katmandu, is the antithesis of a peaceful, relaxing trek through the mountains. You can find just about anything you need in Thamel, however, including restaurants, hotels, groceries, climbing gear, photo supplies, and night clubs. I recommend finding lodging someplace other than Thamel for a more enjoyable stay and venturing into Thamel when you need to. There are some excellent hotels in more demure parts of the city not far from the hustle and bustle of Thamel.

Gear shops dot the streets of Thamel with real, fake, and secondhand gear. Generally, fake gear is obvious, but if you're in doubt, just ask the proprietor, and they'll be up-front about the authenticity of the product. Counterfeit climbing equipment could be very dangerous to use! Most of these cheaper shops also carry some new brand-name and plenty of secondhand gear. There are also several new shops in Katmandu that do sell new, real name-brand gear such as Mountain Hard Wear from the United States and Millet from Europe. This gear is the same quality that you'd find overseas.

GETTING TO SOUTH-SIDE BASE CAMP

Unlike the north-side base camp, Everest's south-side base camp must be reached on foot—but it is one of the most impressive hikes in the world. See "Climbing Mount Everest," below.

FLYING TO LUKLA

The trek to Everest base camp usually begins with a domestic flight from Katmandu to Lukla, at 9383 feet (2860 m), although climbers can add several days of trekking by taking a bus to Jiri and beginning the hike there. The domestic terminal is attached to the international terminal at Katmandu's Tribhuvan Airport. Several carriers fly into the Khumbu, including Yeti and Agni Airlines. Flights are roughly $280 round trip. Flights are scheduled to leave all day, but weather is usually too poor for afternoon flights. Flights depart from 6:30 AM onward at regular intervals for the thirty- to forty-minute shuttle.

ELIZABETH HAWLEY

Elizabeth Hawley is an American expatriate, journalist, and chronicler of the Himalayan climbing database. Elizabeth was born in Chicago in 1923 and moved to Nepal in 1960, where she has been since working for *Fortune* magazine. She has also worked for Reuters news agency and *Time* magazine. She has been keeping a detailed, complete, and accurate Himalayan database for the Nepal region for more than four decades. Beyond her work on the database, Elizabeth is a colorful character, a wealth of knowledge on all subjects, and a joy to talk to. If you are planning an expedition to climb in Nepal, you will most likely meet Elizabeth or one of her aides. She is doing the Himalayan climbing community an important service by compiling the information in the database, so please give her a few moments of your time. You can purchase Elizabeth Hawley's database by visiting this website: www.himalayandatabase.com.

GETTING TO NORTH-SIDE BASE CAMP

Most climbers approach Mount Everest base camp on the Tibetan side in one of two ways: via Katmandu, flying to Lhasa and then driving from Lhasa to north-side base camp, or driving from Katmandu to Everest's north-side base camp. Both options take a similar amount of time and allow climbers to acclimatize appropriately en route.

The CMA or TMA will make lodging and dining arrangements for you and your team. The accommodations are usually some of the nicest available, which can vary greatly depending on where you are in Tibet. The smaller towns only have very rustic hotels. CMA and TMA always work with the same people, so climbers are unable to choose where to eat or stay.

FLYING TO LHASA, THEN DRIVING TO NORTH-SIDE BASE CAMP

The flight to Lhasa leaves from the international terminal at Katmandu's Tribhuvan Airport and takes about one and a half hours. The flight traverses south of the Himalayas before turning north, giving an amazing view of Everest, Makalu, and Kangchenjunga. Lhasa sits at 11,450 feet (3490 m), about 7000 feet (2100 m) higher than Katmandu, which will be apparent from the shortness of breath you will experience upon arrival. Most teams spend two or more days in Lhasa acclimatizing before the drive west to Everest's north-side base camp.

DRIVING FROM KATMANDU TO NORTH-SIDE BASE CAMP

Driving from Katmandu allows a gradual altitude gain and less chance for acute mountain sickness but by skipping the flight to Lhasa, climbers miss seeing some important Tibetan cultural landmarks. Also, driving from Katmandu can be delayed due to landslides on the road to the border, especially during the postmonsoon season. However, the road to north-side base camp was completely renovated from 2005 to 2010, cutting driving times in half, and is now much less prone to landslides and road closures.

The Friendship Bridge connects China with Nepal between the border towns of Kodari in Nepal and Zhang Mu in China, marking the point of entry into Tibet for climbers driving from Katmandu. The total drive from Katmandu to Everest base camp takes only ten hours but gains 13,000 feet (3960 m) of altitude, forcing teams to acclimatize along the way. Most climbers take at least seven days to make the trip in order to properly acclimatize.

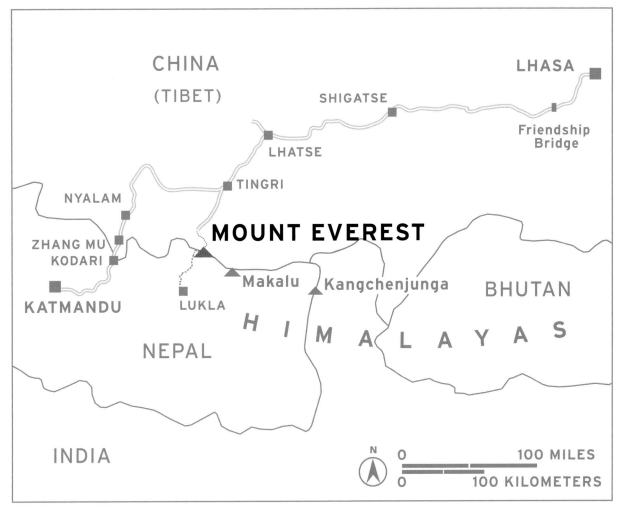

Mount Everest environs

GATEWAY SETTLEMENTS

Small villages en route to Everest are Nepalese on the south side and Tibetan on the north side.

SOUTH SIDE

Lukla is a large town, by Khumbu Valley standards, that sits at the mouth of the valley. Lukla has one of the shortest, steepest, scariest runways in the world—but this amenity provides access for climbers from around the world. Lukla is a mountain town with hotels, restaurants, a post office, and a hospital.

NORTH SIDE

If you fly to Lhasa and drive to the north-side base camp, Lhasa will be the largest town you encounter before base camp. To acclimatize in Lhasa, many climbers sightsee important Tibetan cultural landmarks, such as the Potala Palace (where the Dalai Lama grew up) and the Johkang Temple. It's amazing to experience these revered holy sites that hold an important place in the spiritual lives of Tibetan Buddhists.

If you drive to Everest base camp from Katmandu or Lhasa, you will likely pass through Tingri, at 14,268 feet

SAMPLE RESOURCES: SOUTH RIDGE EXPEDITION 2010

- 85 people total (climbers, guides, cooks, base camp manager, and liaison officers)
- 32 non-Sherpa climbers
- 42 climbing Sherpas
- 12 cooks
- 40,000 pounds (18,000 kg) total of gear, food, fuel, and oxygen
- 600 porter loads to base camp
- 230 bottles of oxygen
- 45 oxygen masks

- 50 regulators
- 4500+ eggs
- 1600 quarts (liters) of kerosene
- 35 cylinders of propane
- 200 canisters of epigas
- 94 tents total (base camp tents and climbing tents)

Data supplied by International Mountain Guides and Ang Jangbu Sherpa, co-owner of Beyul Adventures.

(4348 m), the last Tibetan settlement on the way to Everest's north-side base camp. Tingri sits high on the Tibetan Plateau between Thong La Pass and Pang La Pass. Its services are minimal.

OTHER ACTIVITIES: TREKKING AND WILDLIFE VIEWING

Other popular treks in the Nepalese Himalayas include Annapurna Base and the Annapurna Circuit, both from the bustling city of Pokhara. In southern Nepal, on the border with India, wildlife safaris into Royal Chitwan National Park might include sightings of tigers and rhinoceroses.

CLIMBING MOUNT EVEREST

Mount Everest is the crowning jewel of the Seven Summits. It is widely regarded as the most challenging of the seven and would be a remarkable addition to any climber's resumé. To stand on top of the world is universally recognized as a timeless achievement.

The two main climbing routes on Mount Everest encompass more than 90 percent of all ascents of the peak. The southern route through Nepal, also known as the South Ridge, consists of trekking up the famous Khumbu Valley and surmounting the Khumbu Icefall en

route to the top. The northern route, commonly known as the Northeast Ridge, takes climbers through China up the Rongbuk Valley past Changtse toward the summit. The northern route consists mainly of ridge and face climbing on fixed lines and is often less crowded, whereas the southern route climbs through an icefall and broad valley with some face and ridge climbing toward the summit.

Both routes are technically and physically demanding and consist mainly of moderate to steep fixed-line climbing. The South Ridge Route is considered to have more objective hazard due to the time spent in the perilous Khumbu Glacier exposed to avalanches from Nuptse and the west shoulder. However, summit day

GUIDE TIP

The mountain is more active and dangerous later in the day when the sun begins to melt ice and snow, making rock- and icefall much more common. For safety, travel early in the day (before the sun hits) when it's cold. It's also unbearably hot once the sun hits. The body performs much worse in the heat.

Chilies being sold
at the famous
Namche Bazaar

on the South Ridge is considered somewhat easier and safer. Both routes generally require fifty to seventy days to climb, with a month of this time spent at or above base camp.

ROUTES

There are major differences between climbing Mount Everest from the south side as opposed to the north side, and it's important for climbers to understand what these differences are before deciding which side to climb. The variation in routes includes logistics, politics, safety, and the social atmosphere of the climb, among other factors. One of the things to consider is how much time the route requires a climber to be in the death zone (above 26,000 ft, 8000 m). The "death zone" is a term used for this extreme environment where most climbers need supplemental oxygen, the body gets rapidly weaker, and rescues are extremely difficult.

> ## GUIDE TIP
>
> If you have a headache or feel light-headed from the altitude, you need to spend more time at your current altitude before ascending. If you don't, you risk more serious altitude sickness, which could potentially end your trip. Be careful and take it slow!

SOUTH RIDGE ROUTE FROM NEPAL

The South Ridge Route consists of more technical climbing and greater exposure to objective hazards both in the icefall and on the upper route. Summit day on the South Ridge is considered safer due to less traversing and less time spent in the death zone. It is easier to descend to lower altitudes in the Khumbu Valley in case of a rescue than it is on the high Tibetan Plateau. A nonambulatory climber needing a rescue on summit day has a better chance of survival on the south side because, below the south summit, it's possible to drag someone down the fall line on snow. A critical safety aspect is helicopters.

Modern helicopters can fly patients out of base camp or higher on the Nepal side. The shorter rescue time on the south side is critical in emergency situations.

Teams on the south side tend to be more cohesive, cooperative, and social with each other. Most reputable and tenured guide services operate exclusively on the south side because they have longstanding relationships with outfitters and climbing Sherpas there. These relationships are important in running a smooth expedition.

NORTHEAST RIDGE ROUTE FROM TIBET, CHINA

Rescues on summit day on the Northeast Ridge are extremely difficult due to the combination of altitude and traversing on rocky, stepped terrain. Climbers on the north side are dependent upon human power, yaks, and then four-wheel-drive to reach modern medical care as there are no helicopters. From the north, a long drive either to Katmandu or Lhasa is needed to reach definitive care.

Climbing from China is cheaper, especially for those climbing independently and without Sherpa support. However, on several occasions, China has decided to shut down Tibet to climbing, forcing expeditions to cancel or move to the south side at the last minute.

ACCLIMATIZATION

Climbers attempting to ascend Mount Everest almost always underestimate how much time is spent waiting and resting while acclimatizing. Most Everest climbers are goal-oriented type-A personalities who have become successful by not sitting around being lazy, but often, to be successful on Mount Everest, resting is the single most important thing you can do. The reason the climb takes so long is because of the lengthy acclimatization process.

If climbers were dropped out of a helicopter onto the summit of Mount Everest, even with oxygen, they would die almost instantly, but fully acclimatized climbers can survive! The human body goes through physiological changes when we go to altitude, such as producing more oxygen-carrying red blood cells to combat the effects of

South and Northeast Ridge Routes on Mount Everest

the rarefied air at altitude. Climbing to moderate altitudes like those found on Mount Kilimanjaro in Africa and on Mount Rainier in the United States takes only a little time to acclimatize, but extreme altitudes like those found on Mount Everest take a month or more to acclimate to. Every year climbers rush the acclimatization process and push too hard when they should be resting, and it costs them a successful climb.

Once you are at base camp, for every day spent climbing there is usually a day spent resting, acclimatizing, or recovering from an acclimatization rotation up the mountain. Teams spend two weeks trekking to the south-side base camp in order to acclimatize properly and then make several successively higher rotations up the mountain while climbing with rests in between for the same reason.

WATER, SANITATION, AND GARBAGE

Mount Everest has acquired a reputation for being a dirty mountain, but this is unfounded, especially in recent years when cleanup efforts have intensified and several environmental expeditions have made it their mission to clean up the mountain. Over the years, some trash has accumulated on the flanks of the mountain, most notably at the South Col on the South Ridge Route, but most of this has been removed.

The Nepal government created the Sagarmatha Pollution Control Committee (SPCC) to monitor waste and sanitation issues on the mountain, and this effort has been quite effective. All teams are required to advance a garbage deposit for south-side Mount Everest climbs. This fee is $4000 regardless of whether the permit is full or not.

Beyond collecting garbage deposits and monitoring trash, SPCC offers a set amount of money for all trash and oxygen bottles that are brought off Mount Everest. As trash melts out of the route, it's usually Sherpas who take up the task of collecting this payment, and this has served to clean the mountain substantially over the last few decades. All human waste and trash must be accounted for before you receive your garbage deposit back at the end of the trip.

If teams use common sense at base camp and on the mountain, sanitation is rarely an issue. The most important way to keep teams healthy is to make sure cooks prepare food with high hygiene standards. It's important not to collect drinking water near toilet zones both at base camp and on the mountain and to make sure toilets cannot affect water collection areas. Collect snow and ice for water melt away from camp.

Most teams now use bio-bags (wag-bags) or trash bags, which facilitate easy removal of human waste from the mountain. All garbage from the mountain must be collected and disposed of properly in the lower valleys. Teams hire local porters to collect and move human waste and garbage from base camp.

SAMPLE CLIMBING ITINERARY: MOUNT EVEREST'S NORTHEAST RIDGE ROUTE

Day	Location	Start Elevation	End Elevation	Elevation Gain	Distance
1	Fly from home				
2	In transit to Katmandu				
3	Arrive in Katmandu		4593 ft (1400 m)		
4	Obtain permit from ministry				
5	Extra day in Katmandu				
6	Fly to Lukla	4593 ft (1400 m)	9383 ft (2860 m)	4790 ft (1460 m)	60 miles (96 km)
	Trek to Phakding	8497 ft (2590 m)	8563 ft (2610 m)	63 ft (20 m)	4 miles (6.5 km)
7	Trek to Namche Bazaar	8563 ft (2610 m)	11,457 ft (3492 m)	2894 ft (882 m)	8 miles (13 km)
8	Short acclimazation hike				
9	Rest day				
10	Trek to Deboche	11,457 ft (3492 m)	12,467 ft (3800 m)	1010 ft (308 m)	10 miles (16 km)
11	Acclimatization hike to Tengboche	12,467 ft (3800 m)	12,716 ft (3876 m)	250 ft (76 m)	
12	Trek to Pheriche	12,467 ft (3800 m)	14,271 ft (4350 m)	1804 ft (550 m)	10 miles (16 km)
13	Acclimatization hike above town				
14	Trek to Lobuche	14,271 ft (4350 m)	16,089 ft (4904 m)	1818 ft (554 m)	7 miles (11 km)
15	Rest day				
16	Trek to Gorak Shep	16,089 ft (4900 m)	16,929 ft (5160 m)	840 ft (256 m)	6 miles (10 km)
17	Acclimatization climb of Kala Patthar	16,929 ft (5160 m)	18,208 ft (5550 m)	1279 ft (390 m)	2 miles (3 km)
	Trek to base camp	16,929 ft (5160 m)	17,477 ft (5327 m)	548 ft (167 m)	5 miles (8 km)
18	Rest day				
19	Acclimatization hike to Pumo Ri Camp 1	17,477 ft (5327 m)	19,290 ft (5880 m)	1813 ft (553 m)	3 miles (5 km)
20	Rest day				
21	Climb to icefall and back to base camp	17,477 ft (5327 m)	18,307 ft (5580 m)	830 ft (253 m)	3 miles (5 km)

Day	Location	Start Elevation	End Elevation	Elevation Gain	Distance
22	Rest day				
23	Climb to Camp 1	17,477 ft (5327 m)	19,390 ft (5910 m)	1913 ft (583 m)	3.75 miles (6 km)
24	Acclimatization hike toward Camp 2; sleep at Camp 1	19,390 ft (5910 m)	19,390 ft (5910 m)		
25	Climb to Camp 2	19,439 ft (5910 m)	21,998 ft (6705 m)	2608 ft (795 m)	3 miles (5 km)
26	Rest day				
27	Acclimatization climb to Lhotse Face; sleep at Camp 2	21,998 ft (6705 m)	21,998 ft (6705 m)		
28	Descend to base camp	21,998 ft (6705 m)	17,477 ft (5327 m)	−4521 ft (−1378 m)	6.75 miles (11 km)
29	Rest day				
30	Rest day				
31	Rest day				
32	Rest day				
33	Climb to Camp 1	17,477 ft (5327 m)	19,390 ft (5910 m)	1913 ft (583 m)	3.75 miles (6 km)
34	Climb to Camp 2	19,390 ft (5910 m)	21,998 ft (6705 m)	2608 ft (795 m)	3 miles (5 km)
35	Rest day				
36	Climb to Camp 3	21,998 ft (6705 m)	24,015 ft (7320 m)	2017 ft (615 m)	1.6 miles (2.5 km)
37	Descend to Camp 2	24,015 ft (7320 m)	21,998 ft (6705 m)	−2017 ft (−615 m)	1.6 miles (2.5 km)
38	Descend to base camp	21,998 ft (6705 m)	17,477 ft (5327 m)	−4521 ft (−1378 m)	6.75 miles (11 km)
39	Rest day				
40	Rest day				
41	Rest day				
42	Rest day				
43	Rest day				
44	Climb to Camp 2	17,477 ft (5327 m)	21,998 ft (6705 m)	4521 ft (1378 m)	6.75 miles (11 km)
45	Rest day				
46	Climb to Camp 3	21,998 ft (6705 m)	24,015 ft (7320 m)	2017 ft (615 m)	1.6 miles (2.5 km)
47	Climb to Camp 4 (South Col)	24,015 ft (7320 m)	26,000 ft (7925 m)	1985 ft (630 m)	1.2 miles (2 km)
48	Climb to summit	26,000 ft (7925 m)	29,035 ft (8850 m)	3035 ft (925 m)	3 miles (5 km)
49	Descend to Camp 4 (South Col)	29,035 ft (8850 m)	26,000 ft (7925 m)	−3035 ft (−925 m)	3 miles (5 km)
50	Descend to base camp	21,998 ft (6705 m)	17,477 ft (5327 m)	−4521 ft (−1378 m)	6.75 miles (11 km)
51	Trek to Pheriche	17,477 ft (5327 m)	14,271 ft (4350 m)	−3206 ft (−977 m)	12 miles (19 km)
52	Trek to Namche Bazaar	14,271 ft (4350 m)	11,457 ft (3492 m)	−2814 ft (−858 m)	20 miles (32 km)
53	Trek to Lukla	11,457 ft (3492 m)	8497 ft (2590 m)	−2960 ft (−902 m)	12 miles (19 km)
54	Fly to Katmandu	8497 ft (2590 m)	4592 ft (1400 m)	−3905 ft (−1190 m)	60 miles (96 km)
55	Sightsee in Katmandu				
56	Fly home				

The Puja ceremony marks the start of an Everest expedition.

THE CLIMB: SOUTH RIDGE ROUTE FROM NEPAL

Trekkers and climbers from all over the world flock to the Khumbu Valley to experience the Himalayas. These mountains provide some of the most awe-inspiring vistas imaginable. Here, trekkers are in the heart of the Himalayan range's highest mountains. The Everest base camp trek is the most popular one in Nepal, which provides its only drawback: it's busy in high season. However, most climbers find this social atmosphere enjoyable.

Base camp lies on a scree-covered section of the Khumbu Glacier at the toe of the Khumbu Icefall. The location of base camp is quite safe, although you will

GUIDE TIP

The Khumbu Icefall is a dynamic and dangerous place. The key to staying safe climbing through the icefall is moving quickly. The more time you spend in the icefall, the more you expose yourself to shifting blocks of ice and avalanches off the west shoulder of Mount Everest. Acclimatize with hikes to Kala Patthar and Pumo Ri Camp 1, and consider a climb of Lobuche before traveling through the icefall. This will allow you to move faster and be safer.

regularly hear large ice- and rockfalls tumbling off nearby Nuptse, Lingtren, Pumo Ri, and Lho La ("Pass"). A few times each season, the base camp gets dusted by avalanche debris off Lho La. There are good opportunities for rest-day ice climbing and artifact hunting on the exposed glacier just outside of base camp.

The south side of Mount Everest offers varied and challenging climbing. Unlike the Northeast Ridge Route, where the climbing doesn't start until about 22,000 feet (6700 m), the South Ridge Route begins climbing immediately out of base camp in the Khumbu Icefall. The icefall is a daunting formation that can be dangerous.

TREK FROM LUKLA TO SOUTH-SIDE BASE CAMP (KHUMBU VALLEY)

From Lukla, most climbers take ten to fourteen days to walk the 50 miles (80 km) to Everest's south-side base camp. Base camp sits about 13,000 feet (3930 m) above Katmandu, making it important to trek in slowly, allowing your body time to acclimatize properly. The trek in to base camp ascends steep river valleys through several ecological zones among some of the most breathtakingly high mountains on Earth.

From Lukla the trek winds north along the east bank of the Dudh Kosi River to Phakding, where you cross the river. A mile or so below Jorsale the path crosses the river again, then enters Sagarmatha National Park at Jorsale. The path crosses the river three more times before the steep climb into Namche Bazaar. Namche, the second largest town on the trek to base camp (Lukla is larger), is the commercial and cultural heart of the Khumbu Valley. The weekly bazaar, or market, is a trading destination for people on both sides of the Himalayan range. Namche consists of houses and hotels extending up the hillsides in a glacial cirque.

A popular acclimatization hike above Namche ascends a steep, rock-covered trail directly above the town to a landing strip and past several rustic homes en route to the Everest View Hotel, which offers an incredible view of Everest, Lhotse, and Ama Dablam. This hike takes

> ## GUIDE TIP
> Often the first night climbers spend at Camps 2 and 3 are rough and they get little sleep because their body is struggling to adjust to the altitude and is plagued by Cheyne-Stokes breathing—rapid breathing common at extreme altitudes. If this happens to you, consider taking 125 mg or less of Diamox to mitigate these symptoms. It usually aids sleep and helps climbers get more rest than they would otherwise.

only a few hours round trip but gains almost 1000 feet (300 m) of altitude. A side trip to the town of Khumjung can be added onto this hike.

From Namche the path heads northeast, up the Imja Khola river valley, with occasional sections of stone steps. You'll pass through Tengboche, Deboche, and Pangboche; an acclimatizing hike to the monastery at Tengboche is a good way to spend a day in this valley. At Pheriche Pass the trail leaves the Imja Khola and heads north again, along the Lobuche Khola river, crossing another pass before dropping into Lobuche.

After climbing Lobuche Pass the path drops into Gorak Shep. A great way to acclimatize on the way into base camp is climbing Kala Patthar, a small peak directly above Gorak Shep with amazing views of Everest and Nuptse. The climb up Kala Patthar (Nepali for "Black Rock"), ascends one of the two obvious trails up the open slope directly opposite Gorak Shep, across a low-lying area of what looks like beach sand. The "summit" of Kala Patthar is just a high point on the south ridge of Sample Climbing Itinerary: Mount Everest's South Ridge Route of Pumo Ri. The climb rises 1500 feet (460 m) and takes two to three hours round trip, leaving enough time to trek into base camp the same day.

I describe a conservative trekking schedule in the sample climbing itinerary for Everest's South Ridge

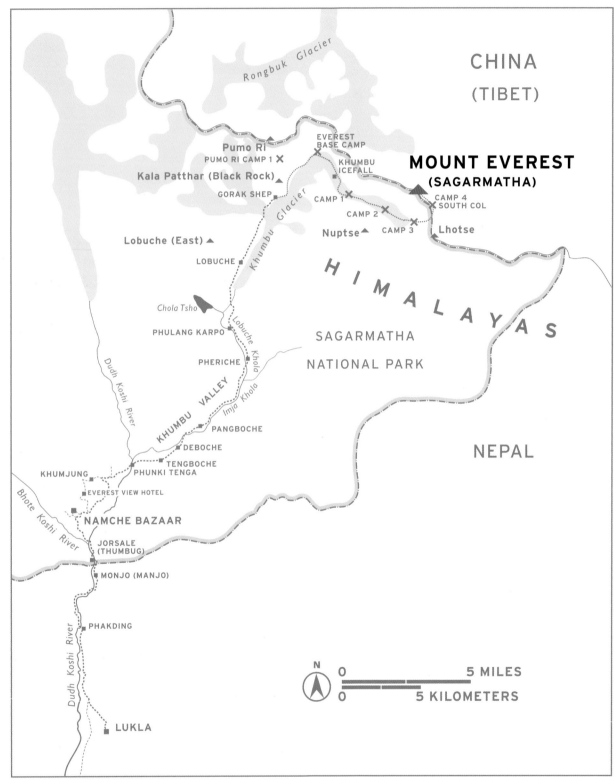

Trek to south-side base camp

Route. This schedule, which is used by most of the larger commercial climbing expeditions, can of course be customized.

SOUTH-SIDE BASE CAMP TO CAMP 1

Beyond base camp, formations of ice that force the route up and down and back and forth, will slow your progress toward the gut of the icefall. After an hour, you begin to climb over loose blocks of ice and steeper pitches of ice on fixed lines. The route steepens in the heart of the Khumbu Icefall, necessitating horizontal and vertical ladders. This section is known as the Popcorn because it's so jumbled. Great towers of ice loom overhead, and you will undoubtedly hear the glacier moving and shifting and ice blocks settling, which will remind you that this area is not very safe. Keep moving!

ICEFALL DOCTORS

The "icefall doctors" are a team of local Sherpas hired each year by the Nepal Ministry of Tourism on behalf of climbing expeditions to create and maintain the route through the Khumbu Icefall as far as Camp 2. They start their work a few weeks before the climbing season begins, usually the first of April, to have the route open by the time climbers start to arrive at base camp. They work tirelessly throughout the entire season to make sure the route is in good condition. After establishing the route, they continue to maintain the route on nearly a daily basis, fixing collapses and melting anchors. The team started as a father-and-son pair but has expanded over the last decade to six or eight "doctors" on any given year. They are paid through permit fees from each climbing team and rely on information from the climbing teams to know when they are needed in the icefall.

GUIDE TIP

Review the summit checklist provided and make sure that every detail of your summit kit has been double- and triple-checked. It's often the small things that prevent climbers from being successful on summit day. Problems such as oxygen system failure, frozen eyes, cold hands or feet, or equipment failure can be catastrophic on summit day.

After two to four hours, climbers reach the Football Field, a flatter, somewhat safer section of glacier. This is the best option for taking a break in the icefall before moving into another jumble of ice blocks called the Upper Popcorn. From the Football Field, it takes two to three hours to exit the Khumbu Icefall and enter the flatter Western Cwm, or valley. From the start of the cwm, climbing is faster; an hour of climbing brings you to Camp 1.

Camp 1 sits at 19,390 feet (5910 m) in the middle of the Western Cwm. Massive, snow-filled crevasses surround the camp on most years. Looking west out of the cwm you'll see the perfectly shaped Pumo Ri drenched in sunlight, and farther up the valley the Lhotse Face offers you a glimpse of the climbing to come. Avalanches, mainly off the West Ridge of Everest, are common in the Western Cwm but rarely affect camps.

CAMP 1 TO CAMP 2

The route from Camp 1 to Camp 2 swings south, close to the base of Nuptse, before swinging back north to the middle of the cwm after several ladder crossings. The gradual ascent takes from two to four hours. Camp 2, which lies at the head of the Western Cwm at the base of the southwest gully on scree, is well provisioned; it is considered to be Advanced Base Camp. Climbers spend as many as ten nights here over the course of several acclimatization rotations prior to the summit bid.

South Ridge Route: base camp to South Col

CAMP 2 TO CAMP 3 (LHOTSE FACE)

The route above Camp 2 consists of gradual glacier walking with minimal obstacles for an hour or two to the base of the Lhotse Face. Climbing the bergschrund at the base of the Lhotse Face can be tricky on drier years. The Lhotse Face averages 40 degrees, with some steeper ice steps.

There are two Camp 3s: an upper and a lower about 500 vertical feet (150 m) apart. Upper Camp 3 offers better acclimatization and makes for a shorter trip to the South Col on the summit rotation, and lower Camp 3 shortens the rigorous day from Camp 2 to Camp 3 and allows a better night's sleep on the Lhotse Face.

CAMP 3 TO THE SOUTH COL (CAMP 4)

Above Camp 3 the route continues up steady terrain directly for 500 vertical feet (150 m) before angling north and traversing toward a feature known as the Yellow Band. Climb the Yellow Band, a short, steep pitch of limestone, and awkwardly crampon up the rock above before getting back on snow. From the top of the Yellow Band, the snow slope angles off and traverses north to a stratified rock-ledge system that is part of the Geneva Spur. Follow fixed lines for half an hour and 300 vertical feet (90 m) on this walkway before climbing a steep pitch of stepped rock 200 feet (60 m) tall and cresting the Geneva Spur. Once on top of the Geneva Spur, follow a relatively flat ledge system for another half hour to the South Col.

The South Col is a broad, flat expanse of scree and ice with room for literally hundreds of tents. Even in the best of weather, this is a miserable place to be. Hypoxia affects everyone, and persistent wind and snow make the experience even worse. Most of the route to the South Summit can be seen from the South Col.

SOUTH COL TO THE SUMMIT

Climbers leave for the summit between 10:00 PM and 2:00 AM, depending on weather conditions and crowds. This means that once you have organized your gear and had a bite to eat, you'll have only a few hours of rest before departing for the top of the world. If you leave too early, it'll be dark and very cold at the summit, and the summit photos won't be as spectacular. The sun rises

around 4:45 AM, so plan your departure time accordingly. Climbers average eight to eleven hours to the summit and about half that back to camp at the South Col, making for twelve to eighteen hours of extreme exertion.

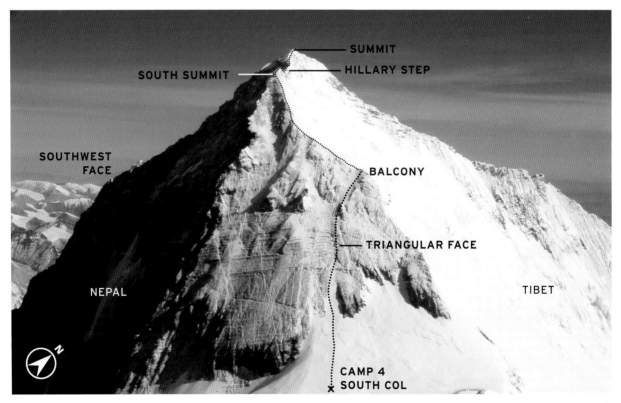

South Ridge Route: South Col to summit (Photo by Greg Vernovage)

The route from the South Col to the summit crosses a broad plateau before ascending the Triangular Face to the Balcony. This stretch consists of 40-degree snow with intermittent rock steps. Beware of rockfall, especially on low snowfall years.

The Balcony is a small snow bench sitting at about 27,500 feet (8380 m) three to four hours above the South Col. Hillary and Tenzing put in a higher camp here, as did many of the early climbing teams, to allow them a shorter summit day and more time to climb in the warmth of the sunlight. This camp is rarely used anymore. The Balcony makes a perfect staging area for changing oxygen bottles and taking a rest before heading up the steeper and more technical climbing above.

Follow the obvious snowy ridge to climbers' left (west) of the Balcony on mellow terrain for half an hour before beginning the steep ascent to the South Summit. The route traverses north before climbing a steep rock and snow pitch on fixed lines, culminating in a few awkward rock moves to the anchor. This is one of the steepest and most arduous pitches of the whole climb. Always check the anchors and the quality of the rope when you reach the top and before rappeling back down this pitch. The rope gets frayed from rubbing on the rocks at the top, and with several climbers weighting this rope at once, it could get dangerous. Replace or fix the rope if necessary.

> ## GUIDE TIP
>
> Check your regulator and the threads on the oxygen bottle before you use them to make sure no dirt or ice is trapped in the threads. Obstructions can cause the regulator to misthread and the oxygen to leak out. I have seen this happen several times, and on most occasions it means an end to the climber's summit bid. Double- and triple-check everything in all your gear!

> ## GUIDE TIP
>
> Use the buddy system to check your oxygen-tank level and your oxygen mask. With your bottle on your back, it's difficult to check your own flow rate and amount of oxygen left. Also, oxygen masks have a tendency to ice up from the moisture from your exhalations as well as that in the ambient air. Have your climbing partner or a Sherpa check your tank and mask for you to make sure there are no mistakes.

Above this almost vertical pitch, the route continues to climb steeply for another hour before cresting the South Summit. At this small flat area, teams will often grab an energy snack and a shot of water before continuing on.

Beyond the South Summit the route drops 20 vertical feet (6 m) and then continues across the obvious cornice traverse, gradually gaining altitude while winding its way around small rock steps. This ridge climb can be quite easy and spacious when the ridge is covered in snow, but in drier years it's very rocky, awkward, and difficult to pass other climbers. From the South Summit to the Hillary Step takes climbers anywhere from one to two hours, depending upon traffic and the condition of the ridge. Congestion is worst at the Hillary Step. This 30-foot (9-m) rock step consists of a short, near-vertical rock pitch followed by a rock move across to a short ledge traverse before ascending the snow on the other side. On snowy years the step might be all snow, and you can ascend directly up to the top without traversing.

From the top of the Hillary Step it's another twenty minutes to the summit. The summit is large enough for ten to twenty climbers to rest just below the true summit.

DESCENT

After the exhilaration of summiting has worn off, you'll be physically exhausted on the descent. Take care while

The South Ridge Route's mighty Lhotse Face

descending and look out for others. Climbers typically descend to the South Col on summit day, to Camp 2 the next day, and to base camp the following day.

The South Col is not a restful place even while you're sleeping on oxygen. Camp 2 is a much safer option, and your body will recover better at a lower altitude. That said, if you are physically pushed to the max, don't risk making a mistake on the Lhotse Face. Spend another night at the Col and descend to Camp 2 in the morning after you've had a chance to rest on oxygen and get some food and water into your system.

From base camp, you'll likely be able to trek out in three or four days to Lukla because you'll be acclimated and going downhill.

TENGBOCHE MONASTERY

This place, the Tengboche valley,
As if descended from the realm of Gods,
The people of the world rush to come and see it.
Encircled by Snow Mountains, open pastures and great forests,
Deer abound in this place, which resounds fresh and peaceful.
Flowing rivers swirl gently by,
Pure water endowed with eight great qualities.
Here the auspiciousness of natural goodness is supreme.
—Ngawang Tenzin Jangpo, Tengboche Rinpoche

More than 350 years ago, Lama Sangwa Dorje brought Buddhism to the Khumbu Valley and established the first monastery in Pangboche. It wasn't until 1916 that a monastery was built in Tengboche by Chatang Chotar, also known as Lama Gulu, as a place monks could follow the Nyingmapa version of Vajrayana Buddhism. It took three years to complete the construction of this now famous structure. The Tengboche Monastery has strong ties with the Rongbuk Monastery on the north side of Mount Everest at the foot of the Rongbuk Glacier. It's rumored that the monks used to travel back and forth over the high mountain passes regularly to exchange information, but due to glacial recession that is now impossible.

The Tengboche Monastery is the center of Buddhist life and education in the Khumbu Valley, hosting as many as fifty lamas at one time. The two high lamas of the Khumbu Valley are at Tengboche and Upper Pangboche. It's possible to tour the monastery at certain times of the day. Taking photos may or may not be acceptable: ask.

In 1989, a fire caused by a heater destroyed the original monastery. The current monastery was erected with the help of many locals, Sir Edmund Hillary, and others who donated time and money to the project. The new building sits on the same plot of land as the last but is made of rock rather than wood to minimize the chance of another catastrophic fire. A team of painters led by master painter Thake-La worked for more than two years to complete the colorful artwork that fills the main prayer hall. The current Rinpoche, or high lama, Ngawang Tenzin Jangpo, was born in 1935 in Namche Bazaar the same day the Dalai Lama was born. Tengboche monks congregate each day for meditation and prayers, usually starting at 6:00 AM and 4:00 PM, and tourists are welcome to view these ceremonies.

SAMPLE CLIMBING ITINERARY: MOUNT EVEREST'S NORTHEAST RIDGE ROUTE

Day	Location	Start Elevation	End Elevation	Elevation Gain	Distance
1	Fly from home				
2	In transit to Katmandu				
3	Arrive in Katmandu		4593 ft (1400 m)		
4	Obtain Chinese visas				
5	Sightsee in Katmandu				
6	Fly to Lhasa	4593 ft (1400 m)	11,450 ft (3490 m)	6858 ft (2090 m)	375 miles (600 km)
Alternate	Drive to Kodari; enter China	4593 ft (1400 m)	7500 ft (2286 m)	2908 ft (886 m)	120 miles (195 km)
7	Sightsee in Lhasa				
Alternate	Drive to Nayalam	7500 ft (2286 m)	12,460 ft (3799 m)	4960 ft (1513 m)	65 miles (105 km)
8	Drive to Shigatse	11,450 ft (3490 m)	12,600 ft (3840 m)	1150 ft (350 m)	175 miles (280 km)
Alternate	Acclimatization day				
9	Acclimatization day				
Alternate	Drive to Tingri	12,460 ft (3799 m)	14,400 ft (4389 m)	1940 ft (590 m)	161 miles (260 km)
10	Drive to Tingri	12,600 ft (3840 m)	14,400 ft (4389 m)	1800 ft (549 m)	180 miles (292 km)
Alternate	Acclimatization day				
11	Acclimatization day				
12	Rest day				
13	Drive to Everest base camp	14,400 ft (4389 m)	17,590 ft (5361 m)	3190 ft (972 m)	25 miles (40 km)
14	Acclimatization day				
15	Acclimatization day				
16	Rest day				
17	Climb to Camp 2 (Intermediate Camp)	17,590 ft (5361 m)	20,300 ft (6187 m)	2710 ft (826 m)	9 miles (15 km)
18	Rest day				
19	Acclimatization hike above Camp 2 (Intermediate Camp)				
20	Climb to Camp 3 (Advanced Base Camp)	20,300 ft (6187 m)	21,300 ft (6492 m)	1000 ft (305 m)	9 miles (15 km)
21	Rest day				
22	Acclimatization hike above Camp 3				
23	Climb toward North Col; descend to Camp 3	21,300 ft (6492 m)	22,300 ft (6797 m)	1000 ft (305 m)	3.75 miles (6 km)
24	Rest day				
25	Rest day				

Day	Location	Start Elevation	End Elevation	Elevation Gain	Distance
26	Ascend to North Col (Camp 4)	21,300 ft (6492 m)	23,000 ft (7010 m)	1700 ft (518 m)	2.5 miles (4 km)
27	Rest day				
28	Climb toward Camp 5; descend to North Col (Camp 4)	23,000 ft (7010 m)	24,000 ft (7315 m)	1000 ft (305 m)	1.25 mile (2 km)
29	Descend to Camp 3 (ABC)	23,000 ft (7010 m)	21,300 ft (6492 m)	−1700 ft (−518 m)	2.5 miles (4 km)
30	Rest day				
31	Rest day				
32	Rest day				
33	Climb to Camp 4 (North Col)	21,300 ft (6492 m)	23,000 ft (7010 m)	1700 ft (518 m)	2.5 miles (4 km)
34	Rest day				
35	Ascend to Camp 5	23,000 ft (7010 m)	24,600 ft (7498 m)	1600 ft (488 m)	0.6 mile (1 km)
36	Climb above Camp 5; descend to North Col (Camp 4)	24,600 ft (7498 m)	23,000 ft (7010 m)	−1600 ft (−488 m)	0.6 mile (1 km)
37	Descend to Camp 3 (ABC)	23,000 ft (7010 m)	21,300 ft (6492 m)	−1700 ft (−518 m)	2.5 miles (4 km)
38	Descend to base camp	21,300 ft (6492 m)	17,590 ft (5361 m)	−3710 ft (−1131 m)	18 miles (30 km)
39	Rest day				
40	Rest day				
41	Rest day				
42	Rest day				
43	Rest day				
44	Climb to Camp 3 (ABC)	17,590 ft (5361 m)	21,300 ft (6492 m)	3710 ft (1131 m)	18 miles (30 km)
45	Rest day				
46	Climb to Camp 4 (North Col)	21,300 ft (6492 m)	23,000 ft (7010 m)	1700 ft (518 m)	2.5 miles (4 km)
47	Climb to Camp 5	23,000 ft (7010 m)	24,600 ft (7498 m)	1600 ft (488 m)	0.6 mile (1 km)
48	Climb to Camp 6 (High Camp)	24,600 ft (7498 m)	27,230 ft (8300 m)	2630 ft (802 m)	0.6 mile (1 km)
49	Climb to summit	27,230 ft (8300 m)	29,035 ft (8850 m)	1805 ft (550 m)	1 mile (1.5 km)
	Descend to Camp 4 (North Col)	29,035 ft (8850 m)	23,000 ft (7010 m)	−6035 ft (−1840 m)	2.25 miles (3.6 km)
50	Descend to Camp 3 (ABC)	23,000 ft (7010 m)	21,300 ft (6492 m)	−1700 ft (−518 m)	2.5 miles (4 km)
51	Descend to base camp	21,300 ft (6492 m)	17,590 ft (5361 m)	−3710 ft (−1131 m)	18 miles (30 km)
52	Rest day				
53	Pack up				
54	Drive to Nayalam	17,590 ft (5361 m)	12,460 ft (3799 m)	−5130 ft (−1562 m)	175 miles (280 km)
55	Drive to Katmandu	12,460 ft (3799 m)	4593 ft (1400 m)	−7868 ft (−2399 m)	186 miles (300 km)
56	Sightsee in Katmandu				
57	Fly home				

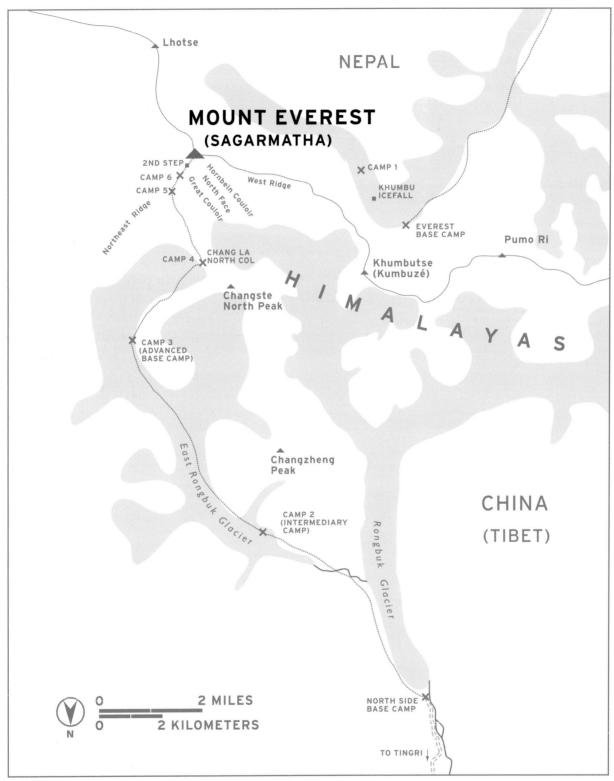

The Northeast Ridge Route

THE CLIMB: NORTHEAST RIDGE ROUTE FROM TIBET, CHINA

Climbing Mount Everest from the north offers a unique cultural experience and a beautiful ascent in rugged Tibetan alpine terrain. Most of the climbing on the lower mountain is easier than that on the south-side route but is technically challenging higher on the mountain.

NORTH-SIDE BASE CAMP TO CAMP 2 (INTERMEDIATE CAMP) AND CAMP 3 (ADVANCED BASE CAMP)

The "climbing" from the north-side Everest base camp to Advanced Base Camp (ABC) consists of gentle trekking up the broad Rongbuk Glacier valley flanking Mount Changtse to the west. The trek gains roughly 3700 feet (1130 m) over 18 miles (30 km) of terrain. There are no technical difficulties along the route. Most teams use an Intermediate Camp (Camp 2) that lies halfway between the base camp and Advanced Base Camp (Camp 3).

It's easy to forget that ABC sits at an extreme altitude due to the easy hiking to reach it. Camp 3 (ABC) on Everest's south side is much different from Camp 3 (ABC) on the north. The climbing to reach ABC on the south side is more technical, committing, and dangerous, making it feel much higher on the mountain when it is only 650 feet (200 m) higher than ABC on the north side.

Camp 3 (ABC) sits on a scree-covered glacier below where the steeper climbing begins. The camp is windy, dry, and inhospitable, but it is where climbers spend the majority of their time. It is possible to see part of the upper route from this camp.

CAMP 3 (ABC) TO CAMP 4 (NORTH COL)

The route from Camp 3 to the North Col camp (Camp 4) crosses gradual, glaciated terrain before beginning a steep, rolling ascent on fixed lines to 23,000 feet (7010 m). This section takes four to six hours on the first rotation.

Camp 4 sits at a low spot on the lower North Ridge. Large enough to hold thirty to forty tents, it provides

> ## GUIDE TIP
>
> Find a slow, comfortable rhythm while climbing. If you lose this rhythm or try to push too fast you'll go into oxygen debt and be much less efficient. Becoming anaerobic by rushing increases your risk of pulmonary edema and will make you more tired in the coming days. Taking a certain number of breaths per step will facilitate keeping your rhythm.

some protection from the wind. Much of the upper route is visible from here. Finally climbers feel as though they are on the mountain and can see what obstacles lie ahead.

CAMP 4 TO CAMP 5

Above the North Col, the route climbs moderately steep snow slopes on fixed lines for 1400 feet. Camp 5 is perched on the slope at the end of the snow at 24,600 feet (about 7500 m). Camp 4 to Camp 5 takes four to six hours. The mighty North Face and Great Couloir loom to the west of camp. Teams climbing the Great Couloir, including the 1983 American team that placed Phil Ershler on the summit, often traverse into the north-side route from this point.

CAMP 5 TO HIGH CAMP (CAMP 6)

Above Camp 5 the route continues up the broad Northeast Ridge, steeply climbing rock and snow, depending on the amount of snowfall. Camp 6 (High Camp) sits at 27,230 feet (8300 m) on rock terraces on the Northeast Ridge 300 feet (90 m) below where the ridge joins the North Ridge proper. High Camp is typically used only during the summit push because of its extreme altitude. Camp 5 to Camp 6 takes four to six hours.

CAMP 6 TO THE SUMMIT

After an uncomfortable night at High Camp, start for the summit by traversing southwest on rock benches around small buttresses, gradually gaining altitude

Looking towards the
Hillary Step from the
South Summit

just below and north of the North Ridge crest. Exposed climbing traverses loose rock on fixed lines en route to the first step at 27,890 feet (8500 m).

Above the steep climbing of the first step the route continues its gradual traverse toward the Great Couloir. The second step lies 260 vertical feet (80 m) and an hour's climb above the first step. Another hour or two of climbing brings you to the last real obstacle, the third step. Above this, the exposed traversing continues for another two to four hours up steeper and snowier terrain to the highest point on Earth!

DESCENT

Reserving enough energy to descend safely is even more important on the north side than on the south side of Mount Everest. The large amount of traversing and long periods of time spent above 26,000 feet (8000 m) make summit day very physically demanding even though the altitude gain isn't great. Most climbers descend to Camp 4 at the North Col if possible, drop down to Camp 3 (ABC) the following day, and reach base camp the next day.

MOUNT EVEREST GEAR LISTS

Everest has a pretty extensive gear list; don't forget the camera!

TRAVEL AND TREKKING GEAR

- Passport (obtain visa upon arrival for most countries)
- Travel wallet to store passport, money, and travel documents
- 2 large duffel bags: 1 rolling, 1 nonrolling
- 1 small duffel bag for storing street and casual clothes in Katmandu
- 3 locks for duffel bags
- Day pack for travel and trekking
- 2 collapsible trekking poles
- Sleeping pad (can be nice to put on teahouse beds)
- Sleeping bag rated to 0°F (-18°C)—doubles as extra bag on the mountain

> **GUIDE TIP**
>
> Very little oxygen is needed when the body is at rest compared to when you're climbing. A minimal oxygen flow of 0.5 to 1 liter per minute is plenty for sleeping. This flow rate will allow you to get a restful sleep without burning through your oxygen reserves. Save the high flow rate for when you need it most: the summit climb!

- Midweight trekking boots
- Sneakers for teahouses and around town
- Casual and city clothes
- Trekking clothes
- Garbage bags to waterproof your gear

CLIMBING GEAR

- Climbing pack for on the mountain
- Pack cover (make sure it fits your pack)
- Alpine ice ax
- 12-point crampons with a good fit
- Helmet
- Harness with releasable leg loops and belay loop
- Ascender
- 3 locking carabiners
- 6 nonlocking carabiners
- 4–5 slings
- 2 prusik loops
- Figure-eight device (works best for rappeling)

CLOTHING

Make sure you're familiar with all your clothing systems before the expedition.

FOOTWEAR:

- Triple climbing boots for summit climbing
- Down booties for high camps
- 4 pairs climbing socks of varying weights

GUIDE TIP

Wear a Buff, a thin tube of cloth that is worn over the nose, mouth, and neck. Humidify and warm the air by wearing your Buff over your face to prevent a sore throat while sleeping. I live in my Buff above base camp.

LOWER-BODY LAYERS:

- Waterproof, breathable shell pants with a full zipper
- 2 pairs climbing pants of different weights made of soft shell material
- Midweight insulated pants for in camps (down or synthetic)
- 1 pair jeans for base camp
- 3 sets underlayers of different weights (synthetic or merino wool)

UPPER-BODY LAYERS:

- Waterproof breathable, lightweight shell jacket
- Heavy down suit for climbing to the summit
- Heavy down parka with a hood
- 3 midweight pile layers, preferably with hoods
- 3 underlayers (synthetic or merino wool)
- A few cotton T-shirts, for base camp

HEADGEAR AND HANDWEAR:

- 1–2 heavy ski hats
- Balaclava
- Face mask
- Sun hat or baseball cap
- 2 Buffs
- Heavy climbing gloves
- Heavy down mitts (must fit over base-layer gloves)
- Base-layer gloves for trekking and warm climbing
- Several pairs hand warmers

PERSONAL GEAR

- Ten Essentials
- Sleeping bag rated to at least -20°F (-29°C)

- 2 pairs glacier glasses
- 2 pairs goggles: 1 clear, 1 dark
- 30+ SPF sweatproof sunscreen
- 2 headlamps with extra batteries
- Altitude watch
- 2–3 1-quart water bottles
- 2–3 water bottle jackets
- Water treatment (iodine or chlorine)
- 1-quart thermos
- Snacks and specialty climbing and comfort food
- Multitool (with pliers)
- Prescription medications
- 1-quart pee bottle
- Camera
- Several books (can trade with others at base camp)

GROUP GEAR

- Permit
- Base camp tents for lounging at Base Camp and Camp 2
- 4-season tents
- Cookstoves and fuel for base camp and mountain
- Expedition food
- American or Russian oxygen bottle systems
- Oxygen masks
- Regulators for oxygen systems
- Fixed line (to fix yourself or give to the fixing team)
- Pickets and ice screws
- Gear duffels or barrels

SUMMIT CHECKLIST

Bring only what you need and not more!

- 2700–3300 cubic-inch (45–55 liter) backpack
- Sleeping bag and pad
- Down suit
- Balaclava or face mask
- Down mitts
- Warm glove system with a liner glove
- Hand and foot warmers
- Triple Everest boots

- Helmet
- Oxygen mask and regulator
- Harness and climbing gear
- Ice ax with leash
- Goggles
- Glacier glasses
- Sunscreen and lip balm
- Headlamp with extra batteries
- Radio with new batteries
- Lighter and/or matches

- 2 1-quart water bottles with insulators
- Thermos
- Electrolyte replacement drink
- Palatable snacks
- Small medical kit with drugs for high altitude
- Foot powder
- 1-quart pee bottle
- Stuff sack to organize gear
- Summit banners
- Camera

The view below the South Summit with the Balcony in the distance (Photo by Jane Lee)

MOUNT KILIMANJARO

ALTITUDE
19,340 feet (5895 m)

DIFFICULTY RATINGS
Technical: 1-2
Physical: 2-3

SUMMIT GPS WAYPOINTS
S 03 04.585
E 37 21.240

ELEVATION GAIN
(base camp to summit)
Machame Route: 13,403 feet (4085 m)
Marangu Route: 13,109 feet (3995 m)

DISTANCE
(base camp to summit)
Machame Route: 28 miles (45 km),
plus 15 miles (24 km) descent
(total 43 miles, 69 km)
Marangu Route: 25 miles (41 km)
one way

TIME
(door-to-door)
16 days (including safari)

SEASON
January-mid-March
June-mid-October

Kilimanjaro looms behind a senecio forest en route to Karanga camp on the Machame Route.

CHAPTER 4
MOUNT KILIMANJARO

AFRICA'S HIGHEST SUMMIT

AS WIDE AS ALL THE WORLD, GREAT, HIGH, AND
UNBELIEVABLY WHITE IN THE SUN . . .

—ERNEST HEMINGWAY, *THE SNOWS OF KILIMANJARO* (1936)

The tallest mountain on the continent of Africa, Mount Kilimanjaro sits 200 miles (322 km) south of the equator in Tanzania, a country located approximately halfway up the eastern seaboard of Africa. Kilimanjaro's summit, an incongruous island of rock and snow, rises more than 17,000 feet (5100 m) out of the arid plains below, just a short distance south of the border with Kenya. Viewed through the hazy heat waves of the equatorial plains below, the anomalous glaciated terrain of the mountain seems almost surreal. The mountain lies in Kilimanjaro National Park, which encompasses 756 square miles (1957 sq km) of terrain above the 9000-foot (2700 m) contour line. The lands below this delineation are inhabited by local Chagga tribespeople. The park was established in 1973 and officially opened in 1977.

Kilimanjaro, by far the most popular of the Seven Summits, is one of the most popular climbs in the world; more than 25,000 climbers attempt its summit annually, with half that number reaching the top. Most of these climbers are not interested in climbing the Seven Summits but are aiming instead to simply challenge themselves on this picturesque, iconic mountain. Some have said that with all the traffic, we are "loving Kilimanjaro to death," which isn't really true. Kilimanjaro National Park has done a good job creating an infrastructure for responsible and sustainable usage while allowing the local economy to benefit greatly from the popularity of the peak. For the amount of traffic the mountain receives, its natural environment is surprisingly well preserved.

NATURAL HISTORY

Around 750,000 years ago, the fault line below Kilimanjaro began to fracture, releasing lava that created the giant massif of Kilimanjaro. Three individual peaks formed along the fault, constituting what we now know as Kilimanjaro's three main dormant volcanic summits: Shira to the north, 13,000 feet (3962 m); Kibo (Uhuru) in the middle, 19,340 feet (5896 m); and Mawenzi to the south, 16,896 feet (5150 m). After Tanzania gained

independence, Kibo summit was given another oft-used name: Uhuru, which means "freedom" in Swahili; today, many refer to the highest point on Kibo as Uhuru Point or Peak.

These dormant volcanoes lie in a northwest-to-southeast orientation spanning 37 miles (60 km). Shira was the first of the three volcanoes to die out, around 500,000 years ago, and it subsequently collapsed in upon itself. Mawenzi later died and eroded, leaving Kibo, the highest of the three, the only active volcano. Around 360,000 years ago, Kibo erupted one final time, filling the Shira caldera and creating the Shira Plateau, the second camp on the Machame Route. Climbers on the Shira Plateau will notice the dark lava rock composed of rhombic, or diamond-shaped, crystals called rhomb porphyry lava.

At one point Kibo was almost 19,500 feet (5944 m) tall before the entire mountain began to sink. About 100,000 years ago, a huge landslide on the flanks of Kibo carried away a large section of the summit pyramid. This landslide, which is still very apparent today, accounts for the most technical climbing on the Machame Route: the Barranco Wall. The third camp on this route sits in the debris of this major landslide.

Including the agricultural lands driven through on the approach to the mountain, climbers pass through six major ecosystems, and with each new ecosystem there is a change in flora and fauna. From lowest to highest on the mountain, these ecosystems are as follows:

Cultivation zone: 4000–6000 feet (1200–1800 m); this terrain used to be shrubbery and dense forest but is now mainly used for agriculture. This land is highly productive due to the volcanic soils. Animals you might see are the tree hyrax and the greater galago.

Forest: 6000–9200 feet (1800–2800 m); this ecosystem is characterized by lush vegetation, high rainfall, and dense foliage. Typical plants are the massive *Olea kilimandsh* and *O. africana* trees and beautiful flowering *Impatiens kilimanjari*. Animals include blue monkeys, colobus monkeys, and leopards. Small squirrels and antelope also roam the forests.

MOUNT KILIMANJARO FAST FACTS

- Kilimanjaro lies in northern Tanzania just south of the border with Kenya.
- There are five distinct climatic zones on Kilimanjaro.
- Kilimanjaro is the closest of the Seven Summits to the equator.
- Scientists predict that all the glaciers on Kilimanjaro will be gone by 2030 to 2050.
- The second-tallest mountain in Africa is Mount Kenya at 17,057 feet (5199 m).
- Kilimanjaro is an inactive volcano.

Heather: 9200–10,800 feet (2800–3300 m); this "in-between" ecosystem connects the wet forests to the arid moorland above. It is characterized by fog near the forests and heathlike shrubs as one climbs higher. Common shrubs are *Erica arborea* and *Philipia excelsa*. You may see eland, Klipspringer, four-striped grass mouse, and the streaky seed-eater (a finch) in this transitional environment.

Moorland: 10,800–13,100 feet (3300–4000 m); this is where climbers spend most of their time on the Machame Route. It's drier, colder, and windier due to the lack of high foliage and increased altitude. Frost can occur at night. Flora is small except for the large *Senecio kilimanjari* tree and smaller *Lobelia deckenii*. Notable fauna include elands, grass mice, and several types of buzzards.

Alpine desert: 13,100–16,000 feet (4000–4900 m): cold and dry with lots of sun. Large daily temperature fluctuations are common; water is scarce. Vegetation is almost nonexistent. Mosses, lichens, and a few species of small flowers survive here. The few animals venturing into this terrain include servals, insects, and the occasional African hunting dog.

Arctic conditions: 16,000 feet (4900 m) and above; there is little precipitation in this ecosystem, and temperatures drop below freezing at night. Plants and animals are scarce. A few lichens survive.

The upper ecosystems on Kilimanjaro are home to some unique species of plants and animals.

Simba, king
of the jungle

CULTURAL AND POLITICAL BACKGROUND

Humans have long lived below this giant peak. Scientists have found evidence such as very old stone bowls and obsidian tools that lead researchers to believe the region around the mountain has been inhabited since ancient times.

The Wachagga (Chagga) tribespeople have lived in the highlands for at least 250 years. They are mainly agriculturalists who have adapted their techniques to match their unique environment. You will most likely be working with the Chagga as porters and guides on the climb, and they can tell you more about their culture.

Kilimanjaro's name's origin is somewhat of a debate. The local Wachagga say they didn't have a name for the mountain, only the two individual peaks. Most believe the name comes from a combination of two words: *kilima* coming from *mlima*, meaning "mountain," and *njaro*, which traders used to refer to the demon of the cold. It could also derive from the word *kilimajyaro*, which Waswahili caravan people used to mean "landmark."

Tanzania was a German protectorate captured by the British during World War II and renamed Tanganyika. In 1961 it achieved independence and, united with Zanzibar, was renamed the United Republic of Tanzania. Its seat of government is Dar es Salaam, on the coast, but its designated capital is Dodoma in the interior.

MOUNT KILIMANJARO TIMELINE

1861-62 German Baron Karl Von der Decken and various companions make two attempts to climb the mountain.

1888 German Otto Ehlers says he summited but later rescinds this statement.

1889 First ascent of Kilimanjaro, Kibo Peak, is made by another German—Hans Meyer.

1912 Germans Fritz Klute and Edward Oehler make first ascent of Mawenzi Peak.

CLIMBING HISTORY

Although humans have lived on the slopes of Kilimanjaro for perhaps thousands of years, it wasn't until the mid-1800s that people began trying to reach the top. By the late nineteenth century, several expeditions had been mounted, culminating in the first ascent of the peak, by Hans Meyer in 1889. After this successful climb, many alternative routes were climbed on the mountain and increasing numbers ascended the peak. Today, it is the center of a thriving climbing industry in Africa.

CLIMBING CHALLENGES

Kilimanjaro is generally considered to be one of the easiest of the Seven Summits to climb because there are several nontechnical routes to the summit, because its summit altitude is moderate, and because it's the most climbed. Kilimanjaro, however, is still a large mountain and a serious challenge to climb. Although it's a nontechnical climb, summit day is long and will physically push even Mount Everest summiters to reach its top. A climb of Kilimanjaro should not be underestimated.

Although altitudes reached on Kilimajaro are only moderate and not nearly as extreme as those found on a Mount Everest or Aconcagua climb, many climbers still run into trouble. Because of its accessibility and quick increase in altitude from base to summit, climbers underestimate the effects of altitude and climb the mountain too quickly. Rushing a Kilimanjaro climb can result in serious consequences such as altitude illness, cerebral and pulmonary edema, and death. The climb should be taken seriously, and climbers should set a safe acclimatization schedule before the climb and stick to it even if they feel like they can climb faster once on the mountain.

Climbing Kilimanjaro is still quite physically challenging. Although climbers aren't carrying heavy loads (just 10–30 lbs, 6–14 kg) as on other mountains, summit day is long and strenuous. Weather can be poor—cold, rainy, and windy—further challenging a climber's body.

Logistically, climbing Kilimanjaro can be a challenge. Since climbers are not allowed on the mountain without local porters and guides, a logistics service must be hired. Many logistics providers offer a wide variety of services, but it can take some effort to match your climbing style and budget to a company.

SUMMIT ON THE SUMMIT

Mountains represent adventure, challenge, beauty, and mystique for people all over the world. In early 2010, a musician and philanthropist known simply as Kenna focused on the element of challenge in ascending a mountain and how closely that endeavor mimics the challenges people around the world face to get clean water. Kenna started Summit on the Summit, a conversation around a goal, around challenge. A few months after the idea was born, a group of activists (including Alexandria Cousteau) and influencers (including Jessica Biel and Lupe Fiasco) came together with educators (Elizabeth Gore, Dr. Greg Allgood, and me!) to climb the highest point in Africa, Mount Kilimanjaro, while learning about the global clean water crisis so we could all share this information with others. Thus was Summit on the Summit (or SOTS, as it is known) launched.

Climbing a 19,341-foot (5895 m) mountain is hard. About the only way to make it harder is to take a group of people who have never slept outside before and add to that a giant camera crew to document the experience. To say the least, I was nervous about it. But I knew that Kilimanjaro held special meaning to Kenna: he was born in Ethiopia and had attempted to climb Kili in the past few years. He suffered from some altitude sickness and so he came back, with a goal bigger than the summit and with the friends he knew would support him.

One of the nicest things about climbing Kilimanjaro is traveling around Africa before or after the climb on safari to see the animals. We took a different type of safari on SOTS, journeying to schools and homes of people who live in Masai villages and hearing about the challenge they face to get clean water. Seeing the mud puddle they pull water from and witnessing the illness that follows was in our faces and real, a good thing to keep in mind while climbing and facing our own challenge.

Our group took seven days to attempt the summit in early January. During the climb, we tweeted and appeared on CNN and the BBC, begging people to "send water" via a text message that would donate funds for the UN HCR to manage. By Day 6 of the climb, we had seen more rain than the mountain had seen in the previous year. All we could do was laugh—water was being sent, all right!

Summit day on Kilimanjaro is the most challenging: high altitude, cold temperatures, and a long day. All forty-five climbers persevered, and at around 10:00 AM, we stood atop the roof of Africa, tired but content.

In the months that followed our return to our various homes, we continued to tell the stories of the struggle for clean water, not just in Africa but globally. Our attempt to raise awareness was so successful that Kenna decided to make SOTS an annual event, challenging climbers and creating a conversation to remind us that so many people go through a similar challenge each day for the simple necessity of water. Climbing Kilimanjaro can be more than just another summit to check off your tick list!

MELISSA ARNOT

THREE-TIME EVEREST SUMMITER, SENIOR GUIDE FOR RAINIER MOUNTAINEERING INC, AND WILDERNESS-MEDICINE INSTRUCTOR

PLANNING AN EXPEDITION

Because Kilimanjaro sees tens of thousands of ascents per year, an entire industry for climbing has sprung up in the towns and cities surrounding the mountain. There are many climbing outfitters and guide services to choose from. Climbers must match their price range and climbing style with one of a wide variety of companies. This will take some time and research if you are making your own arrangements to climb Kilimanjaro. For those climbing with a guide service, this work is done for you.

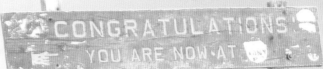

The author and a team he led to Uhuru Peak on Kilimanjaro

KILIMANJARO PORTERS ASSISTANCE PROJECT

The Kilimanjaro Porters Assistance Project (KPAP) is a nongovernmental organization that was created in 2003 to help better the working conditions of porters working on Kilimanjaro. It's an initiative of the International Mountain Explorers Connection based out of Boulder, Colorado, in the United States. They pursue their mission in the following ways:

- Lending clothes free of charge to porters
- Offering free education in English, first aid, money management, and HIV/AIDS
- Instituting guidelines for proper porter treatment
- Educating the public about the porters' conditions

If you're interested in finding out more, log on to www.kiliporters.org or stop by their office in downtown Moshi.

Regardless of your approach, begin planning your Kilimanjaro climb at least six months in advance of the climb date in order to secure plane tickets, book with a logistics provider, get immunizations, train, and organize to be away for several weeks. Almost all Kilimanjaro climbers conclude their trip with a Serengeti safari, which requires additional planning and preparation.

Plan to spend about a week on Kilimanjaro to allow proper acclimatization to reach the summit. In addition, you will want to add several days for travel to and from the mountain, plus a day on each end of the climb for organization, sightseeing days, time for a safari, and time for any additional travel in Africa. Most climbers count on two weeks door-to-door for Kilimanjaro.

GUIDED TRIP VERSUS INDEPENDENT CLIMB

Kilimanjaro National Park requires that everyone climb with a local outfitter and a registered guide. Independent climbing is prohibited. This regulation was put in place to provide work for local porters and guides and to help the local economy. Locals usually do a great job and work very hard. Climbing with them is an excellent way to learn about the mountain and the Chagga culture. If you are looking to "solo" Kilimanjaro, however, you're out of luck.

Most local companies do a good job, but it's important to do your homework before signing up with a company. Non-Tanzanian guide services work with local outfitters they know and trust to offer clients western-style guiding combined with local knowledge. Service provided by local outfitters usually includes the following:

- Ground transportation
- Food
- Group camping and cooking gear
- Hut accommodation
- Park fees
- Local guides
- Porters

Carefully research all the guide services available to find the one best suited to your style and experience.

CLIMBING SEASONS AND WEATHER

Weather on Kilimanjaro is unique for Africa. Major changes occur due to seasonal patterns, but weather also varies depending on altitude and the type of ecosystem you're in. Almost no one climbs during the two rainy periods. During the nonrainy seasons (January through mid-March and June through mid-October),

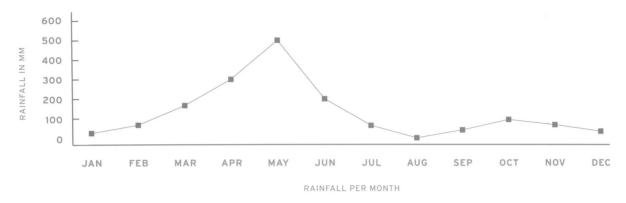

Kilimanjaro Precipitation Chart. From "Kilimanjaro National Park" by Tanzania National Parks, written by Jeanette Hanby.

the weather ranges from hot and arid equatorial conditions down low to arctic conditions on top, with cool, wet rain forest in between. Climbers pass through six major ecosystems en route to the summit, making for an unparalleled ecological experience. The wettest zone on the mountain is from 5900 feet to 9200 feet (1800–2800 m). With a vertical rise of 17,000 feet (5180 m), the temperature difference can be 55 degrees Fahrenheit (30°C) from base to summit on any given day.

The long rains last from the beginning of April to mid-June; the short rains are from mid-November through December. During the long rains, clouds pile up over the mountain and drop their contents; the short rains are more characterized by thunderstorms and constant rain. See the precipitation chart for a better idea of precipitation amounts throughout the year.

January through March is the warmest time of the year, while June through August is the coldest. Other than these major weather trends, few major storms pass over the mountain.

DOCUMENTS

For climbers from most countries, it's not necessary to buy a Tanzanian visa in advance. They can be purchased upon arrival in Tanzania. Visas cost $100; it may be necessary to present your yellow fever immunization card to obtain it.

Permits are necessary for a climb of Kilimanjaro. Guided groups will be asked to fill out the required paperwork that the guides can use to obtain the permit. Permit fees are usually included in a package tour. Check with your climb provider to make sure this is the case. Obtaining permits is an easy process but can take several hours of waiting at the start of the climb, especially if it's a busy day, so be patient.

COSTS

Currency is the Tanzanian shilling; as of 2012, the exchange rate is about 1550 Tanzanian shillings to $1US.

- Logistics provider–guide service (ground transportation, park fees, guides, porters, and on-mountain food and huts): $1000–$5000
- Hotels: $200–$1000
- Food in towns: $100–$200
- Tips: $100–$300
- Safari: $600–$2500

It is customary to tip guides and porters. I use the following guideline (amounts are per local worker) when dispersing tip money from the whole climbing team:

- Porters: $40
- Servers: $60

Kilimanjaro casts a shadow across the lowlands and remaining glacier.

- Cooks: $80
- Assistant guides: $100
- Lead guides: $150+

CONDITIONING

While Kilimanjaro is one of the easiest and most popular of the Seven Summits, don't underestimate it. Summit day is very long and the altitudes are extreme. Climbers attempting the peak need to be fit enough to walk uphill steadily for hours on end several days in a row.

No technical climbing experience is needed. If you haven't camped overnight in a tent before, it will take some getting used to. Do yourself a favor and experience overnight camping at home before getting on the peak (if you're not planning to stay in huts on the Marangu Route). Remember, always take plenty of time to acclimatize.

IMMUNIZATIONS

Plan well in advance to get immunizations, as some courses can take months. Consult your doctor, local travel clinic, or the Centers for Disease Control and Prevention (CDC) at www.cdc.gov. Malaria is a real problem in Africa. Almost a million Africans die from malaria each year, with the majority of those being young children. It is highly recommended that you use a chemoprophylaxis, such as Doxycycline or Malarone, for your Kilimanjaro trip. You can find certain malaria medications in Tanzania, but it's best to buy them before you travel. The best way to avoid malaria, however, is by covering your skin, using insect repellent, and using bug nets for beds. Dengue fever is also a risk. The following immunizations are recommended:

- Diphtheria-tetanus (DPT)—you might have this immunization already but may need a booster
- Polio—you might have it already but may need a booster
- Measles, mumps, and rubella (MMR)—you might have it already but may need a booster
- Rabies
- Typhoid
- Meningitis
- Hepatitis A and B
- Malaria

Some immunizations require starting the course before you arrive in Africa.

COMMUNICATIONS

It's difficult to figure out how to use public phones for international calls in Tanzania. There are some call centers but they're expensive. It may be easiest to make calls from your hotel or with Internet call providers such as Skype. A satellite phone is great to have on the mountain but rarely works in the cities. There is cell service on the mountain, and most guides and porters will have a phone with them, which can be used in case of emergency if your team doesn't have a satellite phone. Consider buying a local SIM card for your cell phone to use while in Tanzania. You can buy cards and recharge minutes at any local store.

GETTING THERE AND GETTING AROUND

Kilimanjaro sits within northern Tanzania close to the border with Kenya and is surrounded by several towns and small cities. Most climbers take the daily Northwest–KLM flight to Kilimanjaro International Airport (KIA) via Amsterdam. Other carriers, such as Ethiopian Air, offer frequent routing from different locations in Africa. KIA,

> ## GUIDE TIP
>
> Kilimanjaro National Park has a reliable, equipped rescue team on the Marangu Route. Rescue service on alternative routes requires that you contact park headquarters (telephone: Marangu 50), which will then send a team of rescuers and experts. A large hospital in the Moshi area, the Kilimanjaro Christian Medical Center, can deal with emergencies (telephone: Moshi 2741).

a moderate-size airport, receives regular traffic from Europe, Dar es Salaam in Tanzania, Nairobi in Kenya, and Adis Ababa in Ethiopia. International and domestic flights can fill early so reserve seats well in advance, especially for the smaller planes flying to the Serengeti. It never hurts to arrive a day in advance in case of lost luggage.

Dar es Salaam and Nairobi are both major cities that are crowded and energetic. They both offer a variety of tourist activities, so consider making a layover there before or after the climb.

KIA sits approximately an hour from the mountain near the small city of Arusha. Once at KIA, climbers take a transport to either Moshi or Marangu, small towns at the base of the mountain, or to Arusha to stage their climbs, depending on their logistics service. Guide services and logistical companies usually provide safe transport to and from the airport as part of their service.

GROUND TRANSPORTATION

Since so many climbers flock to the Kilimanjaro region each year, organizing transportation is quite easy. If you are traveling on your own, it's important to arrange transportation from KIA to your hotel ahead of time. From Arusha or Moshi to the mountain, or back to the airport, it's easy to find a cab without prior notice. A taxi to KIA from Moshi costs $40 to $60.

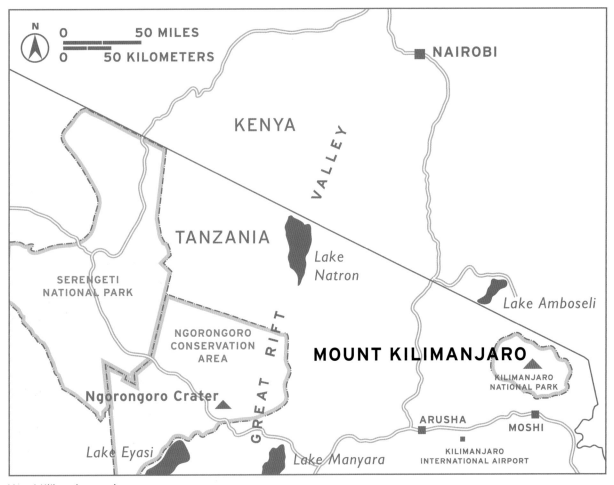

Mount Kilimanjaro environs

GATEWAY SETTLEMENTS

Two small cities that climbers stay in before and after the climb are Moshi (2663 ft, 812 m) and Arusha (4592 ft, 1400 m). Moshi lies 40 miles (64 km) to the east of Kilimanjaro International Airport, and Arusha sits 25 miles (40 km) east. Arusha is larger than Moshi, offering more amenities such as shops, restaurants, and higher-end hotels, but is farther from the mountain.

The main tourist attraction in Moshi and Arusha is markets where locals sell handmade goods. It's important to use street smarts when touring these towns, especially after dark. Drinking bottled rather than tap water is prudent. If you are climbing the Marangu Route,

it's possible to stay at the Marangu Hotel in the small town of the same name on the southeastern flank of the mountain.

OTHER ACTIVITIES: SAFARI

Most people who come to Kilimanjaro choose to do a safari after the climb. It's a great way to unwind from the climb and experience game viewing at its best. The main attractions are Serengeti National Park and Ngorongoro Crater Conservation Area, both in Tanzania. Viewing is great year-round but peaks during the migrations in January and February. Lions, black rhinos, elephants, leopards, zebras, and wildebeest can all be seen. Three days of game viewing is enough for most people, but if you're a serious photographer, you may want to stay longer.

CLIMBING MOUNT KILIMANJARO

Kilimanjaro is one of the most well-known and widely climbed mountains in the world. It has captivated climbers for decades because of its exotic nature and dramatic features. It is the highest point on the African continent but is a relatively easy climb compared to other continental high points, a fact which entices climbers from around the world to ascend its heights. A climb of Kilimanjaro also serves as a great excuse for those of us not from Africa to experience the continent. Whatever your reason for attempting to climb Kilimanjaro, standing on its summit is a noteworthy accomplishment.

Kilimanjaro offers little technical difficulty on the main routes but it does make for a strenuous climb physically. Most people who train for it appropriately can make it to the top. Weather on the mountain can be bad, especially in the shoulder seasons when there's more rain, and summit day is always very cold. Climbing Kilimanjaro should not be taken lightly.

Due to Kilimanjaro's popularity, there are many routes to the summit on every aspect of the mountain, although a few are much more popular than the rest. More than ten main routes and variations are all in use. The majority of traffic climbs the Marangu or "Coca-Cola" Route, but increasingly a significant percentage of climbers are choosing the less direct Machame Route.

A climb of Kilimanjaro takes a week with built-in acclimatization rest days. With travel, organization days, and a possible Serengeti safari, most climbers are gone from home for two weeks in all, a week of that actually spent on the mountain.

ROUTES

The two routes described in this book are the Machame and the Marangu. They are the two most popular climbs on the mountain for very different reasons. Both routes are on the south aspect of the mountain, the area closest

> ### GUIDE TIP
> Don't underestimate the cold on summit day. Bring all your warm clothes, especially a warm parka with a hood. Even though it won't be raining at such a high elevation, bring your rain shell for added warmth and wind protection. Keep your water bottles inside your pack against your back to keep them from freezing.

to the major towns and the airport. The north side of the mountain does get climbed via other routes, such as the Rongai. The Machame and Marangu Routes are technically easy, unlike the Breach Wall above the Machame traverse, which offers some internationally recognized difficult high-altitude climbing. Reinhold Messner made an ascent on the Breach Wall.

MACHAME ROUTE

The Machame Route ascends the west aspect of Kilimanjaro before traversing south and east, circumnavigating part of the mountain and summiting from the southeast, near the Marangu Route. The Machame Route offers a longer hiking distance and views of more of the mountain in a more natural approach to acclimatization. On the Machame Route climbers move camp each night, circumnavigating the south side of the mountain as they acclimatize. The Machame Route is more scenic because it covers more ground that offers views of more of the mountain, and it's less crowded. The Machame Route requires climbers to camp in tents.

MARANGU (COCA-COLA) ROUTE

The Marangu Route is very direct with a lot of infrastructure, unlike the Machame. The Marangu Route ascends directly up the southeastern aspect of the mountain, eventually joining the same summit-day trail as the Machame Route. Rest days are incorporated into the Marangu Route schedule to ensure proper acclimatization. The Marangu Route is more direct, so climbers can

A dream achieved: the roof of Africa

climb it faster than the Machame Route; this makes it a quicker option. However, a short Kilimanjaro climb can spell altitude illness, so opting for a faster climb is not advised. Because the Marangu offers hut accommodations, climbers looking for a more social atmosphere with more creature comforts should consider the Marangu Route.

ACCLIMATIZATION

Acclimatizing properly is a very important aspect of climbing Kilimanjaro. Since it is such an accessible peak and so many novice climbers with little knowledge of altitude sickness attempt the peak each year, many climbers suffer from acute mountain sickness (AMS), and some even experience more serious problems including high-altitude cerebral edema (HACE) and high-altitude pulmonary edema (HAPE), or even death. A slow climbing schedule that allows ample time to acclimatize is the most effective way to avoid altitude illness. If anyone on your team experiences altitude illness, it's important not to move higher until the illness subsides or to descend if it gets worse.

A slow ascent of five to seven days is a reasonable climbing schedule on Kilimanjaro. Even at this conservative pace, climbers can get sick, so this schedule must be adapted for each individual climber. Consult the ascent schedules in this chapter and read more about altitude illness in the medical section at the beginning of this book.

WATER, SANITATION, AND GARBAGE

Toilet facilities on Kilimanjaro are basic and often unsanitary. The park supplies wooden toilets at each camp for climbers to use. They are moved periodically but not cleaned very often, making the experience less than ideal. Some guide services carry their own toilet tents with portable seats to avoid using public toilets.

As with other mountains, all garbage must be carried off with you. If we all do our part to carry out our garbage, the mountain will remain a pleasant climbing experience for generations to come.

There is a clean water source at each of the camps except for high camp, Barafu Camp. Porters bring water to Barafu Camp from Karanga Camp for the summit bid.

Most teams descend below Barafu Camp to spend the night after their summit bid because of this. The porters and guides know where the water sources in the camps are, as they are the ones who collect it for the team. The water is potable but it's best to treat all water on Kilimanjaro before drinking it.

THE CLIMB: MACHAME ROUTE

The Machame Route circumnavigates Kibo Peak to the south and west, offering some of the finest views of the steep summit glaciers. Its extended length allows climbers to acclimatize properly and safely, giving them the best chance of summiting. The Shira Plateau, Breach Wall, and Barranco Wall are impressive geologic structures that climbers on other routes don't get to see.

The route begins at the Machame Gate on the southwestern flank of the mountain. To reach the gate, climbers traverse agricultural lands, passing through Chagga villages. This is a popular starting point, and it takes some time to acquire the permit, so arrive early. Teams use a large parking lot to organize gear and wait out of the rain in a bathroom-park registration complex.

SAMPLE CLIMBING ITINERARY: MOUNT KILIMANJARO'S MACHAME ROUTE

Day	Location	Start Elevation	End Elevation	Elevation Gain	Distance
1	Fly from home				
2	Arrive at KIA; travel to Arusha	2658 ft (810 m)	4592 ft (1400 m)	1934 ft (590 m)	
3	Market sightseeing				
4	Drive to Machame Gate	4592 ft (1400 m)	5938 ft (1810 m)	1346 ft (410 m)	
	Climb to Machame Camp	5938 ft (1810 m)	9774 ft (2979 m)	3836 ft (1169 m)	8 miles (13 km)
5	Climb to Shira Plateau	9774 ft (2979 m)	12,424 ft (3787 m)	2650 ft (808 m)	5 miles (8 km)
6	Traverse to Barranco Camp	12,424 ft (3787 m)	12,651 ft (3856 m)	227 ft (69 m)	7 miles (11 km)
7	Traverse to Karanga Camp	12,651 ft (3856 m)	13,051 ft (3978 m)	400 ft (122 m)	3 miles (5 km)
8	Traverse to Barafu Camp	13,051 ft (3978 m)	15,200 ft (4633 m)	2149 ft (656 m)	3 miles (5 km)
9	Climb to summit	15,200 ft (4633 m)	19,341 ft (5895 m)	4141 ft (1262 m)	2 miles (3 km)
	Descend to Lower Mweka Camp	19,341 ft (5895 m)	9934 ft (3028 m)	-9407 ft (-2867 m)	10 miles (16 km)
10	Descend to Mweka Gate	9934 ft (3028 m)	5602 ft (1707 m)	-4332 ft (-1321 m)	5 miles (8 km)
	Drive to Moshi	5602 ft (1707 m)	2658 ft (810 m)	-2944 ft (-897 m)	
11	Drive to Safari camp				
12	Safari				
13	Safari				
14	Safari				
15	Fly home				

MACHAME GATE TO MACHAME CAMP

The first day of the climb is one of the longest, covering 8 miles (13 km) and gaining 3836 feet (1169 m). Most of the day is spent in the forest, with camp sitting just at the upper border where forest turns into high plains. This day is typically wet and muddy. Climbers can expect to see a wide array of plants and animals residing in the dense, lush forests.

The trek leaves the parking lot at 5938 feet (1810 m) heading northeast through wet forests on muddy trails. High-top boots and gaiters are useful. The old road soon turns into a wide hiking trail at an outhouse an hour into the hike. There are three toilets at regular intervals along the day's route. The route can be very slippery, especially following a rainstorm. Be careful and use ski poles for balance. From here the route gets a little more rugged but is always well defined and maintained. A gradual ascent gives way to steeper terrain after a few hours.

The trail gains a small, broad ridge and begins to climb out of the forest just below the first camp. The ridge offers nice views of the mountain. Above the forest, the weather gets drier and cooler. Camp sits at 9774 feet (2979 m), just below the obvious ranger station just off the trail. Machame Camp is often wet and muddy but offers excellent views of the mountain. This is one of the longer days, consisting of six to eight hours of hiking.

Rain is common on this first day through the forest, so be prepared for a wet hike. Rain shells are appropriate wear, and some climbers bring umbrellas and big rain ponchos to cover their whole packs.

MACHAME CAMP TO SHIRA PLATEAU CAMP

The second day ascends through higher forest and shrublands rising above the denser forests 2650 feet (808 m) in 5 miles (8 km). The heavy rains of the forests are not as common here. The hiking is much less muddy than the previous day. This second day is shorter than the first but still covers a lot of ground.

Begin with a steep climb out of camp for an hour. Soon you'll be above the trees and into the heather, which later

> ### GUIDE TIP
>
> It rains often in the forests even when it might be dry elsewhere. Raingear works great, but I find a poncho works really well on hot days. It allows air to flow through and it doesn't stick to your skin as much. If you buy one big enough, it can also cover your pack as an extra waterproof layer.

gives way to moorlands. The trail is drier and rockier and works its way up dirt trails and rock steps, around rock pinnacles, and through boulders as it traverses several broad ridges. Beautiful highland plants endemic to Kilimanjaro, such as lobelia and the senecio tree, begin to appear. The trail eases off over a series of rocky ridges with several flat areas that make for nice break spots. A short, steep rise with a few rock moves gains the Shira Plateau, and from here it's a short downhill walk into camp. The total hiking time is four to five hours.

Shira Plateau Camp is drier and more open than Machame Camp. The Breach Wall looms above camp. It is possible to start the summit climb here at Shira Camp and save a few days but, with an elevation gain of 12,424 feet (3787 m), this would be a good recipe for altitude sickness.

SHIRA PLATEAU CAMP TO BARRANCO CAMP

The third day is one of the longer days of the climb. It traverses high moorlands in mostly open terrain in plain view below the steep, rocky upper slopes on Kilimanjaro. The day begins with a long, gradual ascent before finishing with a shorter, steeper descent into camp after gaining a significant amount of altitude. Most climbers feel the effects of altitude on this day if they haven't already felt it in the previous two days. The route covers 7 miles (11 km) and gains two thousand feet before losing nearly all of it on the descent to Barranco Camp.

The trail leaves Shira Plateau Camp heading south toward the Lava Tower, a large structure made of volcanic

Masai warriors perform a traditional dance.

rock that's quite obvious. The trekking is gradual until the tower, two hours beyond camp. Most climbers begin to feel the altitude by the time they reach the tower and may even experience a headache. At an intersection just before the lava tower, both routes lead to camp, one trail hiking above and one below. If you want to climb the tower and are feeling comfortable with the altitude, venturing above the tower is an option. If you're looking for the quickest way to camp or you are feeling the effects of altitude, then stay low. The lower route traverses gradually down, while the upper route climbs another few hundred feet before a steep descent on the far side of the tower.

Past the tower it's all downhill! It's another two to three hours of hiking to reach Barranco Camp at 12,651 feet (3856 m). After the steep Lava Tower descent, it's a gradual descent the rest of the way. The trail meanders through groves of senecio trees, including some of the oldest in the park.

Barranco Camp lies just below the Barranco Wall, providing good views of the challenging climbing ahead. There are also incredible views of the Breach Wall from here.

BARRANCO CAMP TO KARANGA CAMP

The climb to Karanga Camp consists of a short, steep climb up the Barranco Wall with a slightly more gradual, undulating descent. The terrain is rough, rocky, and somewhat exposed climbing the Barranco Wall and consists of an easy dirt trail beyond the wall. The route winds through high moorlands in open terrain offering excellent views of the Breach Wall and the summit in good weather. The Barranco Wall ascends 1500 feet

A chaotic scene loading the busses at Mweka Gate

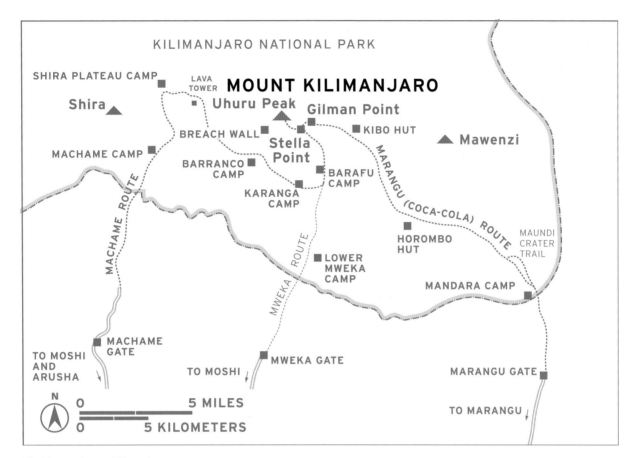

Climbing routes on Kilimanjaro

(457 m) in little over a mile. Almost all of this altitude gain is lost on the gradual descent, with Karanga Camp being only 400 feet (122 m) above Barranco Camp.

The route begins climbing immediately, heading north and then traversing east out of Barranco Camp. Ascend the Barranco Wall, climbing the obvious trail and traversing rocky ledges and up short bulges. Porters, after taking down camp, will rush by with heavy loads on their heads to set up the next camp, so give them room. It's busy and crowded, and there's not a lot of room to pass on the Barranco Wall, so climb safely and get an early start. The climbing can be exposed in places and requires a few very easy rock moves. Your guides can help with this section.

After one to one and a half hours of climbing, the route crests the top of the Barranco Wall. This vantage point is one of the best view spots on the mountain. If the weather is clear, it's a great spot to take a break and fire off some photos.

The route starts to descend immediately, heading southeast below this rest area. Another hour of walking with a short, steep uphill at the end gains Karanga Camp.

Karanga Camp, at 13,051 feet (3978 m), is exposed to wind and rain and is muddy. As in the other camps on the mountain, the toilets are quite rustic. Temperatures can drop below freezing at night, and flat tent spots are few and far between. Total hiking time is four hours, and the route covers 3 miles (5 km).

KARANGA CAMP TO BARAFU CAMP

A short day of one to two hours leads you to high camp. The route leads climbers up a gradual, broad slope heading east through moorlands and open terrain for 2 miles

Typical rocky terrain
above Barafu

(3 km) before gaining a steeper ridge where high camp sits. The day consists of easy hiking on a dirt trail gaining 2149 feet (656 m) in 3 miles (5 km).

Water for the summit bid is carried from the stream below Karanga Camp since there is no water source at high camp (Barafu). The trail from Karanga heads north, gradually climbing the broad slopes above Karanga. After an hour, descend off a small ridge. High camp is visible from here on top of the next obvious ridge. Another hour of moderate hiking brings you into camp.

Barafu Camp sits on top of a steep ridge at 15,200 feet (4633 m). There is a large park presence here since it's the high camp for several routes. It's a busy camp, with ample room to set up tents and about ten toilets.

BARAFU CAMP TO THE SUMMIT

Summit day consists of more than 4000 feet (1200 m) altitude gain and an even bigger altitude loss to reach a lower camp after summiting. This is the biggest day of the trip in every aspect: altitude gain, physical exertion, distance covered, and effects felt by the altitude. To summit and descend, climbers cover more than 12 miles (19 km). The climbing is of only moderate steepness but it is persistent and seemingly never-ending in the dark of the night climbing toward Stella Point. The route climbs rocky steps and a loose dirt trail winding toward the summit around rock pinnacles and up broad scree slopes. Once you have attained Stella Point, and the crater rim, the terrain flattens out as the route winds around the crater toward the true high point, Uhuru Peak.

Summit day begins very early, usually around 2:00 AM. Climb the steep, rocky hill immediately above Barafu Camp climbing north, beginning to the right and angling back left. After thirty minutes, the trail levels out onto flats shortly before beginning to climb again up a second hill. The route maintains a steady angle, zigzagging back and forth across the broad, rock-strewn slope most of the way to the summit. Footing is always good and the trail is well maintained.

The route gains Stella Point, the spot on the summit crater rim closest to camp, at nearly 19,000 feet (5700 m)

after five to seven hours of climbing. The sun should be cresting the horizon at this point, offering breathtaking views of the expansive African plains below and some much-needed warmth.

Another hour of walking around the west side of the crater rim brings you to Uhuru (Freedom) Peak, the high point of Africa. This last stretch is slow and difficult climbing, at nearly 20,000 feet (5900 m), despite easy terrain.

DESCENT TO LOWER MWEKA CAMP

The descent takes a third of the time the ascent takes. It may be possible to take a more direct route and "ski" the loose gravel part of the way back to Barafu Camp.

Pack up quickly once back at camp and begin the descent to Lower Mweka Camp. Since there is no water at Barafu Camp, it's necessary to drop lower down on the route to a camp with accessible water. The final hour of this two- to three-hour descent, which passes the smaller Upper Mweka Camp and ranger station, is on slick mud that can be dangerous. Lower Mweka Camp is muddy and crowded and it's often difficult to find tent spots. However, you will be glad to be off the mountain and out of the rarefied air.

LOWER MWEKA CAMP TO MWEKA GATE

This last day of the trip covers 5 miles (8 km) of terrain and loses 4332 feet (1321 m), descending back through wet, muddy forests on rough, slick, stepped trails before attaining a wider but equally muddy access road. Again, it often rains heavily through the lower forests, so be prepared with your raingear. The route down is steeper at first and then levels out for the last half of the descent, traveling in a southern direction.

From Lower Mweka Camp it's a short hike out the next morning, albeit a slippery one. Even the most experienced porters slip on this mud that's slick as shortening. The Mweka Gate, two hours' trekking below camp, has a checkout point, bathroom facilities with running water and flush toilets, and some cold drinks. Moshi is another twenty minutes from the Mweka Gate by car.

THE CLIMB: MARANGU (COCA-COLA) ROUTE

Marangu, also known as the Coca-Cola Route, is the most popular route on Kilimanjaro mainly because it's the easiest climbing and most straightforward way to the top. As many as 90 percent of all Kilimanjaro climbers use this route. Because of this, it can be very crowded. Often climbers don't take enough time to acclimate on the route, because of its short length and easy climbing, and develop altitude problems. It is a beautiful route, however, and positives of the route include huts to stay in rather than sleeping in tents at camps and the availability of cold beverages. There is a lot of infrastructure on the Marangu Route that cannot be found elsewhere. Climbers looking for a faster, relatively easy climb to the summit should consider the Marangu Route.

The Marangu Route ascends the southeast aspect of the mountain. It begins low on the wet forests and, like the Machame Route, ascends through several distinct ecosystems en route to the summit, traveling northwest. The route connects with the Machame Route an hour below the true summit at Stella Point on the crater rim. Terrain consists of everything from wet, muddy ground to loose scree, rock, and sometimes even snow.

SAMPLE CLIMBING ITINERARY: MOUNT KILIMANJARO'S MARANGU (COCA-COLA) ROUTE

Day	Location	Start Elevation	End Elevation	Elevation Gain	Distance
1	Fly from home				
2	Arrive at KIA; travel to Arusha	2658 ft (810 m)	4592 ft (1400 m)	1934 ft (590 m)	
3	Market sightseeing				
4	Drive to Marangu Gate	4592 ft (1400 m)	6232 ft (1900 m)	1640 ft (500 m)	
	Climb to Mandara Camp	6232 ft (1900 m)	8856 ft (2699 m)	2624 ft (799 m)	6 miles (10 km)
5	Climb to Horombo Hut	8856 ft (2699 m)	12,136 ft (3699 m)	3280 ft (1000 m)	8 miles (13 km)
6	Rest day				
7	Climb to Kibo Hut	12,136 ft (3699 m)	15,416 ft (4699 m)	3280 ft (1000 m)	8 miles (13 km)
8	Rest day				
9	Climb to summit	15,416 ft (4699 m)	19,341 ft (5895 m)	3925 ft (1196 m)	3 miles (5 km)
	Descend to Horombo Hut	19,341 ft (5895 m)	12,136 ft (3699 m)	−7205 ft (−2196 m)	11 miles (18 km)
10	Descend to Marangu Gate	12,136 ft (3699 m)	6232 ft (1900 m)	−5904 ft (−1799 m)	14 miles (23 km)
11	Drive to Moshi	6232 ft (1900 m)	2658 ft (810 m)	−3574 ft (−1090 m)	
	Drive to safari camp				
12	Safari				
13	Safari				
14	Safari				
15	Fly home				

MARANGU GATE TO MANDARA CAMP

Drive past large baobab trees and the town of Marangu to the Marangu Gate at 6232 feet (1900 m) and register your climb. This gate can be very busy so get there early. It may take up to two hours to get the permit, so be prepared to wait.

This first day of the climb winds through wet forests. Be prepared for rain and wet, muddy conditions. The trek is a moderate effort and is perhaps a bit shorter than the rest of the days, climbing 2624 feet (799 m) over 6 miles (10 km) heading north. The first day climbs up gradual terrain into camp.

The trail begins on a paved road that turns into a dirt road. The first few hours of hiking can be very muddy and slick; wearing high-top hiking boots and gaiters is smart. You may see blue monkeys that populate the forests along the winding trail.

The last section to camp climbs steeply up drier trail into Mandara Camp. This camp lies on the border of the forest and moorlands above and is fairly large.

MANDARA CAMP TO HOROMBO HUT

The trail leads up through forest before exiting into the drier, sparse heather. This is a longer day, climbing 3280 feet (1000 m) in 8 miles (13 km) traveling northwest. A little way up the trail is a sign for the Maundi Crater. The Maundi Crater side route makes for a nice detour, which rejoins the regular trail after 2 miles (3 km). The route meanders through heather, passing a large burned area from a fire in 1997 and climbing short, steep sections before arriving at Horombo Hut (12,136 ft, 3699 m).

There are many huts around camp that climbers can stay in. Campers find room on the hillside above the huts. This is always a relatively large camp.

Some people continue up to Kibo Hut the following day, but I strongly recommend spending at least one day at Horombo Hut to acclimate and rest, especially if it's your first time at altitude. Acclimatizing will greatly increase your chance of summiting and make you feel better. Go for a short hike to scout the next day's route, or just take a stroll around camp to get the blood flowing, aiding in the acclimatization process.

HOROMBO HUT TO KIBO HUT

Day 4 is similar to Day 2 in distance and elevation gain, rising 3280 feet (1000 m) in 8 miles (13 km). The route traverses drier, rocky, more open terrain, again traveling northwest. Continue gradually climbing through moorland for an hour before arriving at the Maua River crossing. This is the best place to fill water bottles for the hiking to come. Eventually the trail gains the saddle between Mawenzi and Kibo (Uhuru) peaks, leaving the moorlands behind. There are excellent views of the summit slopes from here. Another few hours of hiking bring you to high camp on the Marangu Route: Kibo Hut.

Climbers may be reeling from a headache when they arrive at Kibo Hut or just suffering from mild acute mountain sickness (AMS), but almost everyone suffers from AMS at this camp. This can make for a rough night with little sleep. Consider taking Diamox (acetazolomide) if you are feeling the altitude.

The following day is another great opportunity to improve your chances of success by spending time acclimatizing and resting before going for the summit. If you have a headache from the altitude, it's a must. Summit day is long and gains a lot of altitude, so if you are hurting at the altitude of this camp, it will be much worse at the top and potentially dangerous. Grab a soda and scout the summit route a bit—the movement will help your body acclimatize.

KIBO HUT TO THE SUMMIT

Summit day is a long day of ascending, taking climbers up 3925 vertical feet (1196 m) of terrain and back down again to Horombo Hut in 14 miles (23 km). The route climbs scree and rocky, open landscapes toward the summit. The Marangu Route reaches the crater rim below the summit east of the intersection with the Machame Route at Gilman's Point on the southeast side before circling west past Stella Point then north to attain the true Uhuru Peak.

Climbers need to start early (2:00 AM) up the steep slopes above Kibo Hut. Summit day can be brutally cold and windy, often entailing hiking through snow. The trail winds uphill, traveling northwest for four to seven hours to Gilman Point on the crater rim at 18,640 feet (5681 m). Another two hours of gradual climbing around the edge of the crater traveling first west then north gains Uhuru Peak, the highest point in Africa. Uhuru is the apex of a broad, flat plateau that's part of the crater rim.

DESCENT TO HOROMBO HUT

The descent should take one-third to one-half of the time it took to ascend. After packing up at Kibo Hut and grabbing a quick snack, continue descending to Horombo Hut for the night.

HOROMBO HUT TO MARANGU GATE

Climbers descend the same route they climbed: from Horombo Hut to the Marangu Gate, descending 5904 feet (1799 m) over 14 miles (23 km) traveling southeast back through forests and mud. At the Marangu Gate, the transport will deliver you back to your hotel to celebrate the climb.

MOUNT KILIMANJARO GEAR LISTS

Gear for Kilimanjaro is pretty standard but make sure you're prepared for some serious precipitation.

TRAVEL GEAR

- Passport (must be valid for at least six months after the trip, with empty pages)
- Passport photos for visa
- Travel wallet
- Cash
- 2 large duffel bags (waterproof is preferable)
- 2 locks for duffel bags
- Carry-on bag or backpack
- Casual clothes
- Sneakers
- Camera

SAFARI GEAR

- Dress clothes (lodges are more upscale, so one set of nicer clothes is handy: collared shirts and slacks for men, a blouse and skirt or slacks for women)
- Casual clothes (long pants and long-sleeved shirts to prevent mosquito bites)
- Warm jacket (it gets chilly in the evenings)
- Sunglasses
- Sunscreen
- Lip balm
- Insect repellent
- Water
- Binoculars
- Camera with telephoto lenses

CLIMBING GEAR

- Medium-size backpack, for day hikes on the climb
- Pack cover (must fit your pack)
- Medium-weight hiking boots with high tops
- Gaiters, for mud and scree on summit day
- Collapsible trekking poles
- Rain poncho and/or umbrella

CLOTHING

Don't underestimate the cold temperatures higher on the mountain, and keep raingear handy at the lower elevations.

FOOTWEAR:
- Camp shoes (sneakers or other)
- 2 pairs climbing socks of different weights

LOWER-BODY LAYERS:
- Waterproof, breathable rain pants with full zipper
- 1 pair medium-weight climbing pants
- 1 midweight pile layers
- 1–2 underlayers

UPPER-BODY LAYERS:
- Waterproof, breathable raingear
- Warm down parka with a hood

- 2 midweight pile layers
- 1–2 underlayers

HEADGEAR AND HANDWEAR:

- Warm winter hat
- Buff
- Sun hat or baseball cap
- Heavy climbing gloves
- Lightweight trekking gloves

PERSONAL GEAR

- Ten Essentials
- Sleeping bag rated to 0˚ F (-18˚ C) or lower
- 2 sleeping pads: 1 inflatable, 1 closed-cell foam
- 30-plus SPF sweatproof sunscreen
- Dark sunglasses
- Goggles (optional, but good to have)
- Altitude watch with an alarm
- 2 1-quart water bottles
- Water purification tablets
- Snack food
- Multitool (with pliers)
- Toiletries

- Toilet paper
- Hand disinfectant
- 5 large, strong garbage bags for waterproofing pack and duffels
- Camera

GROUP GEAR

Guides and porters take care of all group gear through the outfitter.

SUMMIT CHECKLIST

- Parka
- Rain layers for wind and cold
- Sunglasses
- Sunscreen
- Lip balm
- Headlamp with extra batteries
- Radios
- Gaiters
- Buff
- Warm gloves
- 2 quarts or more of water
- Food

Climbing to Shira Plateau on the Machame Route (Photo by Jane Lee)

DENALI

ALTITUDE
20,320 feet (6194 m)

DIFFICULTY RATINGS
Technical: 3
Physical: 5

SUMMIT GPS WAYPOINTS
N 63 06.9256
W 151 01.5472

ELEVATION GAIN
(base camp to summit)
12,717 feet (3877 m)

DISTANCE
(base camp to summit)
18 miles (29 km)

TIME
(door-to-door)
31 days

SEASON
Beginning of May-mid-July

Taking the final few steps to the top of Denali's West Buttress

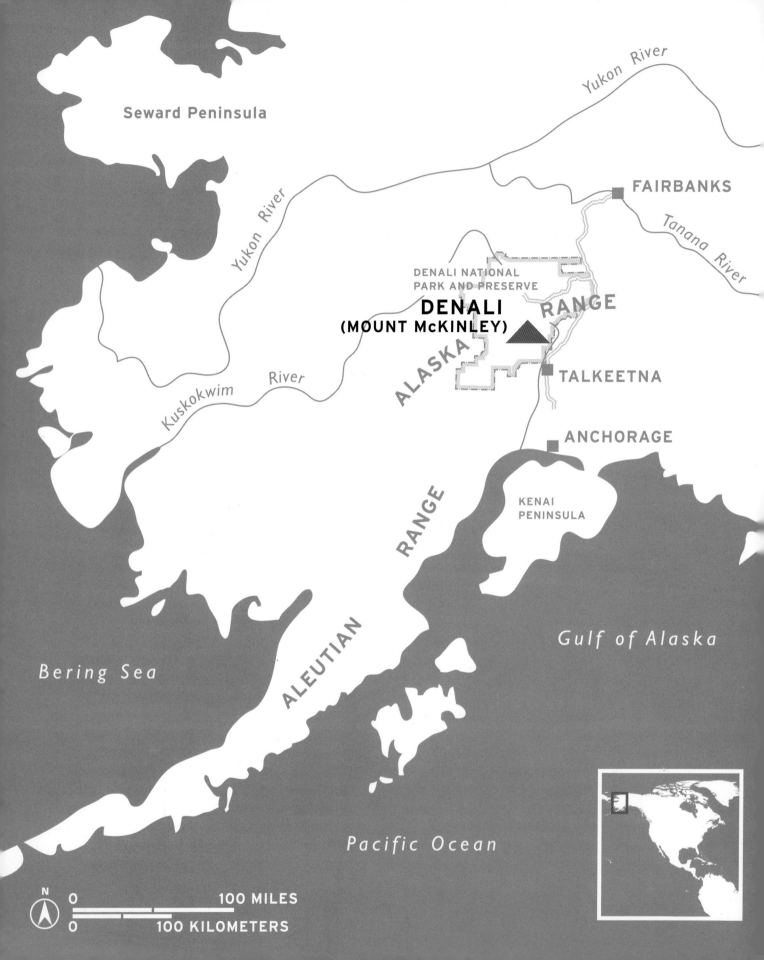

Seward Peninsula

Yukon River

Yukon River

FAIRBANKS

Tanana River

DENALI NATIONAL
PARK AND PRESERVE

**DENALI
(MOUNT McKINLEY)**

ALASKA RANGE

TALKEETNA

Kuskokwim River

ANCHORAGE

KENAI
PENINSULA

ALEUTIAN RANGE

Gulf of Alaska

Bering Sea

Pacific Ocean

N

0   100 MILES

0   100 KILOMETERS

CHAPTER 5

DENALI

NORTH AMERICA'S HIGHEST SUMMIT

EVERYTHING WAS COLD. EVEN OUR SOULS WERE COLD.
—DOUGAL HASTON, *IN HIGH PLACES* (1972)

Lying in the heart of the 600-mile-long (960-km-long) Alaska Range, Mount McKinley, or Denali, is the largest mountain in North America, rising 20,320 feet (6194 m) above sea level. Denali towers almost 18,000 feet (5500 m) above the surrounding tundra, giving it more vertical rise than Mount Everest.

The name *Denali* means "the High One" or "the Great One" in Athabascan, the indigenous language of the region. William Dickey, a late-nineteenth-century gold prospector, named the peak Mount McKinley in honor of then-US President William McKinley. In the 1970s, the Alaska Board of Geographic Names officially changed the name back to Denali, although the US Board of Geographic Names continues to recognize "McKinley" as the official name. In 1980, Mount McKinley National Park was renamed Denali National Park and Preserve.

Other large peaks that tower above the Alaska Range's serpentine glaciers include Mount Foraker (17,400 ft, 5303 m) and Mount Hunter (14,524 ft, 4427 m). These three giants—Denali, Foraker, and Hunter—lie completely within the vast 6 million acres (2.43 million hectares) of Denali National Park and Preserve, an area larger than the state of Massachusetts.

Denali is known to have some of the worst weather in the world. At a latitude of 63 degrees north, Denali is just 200 miles (320 km) south of the Arctic Circle. Winter lows regularly drop to -95 degrees Fahrenheit (-71°C) and winds top 150 miles per hour (240 kph).

Every year more than one thousand climbers come from around the globe with hopes of summiting Denali.

Whiteouts are common on the lower Kahiltna Glacier of Denali.

The overwhelming majority use the Normal Route, the West Buttress. The entire Alaska Range is a proving ground for the world's best alpinists, however. Some of the most difficult alpine routes in the world are on Denali, Foraker, and Hunter.

Alaska is an incredibly wild place. Only 700,000 people inhabit more than 663,000 square miles (1,717,000 sq km), more than twice the size of Texas. That's about a square mile per person! The United States purchased Alaska from the Russian Empire in 1867 for $7.2 million, or about two cents an acre, and it became a state in 1959. The name *Alaska* comes from a Russian translation of the Aleut (a tribe native to Alaska) word *alaxsxaq*, roughly meaning "the mainland." Alaskans are known for their pioneering spirit and toughness. Many residents live outside of towns in small cabins off the power grid, in the wilds of the state.

Denali is considered by some climbers to be the most challenging of the Seven Summits. On Denali climbers carry all their own gear, make their own camps, and

FIRST WINTER ASCENT

The first winter ascent of Denali is immortalized in the book *Minus 148°*, by Art Davidson. Most believed climbing Denali in the winter to be impossible at the time. Eight climbers battled brutal cold and almost total darkness during the ascent. Soon after embarking on their expedition, a team member fell into a crevasse and died. Davidson, Dave Johnston, and Ray "the Pirate" Genet (for whom Genet Basin was named) would eventually stand on top on March 7, 1982, before getting trapped in a snow cave just below the summit for six days. All three suffered extensive frostbite but made it off the mountain.

prepare their own food, unlike other mountains where high-altitude porters or beasts of burden help with the work. Fierce storms hammer the mountain year-round. The route covers 18 miles (30 km) from base to summit and gains almost 13,000 vertical feet (4000 m). Temperatures can easily reach -50 degrees Fahrenheit (-46°C) at High Camp in early summer. Crevasse hazard is higher on Denali than on any other of the Seven Summits, except for climbing through the Khumbu Icefall on Everest. That makes Denali an especially dangerous climb for unroped soloists. Every year dozens of climbers take crevasse falls and sustain severe cold injuries.

NATURAL HISTORY

The Alaska Range is several hundred million years old and still rising at a rate of about a quarter-inch (6.35 mm) per year. It extends 1300 miles (2080 km) from the Yukon Territory in northern Canada to the Aleutian Islands. The Alaska Range is a result of the ocean floor being thrust upward and over the continental land as the two collided at the Denali Fault. This fault is still very active, causing frequent earthquakes and volcanic activity.

Denali is mostly composed of granite that intruded through uplifted slate seafloor layers around 56 million years ago. Climbers will notice both of these formations on the upper reaches of Denali. The Ruth Gorge, about 15 miles (24 km) southeast of Denali, is a great example with massive granite walls extending thousands of feet out of the glacier. Mount Dickey's granite face extends nearly a vertical mile above and 4000 feet (1200 m) below

the glacier, making a 9000-foot (2750 m) wall, perhaps the deepest gorge on Earth.

Glaciers began to recede 10,000 to 14,000 years ago, although many large glacier systems still remain. The Kahiltna Glacier is the longest on the mountain at 44 miles (72 km), with the Muldrow a close second at 39 miles (62 km) long.

Plants and animals are scarce on Denali apart from the occasional raven, lichen, ice worm, or lost bear. In fact, a grizzly was once seen just below Camp 3 at 13,500 feet (4115 m) on the West Buttress route. Ravens are commonly seen scouring the high mountain landscape for handouts or food to steal during daylight hours. Sometimes birds and insects get caught in the upflow of warm wind rising through Kahiltna Pass, or migrate through, and can be seen on the lower Kahiltna Glacier.

Below the snow line, Alaska is teeming with life. The northern side of the Alaska Range is a rain shadow,

DENALI FAST FACTS

- Denali is the farthest north of the Seven Summits, at 63 degrees north latitude.
- In mid-summer on Denali it is always light, so you won't need a headlamp.
- In winter, Denali is one of the coldest places on Earth.
- The United States bought Alaska from Russia in 1867 for about two cents an acre.

which accounts for the variation in species between south and north. Animals surrounding the mountain include brown bears (grizzlies), wolf packs, moose, caribou, many species of migratory birds, ravens, golden eagles, and Dall sheep. The grizzlies are omnivorous, feeding mostly on salmon, roots, berries, ground squirrels, and the occasional caribou.

There are more than 650 species of flowering plants in the park, as well as mosses and lichens. These plants have all survived by adapting to the long, harsh winters and short growing seasons. South of the Alaska Range is mostly forested land, whereas the north is taiga and tundra.

CULTURAL AND POLITICAL BACKGROUND

Although Denali is in the middle of the massive and expansive Alaska Range without nearby towns, climbers attempting the West Buttress Route pass through the uniquely Alaskan town of Talkeetna. Talkeetna is a small town centered around climbing, fishing, hunting, and tourism. People from the town are sincere and welcoming and exemplify the pioneering Alaskan spirit.

Alaska is part of the North American mainland but sits to the northwest of Canada and the contiguous United States. The largest city in Alaska is Anchorage and its capital is Juneau. Alaska, the largest of the fifty United States of America, is one of only two states not connected to the contiguous forty-eight states.

CLIMBING HISTORY

Denali's rich climbing history reflects the people that surround it. Many early attempts were made by gold miners and explorers from the north side of the mountain. One of these early climbs was a successful ascent of the lower North Peak on April 3, 1910, by Bill Taylor and Pete Anderson. They hauled a 14-foot-tall (more than 4 m tall) spruce pole along with them, which they planted at the summit! Unfortunately, it wasn't the true summit, and the ultimate Alaska prize still remained. The higher south summit of Denali was finally reached

DENALI TIMELINE

1867 The United States purchases Alaska for just over $7 million.

1906 Americans Dr. Frederick Cook and Edward Barille claim to reach the summit of Denali but actually climb "Fake Peak" at just 5300 feet (1615 m).

1910 Americans Bill Taylor and Pete Anderson of the Sourdough Expedition attain the North Summit.

1913 First ascent of Denali (South Summit) by Americans Hudson Stuck, Harry Karstens, Walter Harper, and Robert Tatum.

1917 US Congress establishes Mount McKinley National Park.

1947 American Barbara Washburn becomes the first woman to summit Denali, ascending via the Muldrow Glacier.

1951 First ascent of the West Buttress, led by American Bradford Washburn.

1951 Famed glacier pilot Don Sheldon makes the first commercial glacier landing, on Denali.

1961 First ascent of Cassin Ridge, by Italians Ricardo Cassin, Romano Perego, Giancarlo Canali, Luigi Alippi, Annibale Zucchi, and Luigi Airoldi.

1967 First winter ascent, by Americans Art Davidson, Dave Johnston, and Ray Genet.

1970 First solo ascent, by Japanese Naomi Uemura.

1984 First winter solo ascent, by Japanese Naomi Uemura; Uemura dies on descent.

1988 First successful solo winter ascent was completed by American Vern Tejas.

2003 Fastest ascent—fourteen hours and twenty-two minutes—by American Chad Kellogg.

The view below
Squirrel Hill

This sign exhibits Talkeetna's rustic charm.

on June 7, 1913, by Hudson Stuck, Harry Karstens, Walter Harper, and Robert Tatum via the Muldrow Glacier. The majority of teams now climb the West Buttress on the opposite side of the mountain which was first climbed by Bradford Washburn and his team in 1951.

CLIMBING CHALLENGES

The first hazard that a Denali climber faces is the flight in. As good as the pilots are, and they are some of the best out there, the flight has inherent risks. Guides call it an "occupational hazard." It's rare that there's a crash, but there have been several over the years.

Crevasse falls happen occasionally on the lower Kahiltna Glacier. For the most part, climbers fall in to their waist or shoulder and crawl out, but sometimes falls are more serious. Make sure your crevasse rescue

skills are honed before starting up the glacier. Because of the crevassed nature of the climbing on Denali, solo climbing is not recommended even for very experienced mountaineers.

Clouds seem to blanket the lower glacier even when skies are clear above the 11,232-foot Camp 2 (3424 m). Bring wands to mark the route, track GPS points on the ascent to follow on the descent, and plug in the GPS points before beginning your climb. On the flat expanses of the lower Kahiltna, it's easy to get off route and turned around.

Avalanches, icefall, and rockfall become a concern above Camp 2. See the route description for more specific details on which slopes should be most watched. The most hazardous spots are the lower flanks of the West Buttress that lie above the route to Windy Corner, just beyond Windy Corner, and on into Genet Basin. Directly in front of Windy Corner is the most rockfall-prone area; do not take a break anywhere near here. You are simply exposing yourself to injury by doing so. I've seen climbers stopped at the corner resting on boulders that have recently fallen off the cliffs above—bad idea! Move quickly and deliberately through here.

Avalanche hazard is a concern on the slopes above Genet Basin while you're climbing the fixed lines. Occasionally a rock or two comes careening down the fixed lines from above, but this is rare. It's not a bad idea to wear your helmet, however.

Climbing above the fixed lines on the buttress, to Denali Pass and on the summit ridge, is steep and exposed. It's important to protect against falls. Placing pickets, slinging rocks, and using natural protection can provide enough security to make it a safe climb.

The windswept and exposed terrain above High Camp is one of the most unforgiving places on Earth. Climbers must brace for cold temperatures and be prepared for dramatic changes in weather.

Climbing Denali is a serious endeavor, not to be underestimated. Load carrying on Denali is very strenuous. Climbers must be able to endure long periods of poor weather. Multiday winter camping and climbing experience are a must. Crevasse rescue, fixed-line ascension, roped glacier travel, placing running belays, cramponing, self-arrest, placing snow and ice anchors, packing and rigging a sled, and tying knots are some, but not all, of the skills climbers need for this ascent. It is advisable to take climbing courses from professional guide services or instructors, to develop or brush up on the necessary skills.

FIRST SOLO WINTER ASCENT OF DENALI

A solo winter climb of Denali? In 1984, I could not have imagined a more audacious idea. After having climbed the mountain many times in prior "normal" summer seasons, I was on vacation in Japan that winter when Naomi Uemura, a Japanese mountaineering hero, was declared lost on Denali during his attempt at the first solo winter ascent of the mountain. Uemura was never found, and I couldn't stop thinking about what had gone wrong. From that point on, I spent almost all of my free time imagining how difficult it would be to pull off a successful solo winter climb of Denali.

On February 15, 1988, the bush plane dropped me on a cold, dark morning on the Southeast Fork of the Kahiltna Glacier near the base of Mount McKinley. When I had first started to conceptualize the project in Japan four years earlier, the challenge of such an undertaking seemed overwhelming. To come to terms with the daunting task, I tried to focus on my major concerns: crevasse fall, carrying only what was absolutely necessary for survival (in other words, the less gear I carried, the more quickly I would be able to move up the mountain), and the extreme weather.

Crevasses are always an issue on Denali, but because I would be by myself, falling into a crevasse was more of a concern than usual. I bought a lightweight aluminum ladder at a local hardware store to wear around my waist while crossing a crevasse field, hoping that it would span any hole I might kick through in a snow bridge over a crack.

Due to weight limitations, I opted to travel without a thermometer. In retrospect, I suspect that my decision was at least in part psychological, as I didn't really want to know how cold it actually was. One may extrapolate by using temperatures in nearby Talkeetna, Alaska, 60 miles (96 km) southeast and calculating standard lapse rate, that I certainly experienced fifty-below temperatures and wind chill that was off the new wind chill chart by the National Oceanic and Atmospheric Administration (-99˚F, -73˚C).

Mid-February on Denali is dark. I received no more than eight hours of sunlight, so I took two headlights powered with lithium batteries. To deal with the cold, I used military-style arctic footwear (bunny boots) and expedition mittens. Over the top of my one-piece down suit, I wore a one-piece nylon wind suit. Even with this clothing, I needed to keep moving vigorously any time that I was outside of my snow shelter in order to avoid hypothermia and frostbite.

After I flew onto the glacier, a relentless series of low-pressure systems started to hammer the mountain with high winds and snow. Because of the weather, I could climb only one day out of every three. In the meantime, I spent most of my time listening to the howling winds while hunkered underground in my dark snow trench. On each storm day, I restricted myself to half rations of food so as not to run out. When there was a lull between storms, I would hastily pack up all of my belongings, load up my backpack and sled, and ski like mad up the mountain to the next suitable campsite. I had to keep moving to keep warm, so I would immediately dig the next trench and dive into it before I cooled down too much and became hypothermic. Once I was sealed inside, the trench would warm up to a temperature that was sixty or seventy degrees warmer than the outside temperature, and I was able to cook, make repairs, and get some sleep.

Progress was slow and laborious. Because of the amount of gear, I had to do double-carries of food and equipment between each campsite until I got to 14,200 feet (4330 m), where I left my ladder. Above that point, I used a very conservative snow bridge crossing technique: I pounded in two snow pickets for protection before crossing a bridge and, after attaching my rope to those pickets, I used my ascender to belay myself across the bridge. Once across, I drove in two more pickets and, on the rope, crossed back over the bridge to pull the original two pieces of protection. I did this for each of the five largest crevasses that I encountered above 14,200 feet. It was time consuming but safe.

On Day Twenty of the climb, after having moved camp eight times above base camp, I finally was positioned within striking distance of the top. After a couple of days waiting for a good weather window, and very low on food, I made a dash to the top. From the summit, I was able to make radio contact with a Citizens Band radio operator, who patched me through to my pilot so that I could arrange for a pickup down at base camp two days later. The next day, however, a major storm hit, stopping me in my tracks and preventing me from descending. I made it down to base camp after a several-day wait, only to be stranded for several more days with no contact with the pilot or anyone else in the outside world. One week later, down to my last candy bar on the twenty-ninth day of the expedition, my pilot (Lowell Thomas Jr.) was finally able to land and pick me up.

Despite the challenges of the expedition—the extreme weather, bouts of starvation, deprivation, and absence of any safety net—I immensely enjoyed the climb and feel that the expedition was one of the most formative and profound experiences of my life (so far!). If you want to read more about the climb, check out *Dangerous Steps* by Lew Freedman.

VERNON TEJAS

SENIOR GUIDE FOR ALPINE ASCENTS INTERNATIONAL, WHO HAS CLIMBED EVEREST
NINE TIMES, DENALI FIFTY TIMES, AND THE SEVEN SUMMITS NINE TIMES

PLANNING AN EXPEDITION

Climbing Denali requires a lot of planning and preparation, perhaps more than any of the Seven Summits. It is a serious, gear-intensive climb that requires plenty of advanced planning to ensure success. Many facets of this climb require attention, including buying, preparing, and becoming familiar with gear and food; applying for permits more than sixty days in advance of the trip date; acquiring specific climbing skills and fitness; organizing visas and travel-lodging arrangements; and hiring a guide service.

Gear is a critical aspect of this climb. It is absolutely essential to have the correct gear and know how to use it in such an extreme environment. Climbers should

CONCESSIONAIRES

There are six concessionaires, or licensed guide services, legally allowed to lead climbs in Denali National Park and Preserve as of 2012. These companies are chosen by the Park Service. This system, which has been in place for several decades, is similar to systems in other national parks in the United States. Other guide services may run trips in conjunction with concessionaires.

If a guide is not working through one of the concessionaires listed below, they are in violation of the park rules and may be subject to penalties such as fines or not being allowed to climb. Concessionaires have established track records on Denali, know the mountain well, and work according to the rules of their concession. Concessionaires are allowed a certain number of clients per two-week period. The concessionaires are:

- Alaska Mountaineering School
- Alpine Ascents International
- American Alpine Institute
- Mountain Trip
- National Outdoor Leadership School (NOLS)
- Rainier Mountaineering Inc.

use their gear on smaller training climbs several times before attempting Denali. Some necessary gear is specific to Denali.

Gear considerations: Pack only the essentials to minimize weight. This doesn't mean skimping, just not bringing unnecessary items. Several extra small items weighing a few ounces each all of a sudden add up to several pounds. Light is right!

Food is also critical. You need the right combination of high-calorie, digestible, light, and mountain-friendly food. Choosing the proper food is very important to a team's success, and knowing what to choose can be difficult without a lot of prior experience on long, glaciated climbs. Those climbing with a guide service have the benefit of experienced guide staff knowledge of what works and what doesn't.

Denali National Park and Preserve requires applying for a climbing permit sixty days prior to the climb date. This requirement forces climbers to get organized early and be fully committed to the climb well before flying onto the mountain.

In addition to climbing permits, a lot of organization must be done before you leave for a three- to four-week expedition, including work arrangements, visas, flights, transportation, and hotels.

A typical Denali expedition lasts slightly less than a month door-to-door, with two to three weeks spent on the mountain, including rest, weather, and acclimatization days. You will spend several days traveling to Talkeetna, organizing in town, and cleaning and drying gear after the trip. Some climbers add several days at the end of the climb for sightseeing around the state.

GUIDED TRIP VERSUS INDEPENDENT CLIMB

To attempt Denali independently, climbers should have a solid skill set of glacier climbing and mountaineering techniques and a strong foundation in multiday winter camping. This serious and potentially dangerous mountain shouldn't be taken lightly. If you want to climb independently, it's best to have experience climbing on similar terrain in the Alaskan Range or Canada; also take glacier travel and Denali preparatory courses from guide services. If you are not an experienced climber, it's prudent to hire a guide service for its Denali-specific expertise. Due to the moderate price of hiring a guide and the seriousness of the climb, the majority of climbers on the West Buttress opt to hire a guide service.

CLIMBING RANGERS AND THE RESCUE HELICOPTER

Denali National Park and Preserve keeps a staff of highly trained climbing rangers on the mountain during the climbing season. Their job is to facilitate the climb, keep the mountain clean, relay weather information, and provide rescue service should climbers need it. Rangers are supported by a helicopter that removes waste from the mountain and assists in rescues. The rangers do a great job and have saved many lives on the mountain. It is very important to be self-sufficient and judicious while on the mountain so the rangers don't have to put themselves at risk unnecessarily.

CLIMBING SEASONS AND WEATHER

The weather on Denali can be some of the worst in the world due to the mountain's height and northern latitude. Denali, at 63 degrees north latitude, is the same latitude as Hudson Bay and central Scandinavia. The mountain is notorious for huge snowfalls and hurricane-force winds. It's rare that a team will climb Denali without experiencing significant weather conditions. Weather dictates the climbing schedule. Unlike the dry cold of Antarctica, Alaska gets large amounts of precipitation; 1 to 4 feet (0.5 to 1.5 m) of snow in a single storm is common. This large amount of snowfall can be dangerous, especially when combined with wind events. Climbers must be prepared for avalanche conditions and know how to evaluate the hazard.

Storms are generally due to two major patterns. The most significant is weather from the Bering Sea to the west or from the Gulf of Alaska and North Pacific to the south. Storms from the Bering Sea are characterized by high wind, whereas those from the North Pacific bring lots of precipitation. Lenticular clouds often form on surrounding mountains such as Foraker,

warning of an approaching system. The second pattern is weather created by the mountain itself. Clouds build throughout the day, often dumping their contents on the mountain in the afternoon.

The National Park Service (NPS) provides daily weather information at 8:00 AM and 8:00 PM on talk-about frequency 1.0. The NPS also displays the weather forecast in front of its camp at Genet Basin.

The best time of year to climb Denali is between the first part of May and mid-July. It is miserably cold before May. The lower Kahiltna Glacier becomes too heavily crevassed, dangerous, and difficult to navigate after the middle of July. Winter temperatures hover between 0 degrees Fahrenheit and -100 degrees Fahrenheit (-18°C and -73°C) in almost constant darkness. The famous account of the first winter ascent is aptly named *Minus 148°*, describing the estimated low temperature while the team was high on the mountain (see "First Winter Ascent" earlier in this chapter).

DOCUMENTS

A US visa is required for non-US residents. Climbers must register with the NPS sixty days in advance of the climb by submitting paperwork, including a climbing resumé and a nonrefundable deposit. Beginning in 2012 the permit fee is $350 per climber. Climbers using guide services may sign up after this sixty-day deadline. For complete Denali climbing regulations, contact the NPS ranger station listed in Resources.

Climbers must check in with the NPS and sit in on a climb briefing when they arrive in Talkeetna. The mandatory briefing, conducted by an experienced climbing ranger, discusses risks, sanitation, climbing schedules, the NPS role, and climbing techniques. Clients of guide services must participate in this briefing as well. Climbers are given cache tags, bio-bags for human feces, and clean mountain cans (CMCs) to be used as portable toilets. Except for at High Camp, bio-bags containing human waste may be tossed into crevasses to minimize the weight of waste hauled off the mountain.

Glacier planes picking up climbers are a welcome sight at base camp after a long Denali climb.

COSTS

US dollars are the local currency.

- Guide service (group climb): $6000–$7000
- Permit: $350
- Hotels: $200–$600
- Food: $200–$400
- Transportation: $100

CONDITIONING

Denali is possibly the most physically challenging climb of the Seven Summits. No porters, yaks, or mules carry loads; no cooks make meals for you—it's up to the climbers to do everything as a team. This can mean leaving base camp with a 60- to 100+ pound (27–45+ kg) load divided between a sled and a pack. One cannot be too fit for a Denali climb!

Long day and multiday hikes at least once a week are the best way to train for Denali. Beyond this, cardio training at a higher heart rate is important. A routine of five or six days of training per week is appropriate.

IMMUNIZATIONS

Visa applicants to the United States are required to have the following immunizations. Make sure your vaccinations are up-to-date, and get boosters well in advance of the trip date if needed.

- Hepatitis A and B
- Influenza and influenza type b (Hib)
- Measles, mumps, and rubella (MMR)
- Meningococcus
- Pneumococcus
- Pertussis
- Polio
- Rotavirus
- Diphtheria-tetanus (DPT)
- Varicella

COMMUNICATIONS

Most climbers prefer simple, cheap UHF talk-about radios. They are light, reliable, and effective. Most are five watts, which is sufficient to communicate from High Camp to Base Camp. They can be purchased at most sporting goods stores. The Park Service gives daily weather updates on talk-about frequency 1.0.

In the past, climbers used VHF radios, but most have switched to lighter, cheaper UHF models. Some people still use VHF radios because of their ability to pick up weather stations from Fairbanks and Anchorage. Dual-band VHF radios have UHF capabilities as well.

Satellite phones are a great option to have on Denali so you can communicate with anyone around the world, not just on the mountain. Analog cell phones used to work at Camp 3 and Camp 4 on Denali, but that service has been shut down. Digital cell signals for some carriers now work on the upper mountain.

GETTING THERE AND GETTING AROUND

A climb of Denali begins from Anchorage, the largest city in Alaska. Most climbers fly to Anchorage International Airport, which has several flights per day to and from Seattle on Alaska Airlines and Continental. It's easy to catch a cab into Anchorage from the airport on the outskirts of town.

It is also possible to drive the Alaska-Canada Highway from Seattle in the continental United States and Canada to Anchorage, which takes five days. Or you could take an Alaskan ferry along the coast from Bellingham, Washington; the ferry takes four days.

Most climbers spend a day or two in Anchorage shopping for food, sorting gear, and buying last-minute supplies. There are several large grocery stores in Anchorage with several locations throughout town. Gear stores include Recreational Equipment Inc. (REI) and Alaska Mountaineering and Hiking (AMH). They lie kitty-corner to each other at the intersection of Spenard Road and Northern Lights Boulevard.

GROUND TRANSPORTATION

It's possible to organize a shuttle ride directly from the Anchorage airport to Talkeetna, the stepping-off point for Denali. (See Resources for shuttle contact information.) You need to call in advance to make a reservation. Talkeetna lies 60 miles (100 km) southeast of Denali. The drive from Anchorage to Talkeetna takes three hours. Most people drive to Talkeetna, but it is also possible to charter a plane and fly, for about $400, cutting off some travel time.

GATEWAY SETTLEMENTS

Talkeetna is a colorful little town with all the character you'd expect from an Alaskan village. It's sleepy in the winter, but in the spring and summer, it becomes overrun with climbers, transients, and tourists from all over the world on bus and train tours. It's the epicenter for climbers flocking to the Alaska Range to test their skill. Alaska Mountaineering School's Pro Shop in Talkeetna has just about everything you need to climb the mountain; it sits just across the train tracks from the center of town.

DOMESTIC FLIGHTS

Once climbers have completed their briefing with the NPS in Talkeetna, they are ready to fly by glacier plane onto the mountain. The forty-minute flight provides incredible views of Denali and the surrounding peaks. "Kahiltna International Airport," as the base-camp landing strip is referred to, lies at 7600 feet (2300 m) on the

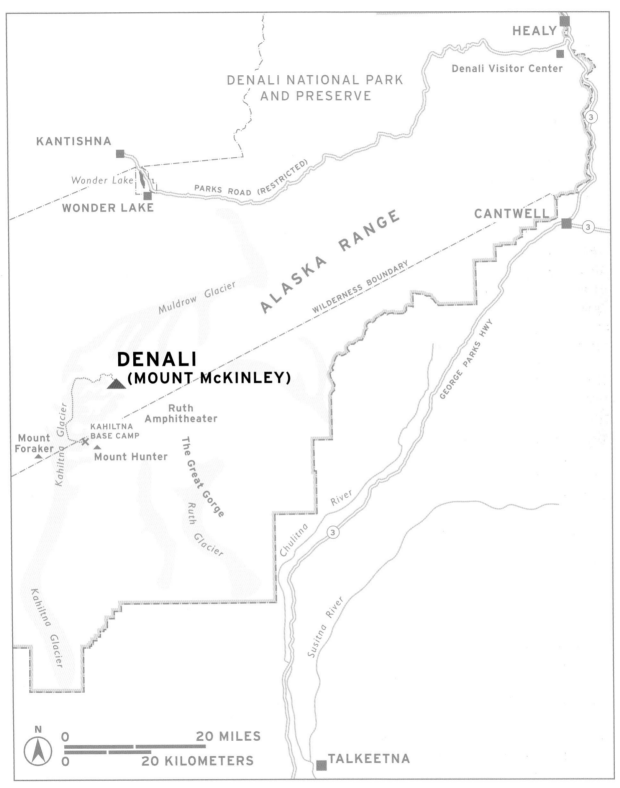

Denali environs

southeast fork of the Kahiltna Glacier. Base camp sits just below the Moonflower Buttress on Mount Hunter and looks across the Kahiltna Glacier at Mount Foraker. It is much cooler on the glacier than in Talkeetna, so plan accordingly.

Before starting up the glacier, climbers must check in with the base-camp manager stationed in the semipermanent tent just off the runway. The base-camp manager records permit numbers and hands out prepurchased white gas.

GUIDE TIP

One skill you will need to know for a Denali climb is how to cache your gear when double-carrying between camps. Several caches will be made: typically at Kahiltna Pass, Windy Corner, and the top of the fixed lines on the headwall, as well as at the camps on the ascent. To make a cache you will need a strong shovel, trash bags, triple wand markers with duct tape, and cache tags. Dig the cache at least 6 feet (1.8 m) deep to ensure ravens don't dig it up and so it doesn't melt out in the summer sun. Conversely, cache markers need to stick high enough out of the snow so they won't be buried by a big Alaskan snowstorm which can deposit 5 feet (1.5 m) or more of snow at a time. Keep caches out of any rockfall zones and record the coordinates of your cache on your GPS device.

OTHER ACTIVITIES: WILDLIFE VIEWING

Because you won't see much wildlife on a climb of Denali, once you're off the mountain consider driving to the entrance of Denali National Park and Preserve (several hours north of Talkeetna), or taking the train. From the entrance, the Park Service shuttle bus will carry you deep into the park, to Wonder Lake or the backcountry lodges. Wildlife often spotted from the road includes moose, grizzly bears, mountain goats, and smaller mammals and birds.

CLIMBING DENALI

Most Denali climbers fly through Anchorage en route to the small Alaskan village of Talkeetna, where they fly by glacier plane to base camp on the Kahiltna Glacier in the heart of the Alaska Range. Here climbers organize their gear before beginning the 18-mile (29-km) march first up the glacier, then up ridges and faces, to the summit of North America.

ROUTES

For several decades, the overwhelming majority of climbers have chosen the West Buttress Route for their ascent. This route was pioneered more than a half century ago and soon after became the normal route on the mountain. Before the West Buttress became popular, the Northern Muldrow Glacier was more commonly used. Today, despite the West Buttress's popularity, classic harder Denali routes such as the Cassin Ridge, the West Rib, and the easier Muldrow Glacier still get several ascents per year.

The West Buttress offers a direct route up and interesting climbing while being one of the easiest routes on the mountain. All of the concessionaires except the National Outdoor Leadership School (NOLS) run the majority of their climbs on this route. The National Park Service has a camp at 14,200 feet (4328 m) on the route and maintains fixed lines on the headwall; flight services use Base Camp at 7600 feet (2317 m) as their main landing strip. This infrastructure facilitates safe climbing, information exchange, and establishing camps.

Climbing the West Buttress takes a month door-to-door, allowing for bad weather days and extra time to acclimatize. Storms in Alaska can be fierce and last for several days or even weeks. Not counting travel and prep time in Talkeetna, the expedition usually lasts two to three weeks.

Snow walls shelter tents from strong winds at Camp 2 on Denali.

SNOWSHOES OR SKIS?

Which is a better way to climb Denali: snowshoes or skis? You will see many climbers on each on the West Buttress. Climbing on skis is similar to snowshoeing, but descending is quite different. You must be a very proficient skier to descend safely with massive Denali-sized loads on your back and in your sled in marginal conditions. If you are at this level of skiing, then it might be the right choice for you but remember your teammates must be at the same level if you plan on climbing and descending together. With snowshoes, it's much easier to maintain control on the descent.

Another consideration is the boot system. Some ski-touring setups allow you to use climbing boots, but they ski poorly. Other ski-specific bindings ski much better, but climbers have to wear ski boots. If climbers plan to use ski boots, they should consider either bringing the extra weight of climbing boots or climbing in their ski boots. Most teams find it is easier to snowshoe.

> PREVENTION, NOT TREATMENT, IS WHAT ULTIMATELY WILL SAVE YOUR LIFE IN THE WILDERNESS.
>
> —DARYL R. MILLER, CLIMBING RANGER, DENALI NATIONAL PARK AND PRESERVE

ACCLIMATIZATION

Denali stands at 20,320 feet (6194 m), which feels several thousand feet higher because of the thinness of the earth's atmosphere nearer the poles due to the planet's rotation. Climbers must acclimatize to the altitude in order not to get altitude sickness and to ensure success. To do this, climbers employ a "climb high, sleep low" approach to climbing the mountain, double-carrying from camp to camp in order to give their bodies extra time to go through the physiological changes needed to acclimatize. Adjusting to this extreme an altitude takes a significant amount of time. Additional rest days are prudent, especially high on the mountain, in order to avoid altitude illness. If a climber exhibits signs and symptoms of altitude illness, the team needs to halt its ascent until the climber improves, or descend if the condition worsens. See "High-Altitude Medicine" in chapter 2 for more information.

WATER, SANITATION, AND GARBAGE

Leave No Trace (LNT) mountaineering has evolved over the past thirty years on Denali. Since the late 1970s, a pack in–pack out policy has been successfully enforced, with climbers removing all their garbage from the Alaska Range. The clean mountain can (CMC) program takes this one step further with the removal of human waste. The CMC was conceived in 2000 by ranger Roger Robinson and the other Denali mountaineering staff for use in the rugged environment on Denali.

Today, Denali National Park and Preserve requires that all human waste be removed from the 17,200-foot (5243 m) High Camp. Use of the CMC remains a high priority for other glacier fly-in base-camp operations throughout the park.

For more information on Leave No Trace mountaineering, consult *Mountaineering in Denali National Park and Preserve*. You can download a pdf of the book at the Denali National Park website here: www.nps.gov/dena /planyourvisit/booklet.htm.

THE CLIMB

The Alaska Range, one of the most breathtaking landscapes on Earth, should be part of every climber's tick list. A climb of Denali is a great way to experience this awe-inspiring place. The West Buttress Route on Denali encompasses a variety of terrain, from low-angle glacier travel to exposed ridge traverses. Weather on Denali can be stable, but just as often climbers find themselves braving snowstorms and cloudy conditions, often accompanied by wind.

You start by flying forty-five minutes in a ski plane to the mountain from the small Alaskan town of Talkeetna to the Southeast Fork of the Kahiltna Glacier at Base Camp (7600 ft, 2320 m). From Kahiltna Base Camp, the

A snow arch in Camp 3 (Genet Basin) frames Mount Foraker in the distance.

route ascends the main branch of the Kahiltna up moderate terrain surrounded by the largest and most forbidding mountains in North America. The route is mainly lower-angle glacier travel heading north until Camp 3, where the pitch steepens as it gains the upper reaches of the mountain, climbing exposed ridges, snow slopes, and smaller glaciers heading north and east. The West Buttress Route climbs nearly 13,000 vertical feet (4000 m) in 18 miles (29 km), making it one of the biggest climbs of the Seven Summits circuit.

Some climbers choose to spend a day at base camp organizing gear and practicing crevasse rescue before heading up the glacier. Any gear left at base camp must be cached and tagged at least 6 feet (1.8 m) deep so it doesn't melt out over the duration of the climb.

During the day, crevasse bridges melt and become dangerous to travel across due to the intense heat of direct sun. It's also very uncomfortable to travel in such high temperatures. Climbers switch to a night schedule to travel during the coldest hours when the crevasse bridges are safest, typically leaving base camp around 2:00 AM. During the Alaskan summer, there is no need for a headlamp at night. The glacier can change significantly from day to day due to the extreme heat of the sun, so don't assume that yesterday's route across a crevasse bridge is still safe today.

SAMPLE CLIMBING ITINERARY: DENALI'S WEST BUTTRESS ROUTE

Day	Location	Start Elevation	End Elevation	Elevation Gain	Distance
1	Fly to Alaska				
2	Arrive in Anchorage				
3	Organize in Anchorage				
4	Drive to Talkeetna	0 ft (0 m)	346 ft (105 m)	346 ft (105 m)	150 miles (240 km)
5	NPS briefing; fly to base camp	346 ft (105 m)	7603 ft (2317 m)	7257 ft (2212 m)	35 miles (56 km)
6	Contingency				
7	Descend Heartbreak Hill	7603 ft (2317 m)	6721 ft (2049 m)	−800 ft (−268 m)	
	Climb to Camp 1	6721 ft (2049 m)	7790 ft (2375 m)	1069 feet (326 m)	5 miles (8 km)
8	Carry to Kahiltna Pass	7790 ft (2375 m)	10,119 ft (3085 m)	2329 ft (710 m)	7 miles (11 km)
9	Contingency				
10	Climb to Camp 2	7790 ft (2375 m)	11,232 ft (3424 m)	3442 ft (1049 m)	5 miles (8 km)
11	Back-carry to Kahiltna Pass	11,232 ft (3424 m)	10,119 ft (3085 m)	−1113 feet (−339 m)	2 miles (3 km)
12	Rest day				
13	Carry to Windy Corner	11,232 ft (3424 m)	13,451 ft (4100 m)	2219 ft (676 m)	3 miles (5 km)
14	Climb to top of Motorcycle Hill	11,232 ft (3424 m)	11,689 ft (3563 m)	457 ft (139 m)	
	Climb to top of Squirrel Hill	11,689 ft (3563 m)	12,420 ft (3787 m)	731 ft (224 m)	
	Climb to Camp 3	12,420 ft (3787 m)	14,235 ft (4339 m)	1815 ft (552 m)	3 miles (5 km)
15	Contingency				
16	Back-carry to Windy Corner	14,235 ft (4339 m)	13,451 ft (4100 m)	−784 feet (−239 m)	2 miles (3 km)
17	Contingency				
18	Carry to top of fixed lines	14,235 ft (4339 m)	16,214 ft (4943 m)	1979 ft (604 m)	1.5 miles (2.5 km)
19	Acclimatize				
20	Climb to bottom of fixed lines	14,235 ft (4339 m)	15,256 ft (4651 m)	1021 ft (312 m)	
	Climb to Camp 4, grab cache	15,256 ft (4651 m)	17,253 ft (5259 m)	1997 ft (609 m)	1.5 miles (2.5 km)
21	Contingency				
22	Climb to Denali Pass	17,253 ft (5260 m)	18,298 ft (5578 m)	1045 ft (318 m)	
	Climb to summit ridge	18,298 ft (5578 m)	20,107 ft (6130 m)	1809 ft (552 m)	
	Climb to summit	20,107 ft (6130 m)	20,320 ft (6194 m)	210 ft (64 m)	3.5 miles (5.5 km)
	Descend to Camp 4	20,320 ft (6190 m)	17,253 ft (5259 m)	−3120 ft (−950 m)	3.5 miles (5.5 km)

Day	Location	Start Elevation	End Elevation	Elevation Gain	Distance
23	Contingency				
24	Contingency				
25	Descend to Camp 3	17,253 ft (5260 m)	14,235 ft (4339 m)	−3018 ft (−921 m)	1.5 miles (2.5 km)
26	Contingency				
27	Descend to Camp 1	14,235 ft (4339 m)	7790 ft (2375 m)	−6445 ft (−1964 m)	8 miles (13 km)
28	Descend to base camp	7790 ft (2375 m)	7603 ft (2317 m)	−187 ft (−58 m)	5 miles (8 km)
	Fly to Anchorage	7603 ft (2317 m)	0 ft (0 m)		185 miles (300 km)
29	Sightsee in Anchorage				
30	Fly home				

BASE CAMP TO CAMP 1

The route from Base Camp to Camp 1 descends 800 feet (268 m), traveling west down the Southeast Fork of the Kahiltna Glacier before connecting with the main branch of the Kahiltna and turning north. First wind west around crevasses on your right and then east, gradually gaining 1069 feet (326 m) to the first camp. Most climbers single-carry (bring all gear and supplies with them in one move) this first day.

Camp 1 sits at the base of Ski Hill, at 7790 feet (2375 m) in a compression zone on the glacier. Make sure to probe thoroughly for crevasses with an avalanche probe before setting up camp.

CAMP 1 TO CAMP 2

Most climbers double-carry (cache a load up high, return to camp, then move up, carrying more gear, the following day) from Camp 1 and above. Climb the moderate slope above Camp 1, traveling east of the obvious crevasses splitting the slope. The route traverses east, climbs north, and then traverses gently west up Ski Hill before heading directly north the rest of the way up the glacier to the cache zone. There may be some large, open crevasses on the first slope above camp.

Once on top of Ski Hill at 8600 feet (2620 m), the route climbs more gradually north toward Kahiltna Pass. The climb from Camp 1 to the pass takes seven to ten hours round trip. Teams cache at Kahiltna Pass (10,119 ft, 3085 m) and return to Camp 1 to sleep before moving to Camp 2 with the rest of the gear. The route above Ski Hill has few crevasses. Camp 2 is another 1100 feet (340 m) above the cache spot. The route turns east at Kahiltna Pass following the glacier in a backward S up a steep, sustained pitch into camp. This last stretch is difficult after a long day carrying a lot of weight in a sled.

Camp 2 is tucked in a basin surrounded by snow and ice walls on three sides. The snow wall to the northeast is Motorcycle Hill, the route up to Camp 3. Camp 2 is relatively protected from the wind, but snow walls are still needed during more aggressive storms that hit the mountain. Several large crevasses pass through camp, so use caution walking around unroped. The large crevasse tucked underneath the wall to the north can be used for depositing bio-bags.

CAMP 2 TO CAMP 3

Most climbers double-carry from Camp 2 to Camp 3, choosing to cache first at Windy Corner (13,451 ft, 4100 m) before moving all the way to Camp 3 the following day. The route steepens (35 degrees) above Camp 2 as it climbs Motorcycle Hill, the pitch just above the 11,200-foot Camp 2. Motorcycle Hill gains 457 feet (139 m) before leveling off briefly. Immediately above Motorcycle Hill the terrain flattens, providing a good break spot before you begin to climb again. Squirrel Hill begins with a long, off-angle traverse before climbing a

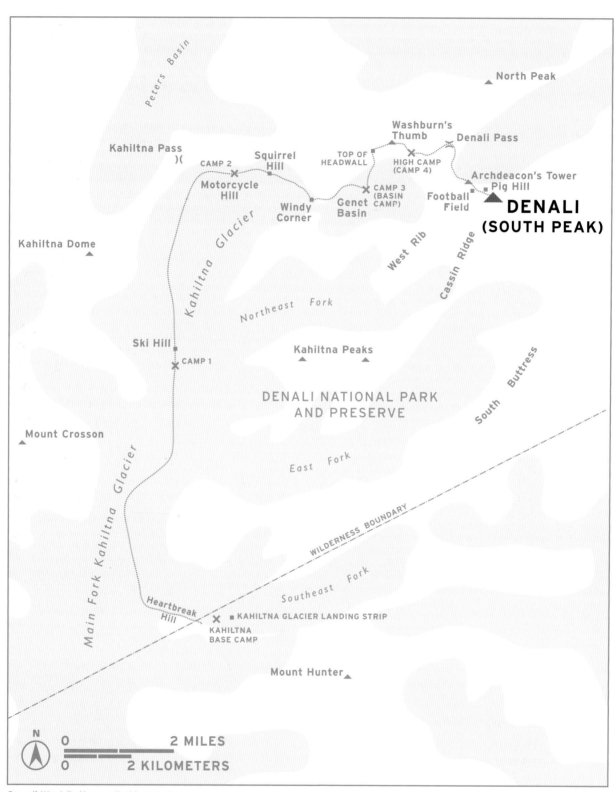

Denali West Buttress climbing route

GUIDE TIP

Avalanches are a very serious concern on Denali due to the amazing amount of snow the mountain receives. Before moving after a large snowfall, assess the snowpack to determine if it's safe to climb. It may be necessary to wait several days for the snowpack to stabilize, especially if a large snowfall has been combined with a wind event.

CAMP 3 TO CAMP 4 (HIGH CAMP)

Teams typically cache gear at the top of the fixed lines above the headwall for two reasons. First, this provides an excuse for climbers to climb high and acclimatize before pushing up to Camp 4 (High Camp). Also, caching gear lightens the load for the difficult push from Camp 3 to Camp 4. Climbers pick up their cache en route to High Camp to avoid back-carrying and climbing on the exposed ridge more than necessary.

steeper slope (35 degrees) for half an hour. In icy conditions, there is a fall hazard down a precipitous face to the north.

Climbing above Squirrel Hill, the route meanders toward the base of the West Buttress before angling southeast across the broad slope leading to Windy Corner. The last half hour below Windy Corner climbs a 20-degree slope to the crest. Most teams cache just beyond Windy Corner in a semicrevassed area below the steep slopes of the lower West Buttress. Be careful of rockfall and crevasse falls through this section.

Above the cache spot, the route winds gently into Camp 3, swinging close to the West Buttress just before entering camp. Many climbers begin to feel the altitude here. The climb to Windy Corner takes three to four hours, and another two hours of climbing brings you to Camp 3.

Genet Basin is equivalent to Advanced Base Camp on Himalayan mountains. It's a relatively safe zone where climbers regroup and acclimatize in order to successfully tackle the upper mountain. Park rangers maintain a camp with a medical tent on the southern side of the basin and post weather daily. Almost the entire route to Camp 4 is within view from this camp, as are the famous Messner Couloir and Upper West Rib, two classic, moderate Denali climbs. Mount Hunter can be seen to the south as well as Mount Foraker to the southwest. Several spots are wanded for peeing, but CMCs must be used for feces.

From Genet Basin to the summit, the climbing becomes steeper and more exposed. Directly above Camp 3, moderately angled slopes lead to the base of the fixed lines at 15,256 feet (4651 m). Park rangers and guides place these ropes at the beginning of each year and maintain them throughout the climbing season. These lines protect the steepest section (45 degrees) of the headwall just below the ridge and run for 960 feet (292 m). There is avalanche potential throughout the entire climb. It takes one and a half hours to reach the base of the fixed lines and another two hours to attain the ridge. I discuss techniques for fixed-line ascension in "High-Altitude Climbing Techniques and Skills" in chapter 2.

There is room for caching gear at the top of the fixed lines as well as on a flat pitch ten minutes farther up the ridge. Descending the fixed lines can be slow and congested, but it's important to be deliberate in order not to fall. It's only forty-five minutes from the base of the fixed lines back to camp.

One of the toughest days of the expedition is moving from Camp 3 (Genet Basin) to High Camp at 17,253 feet (5259 m). The ascent is six to eight hours of strenuous climbing with heavy packs on challenging terrain. This is a great test for how you will do on summit day. The climbing above the fixed lines is steep and exposed but also some of the most enjoyable of the trip. The route winds up the left side of the ridge past rock spires, cresting the ridge in spots. The ridge is easily protected with pickets and natural rock protection. Often the rangers or guide services will leave fixed protection along the

Denali's summit ridge offers incredible views of the Alaska Range below.

route that other teams can use. There is one short section of fixed lines maintained by the Park Service a third of the way up the ridge just below Washburn's Thumb, an obvious rock gendarme.

High Camp lies in a basin just east and south of where the ridge tops out. This camp is one of the most inhospitable camps on Earth due to its exposure to storms and wind. Solid snow-block walls are a necessity here.

CAMP 4 TO THE SUMMIT

The extreme cold of the Alaskan night at this altitude forces climbers to use the heat of the day for climbing. Most parties leave for the summit around 10:00 AM to allow the sun to hit camp and the first climb to Denali Pass. Often there are park rangers at Camp 4 who are a great resource for route information. Climbers average eight to ten hours to the summit, with another three to four hours to descend.

The climb from Camp 4 to the summit of Denali is a long and serious day in a hostile environment. The route above High Camp traverses a broad snow slope called the Autobahn, angling left to the obvious saddle at Denali Pass. This section of the climb covers 1045 feet (318 m) of altitude and takes two hours. It is the most dangerous part of the summit day route. This traverse is protected by large pickets the Park Service puts in place early in the season, although they can be buried by new snow. This slope is very prone to avalanches.

GUIDE TIP

Keep the rope stretched out to full length while traveling on the glacier, but shorten the rope when your team reaches the fixed lines ascending the headwall. This allows better communication and faster movement on this steep terrain. Stretch the rope again on the exposed ridge above to be able to clip the team to more points of protection.

From Denali Pass the route turns south and climbs a 35-degree pitch either to the right or left of a rock outcrop called the Weather Station (because of the weather collection equipment on top). Above this steep step, the route flattens and gradually ascends rolling terrain, staying to the climber's right near the ridge. After an hour of this moderate altitude gain, the route turns left (east) and climbs a small hill, flattens again, climbs another small hill passing south of Archdeacon's Tower, and descends 66 feet (20 m) to the aptly named Football Field at 19,321 feet (5890 m).

Pig Hill gains 500 feet (150 m) above the Football Field before leveling out at the beginning of the summit ridge. Climb gradually, starting on the right side of the ridge, then switching to the left after 845 feet (258 m). The ridge is exposed in places and should be protected as needed.

The true summit is a small snow bump on the ridge crest above a flat area. The South Face falls off 9000 feet (2700 m) just beyond the summit.

DESCENT

Descending to Camp 4 (High Camp) takes roughly a third of the time it takes to climb. Traversing the Autobahn can be dangerous when you are tired. Be careful! Many climbers have slipped here and been seriously injured or killed.

HIGH CAMP TO CAMP 2

The trip back to the airstrip is best broken into two sections. Teams typically descend to Camp 2 the first day, set up camp, and wait for the cooler temperature of nighttime to travel the rest of the way. It takes from seven to nine hours from High Camp to Camp 2.

CAMP 2 TO BASE CAMP

From Camp 2, it takes six to eight hours to reach the airstrip. Plan to arrive at Base Camp around 8:00 AM when the planes start flying and the weather is the most stable. It's common to have to wait, sometimes for days, for planes to be able to get in to pick up climbers because of bad weather.

DENALI GEAR LISTS

Don't skimp on gear for Denali. You need to be prepared for bad weather and emergencies.

TRAVEL GEAR

- Passport and visa
- Travel wallet and cash
- 2 large duffels
- Casual clothes for traveling
- Sneakers for traveling
- Travel documents
- Flight itinerary

CLIMBING GEAR

- Large internal-frame backpack (6000-plus cubic inches, 98-plus liters)
- Lash straps, for attaching hardware to outside of pack
- Skis or snowshoes
- 2 ski poles, for balance when hauling loads with a heavy pack
- Sled and sled rigging
- Alpine ice ax (walking length) with hammer and leash
- Adjustable 12-point crampons that fit your boots with or without overboots on
- Lightweight harness with belay loop
- Belay device
- Chest harness (might be just a double-length runner)
- 9 nonlocking carabiners
- 1 locking D carabiner

> ### GUIDE TIP
> Denali summit day can mean horrendous weather even if the day begins clear. The summit checklist is really the *minimum* of what a climber or team should carry to the top and back.

- 3 locking pear-shaped carabiners
- Gear sling
- Ascender and ascender sling
- Slings
- Prusik cord, for crevasse self-rescue and camp belaying
- Pulleys
- Ice screws

CLOTHING

Temperature changes on Denali on extreme. It can be blistering hot in the sun on the glacier during the day and bitterly cold at night. Cover all exposed skin to avoid both sunburn and frostbite.

FOOTWEAR:

- Double or triple plastic mountaineering boots with plenty of room
- Overboots that fit your boots snugly (only use with plastic double boots)
- Gaiters, to use with double boots without overboots
- Camp booties (synthetic or down) with high cuff and a sole
- 3 pairs rugged, long, synthetic climbing socks: 1 midweight, 2 heavyweight

LOWER-BODY LAYERS:

- Waterproof, windproof, breathable shell pants with a full-length zipper
- Rugged synthetic climbing pants (Scholler™ or soft shell fabric)
- Insulation layer (synthetic or light down) that fits over your climbing pants and base layer and under your shell layer
- 1 midweight synthetic under layer that works with your climbing pants
- 2–3 pairs synthetic underwear

UPPER-BODY LAYERS:

- Windproof, waterproof shell jacket (new lightweight ones work great)

After two long weeks
it's finally time to
celebrate the summit.

- Big, heavy down parka (it's cold! don't skimp) with a hood
- 2 insulating layers that can be worn together: soft shell jacket, pile fleece, micro puff layer, etc.
- 2 base layers

HEADGEAR AND HANDWEAR:

- Winter ski hat
- 2 Buffs
- Sun hat or baseball cap (sun hat with side protection and more coverage is better)
- Heavy climbing gloves (warmest synthetic climbing gloves you can find)
- Midweight fleece gloves that fit underneath your heavier climbing gloves
- Large down overmitts that fit over your heavy climbing gloves
- 2 sets hand warmers

PERSONAL GEAR

- Ten Essentials
- 2 sleeping pads: 1 closed-cell foam, 1 inflatable
- Down sleeping bag rated to at least -20˚F (-29˚C)
- Glacier glasses (darkest you can get) with side shields and UV protection
- Ski goggles (dark lenses) with a vent
- Nose guard
- High SPF, sweatproof sunscreen and zinc oxide
- Altimeter watch
- Cell phone, satellite phone, and/or radio
- Bowl, cup, and spoon
- 2 1-quart water bottles (durable plastic or metal) with a wide mouth
- 4 water bottle insulators (2 for each water bottle)
- Electrolyte replacement drink mix
- Personal lunches and snack food for 21 days
- Multitool (with pliers)
- Nylon cord for tent guy lines and repairs
- 2 rolls toilet paper
- 1-quart pee bottle (and pee funnel for women)
- Lightweight medium-sized duffel for your sled gear

> ## GUIDE TIP
> Cache some beer and hamburgers labeled with your name at base camp when you fly in. There's nothing like an ice-cold beer and a greasy burger when you're waiting for your flight out.

- 2 compression stuff sacks for sleeping bag and other gear
- 2–3 stuff sacks for organizing gear
- Lunch stuff sack for organizing lunch food
- 5 large trash compactor bags for caching gear and waterproofing your pack
- Burgers and beer to cache at base camp!

OPTIONAL GEAR

- Helmet
- Snow study kit and transceiver
- Thermos
- Camera
- Book

GROUP GEAR

- 4-season weatherproof tents
- Large tent for cooking and hanging out
- Cookstoves and white gas fuel bottles
- Stove repair kit
- White gas fuel
- 2 large cookpots (1 for cooking and 1 for melting snow)
- Group food for 21 days
- At least 2 snow shovels (1 is a spare)
- Snow saw
- 25–50 wands
- Avalanche probes for probing campsites
- Glacier travel rope
- Pickets and gear for pickets
- Clean mountain can (CMC) toilet setup
- Biodegradable bags for CMC toilet setup

SUMMIT CHECKLIST

- All cold-weather gear
- Sleeping pad
- Sleeping bag or bivy sack
- Snow shovel
- Snow saw
- Stove, fuel, and cookpot
- Communication device
- GPS device
- Wands
- Medical and repair kits
- Thermos of hot drink
- Water
- Food

A climber rests while taking in the early morning views on the lower Kahiltna Glacier.

ACONCAGUA

ALTITUDE
22,841 feet (6962 m)

DIFFICULTY RATINGS
Technical: 2
Physical: 3-4

SUMMIT GPS WAYPOINTS
S 32 39.13
W 70 00.45

ELEVATION GAIN
(base camp to summit)
Normal Route: 8832 feet (2692 m),
plus 4659 feet (1420 m) on trekking
approach (total 13,500 feet, 4100 m)

False Polish Route: 9163 feet (2792 m),
plus 6050 feet (1845 m) on trekking
approach (total 15,200 feet, 4637 m)

DISTANCE
(base camp to summit)
Normal Route: 7.5 miles (12 km), plus 18
miles (29 km) on trekking approach
(total 25.5 miles, 41 km)

False Polish Route: 9.75 miles (15 km),
plus 25.75 miles (41 km) on trekking
approach, plus 10 miles (16 km) on
traversing descent (total 45.5 miles,
72 km)

TIME
(door-to-door)
Normal Route: 21 days
False Polish Route: 21 days

SEASON
December–February

The tight Relinchos
Valley offers
varied terrain and
beautiful views.

CHAPTER 6
ACONCAGUA
SOUTH AMERICA'S HIGHEST SUMMIT

WHOEVER SAID THIS MOUNTAIN IS AN EASY
WALK-UP IS FULL OF IT.

— MARTY HOEY, FROM *SEVEN SUMMITS* BY DICK BASS, RICK RIDGEWAY,
AND FRANK WELLS (1988)

Aconcagua is the tallest mountain in the Western Hemisphere. It sits entirely within Argentina just east of the border with Chile, some 90 miles (150 km) east of the Pacific Ocean. At 22,841 feet (6962 m), the "Stone Sentinel," as Aconcagua is sometimes called, towers above all the other mountains in the Andes Range, including nearby giants Ameghino, Mercedario, and Tupungato. However, Aconcagua is a mere 204 feet (62 m) higher than its South American rival Ojos del Salado, in northern Chile, which for a time some thought to be higher.

ACONCAGUA FAST FACTS

- Aconcagua is the tallest mountain outside of the Himalayas.
- Several dogs have summited Aconcagua.
- Aconcagua sits at 32 degrees south latitude.
- Argentinean Willie Benegas summited Aconcagua while traversing from Punta de Vacas to the Horcones Valley in one thirty-hour push, a distance of roughly 60 miles (100 km).

The name *Aconcagua* is derived from one of three sources, or possibly a combination of them. The Araucanos, a tribe native to Chile, named the river coming from Aconcagua's west flank Aconca-Hue, meaning "It Comes from the Other Side." The Ayamara people native to the Argentinean side called the mountain Kon-Kawa, meaning "Snowy Mountain." The Incas called the peak Ancocahue, a combination of the words *ancho* for "white" and *cahuac* for "sentinel" in the Quechuan language. The famous South American liberator General Jose de San Martin gathered his army near Aconcagua while planning his attack on the Spanish to liberate Chile in 1817. Even Charles Darwin was aware of massive Aconcagua, having seen the mountain while on land during the *Beagle* voyage.

Aconcagua is the second largest of the Seven Summits. Although the normal routes are technically quite easy, it is physically one of the hardest of the seven to climb due to its altitude and remoteness in the rugged Andes. The Andes Mountains stretch from their northern terminus in Colombia to Cape Horn in Tierra del Fuego at the southern tip of South America.

The area immediately surrounding Aconcagua is home to some of South America's most famous ski resorts. Aconcagua is an equal drive from Chile's largest city, Santiago, and Argentina's wine capital and fourth-largest city, Mendoza. The mountain is part of Aconcagua Provincial Park, which was created in 1990 and encompasses 175,370 acres (71,000 hectares) of land.

Over the last twenty years, climbing on Aconcagua has exploded, to the benefit of the economy of Mendoza, where climbers need to secure their climbing permits. This growth has presented challenges for the mountain and the Aconcagua Provincial Park management regarding sanitation, waste, and overcrowding; however, the park has responded effectively to preserve the mountain environment, educate climbers, and promote responsible practices among climbers.

NATURAL HISTORY

Aconcagua resulted from the subduction of the Nazca Plate (to the west) underneath the South American Plate (to the east) as they collided. Uplifted, stratified rock from this collision is dramatically presented on the eastern walls of the Plaza Francia Valley, which can be seen from the Horcones Valley above Confluencia. Until the Miocene period, Aconcagua was a volcano like Tupungato and Mercedario, two other large mountains in the immediate area. Rocks on Aconcagua are generally either marine sediments or volcanic rocks. The massive approach valleys on either side of the mountain have been shaped by glaciers and dynamic rivers over time.

The highlands of Argentina are similar in climate and feel to those of Tibet. In fact, parts of the film *Seven Years in Tibet* were filmed in the Horcones Valley south of Aconcagua. Filmmakers recreated a traditional Tibetan city that reportedly made Tibetan refugee extras weep because of its resemblance to their homeland.

Above 14,000 feet (4270 m), Aconcagua's plant and animal life are fairly sparse and become more so higher up. The predominant vegetation of the arid steppe are low-lying bushes such as *yareta*, goat horn, and yellow fireweed. There are almost no trees within the climbing region.

Animals able to survive in the harsh climate include sixty varieties of birds, such as the condor and purple eagle, and guanacos, European hares, red foxes, and

A climber celebrates achieving Aconcagua's summit with some breakdancing.

mountain rats. It is also said that there are a few pumas in the park that periodically take down the guanacos.

CULTURAL AND POLITICAL BACKGROUND

The unique and welcoming people of Argentina, the gateway to Aconcagua, have a culture known for its great steaks and wine, relaxed nature, and hospitality. Many remark that Argentinean culture feels very European in atmosphere. This makes sense, considering Argentina's heritage. Obviously, the Spanish played a large role in the development of Argentina, as did Germans, Italians, and Portuguese, in addition to the significant impact of

native cultures before Europeans began exploring the area. Today, Argentina is a federal republic with twenty-three provinces and a federal district.

CLIMBING HISTORY

Although there is no proof that the Incas summited Aconcagua, there is evidence that they spent time high on the mountain. There are also Incan artifacts and burial sites on the summits of many other Andean mountains. A well-preserved mummy was found at 17,060 feet (5201 m) along Aconcagua's Southwest Ridge.

The first nonnative expeditions to the mountains didn't begin until 1833 when a prominent German

ACONCAGUA TIMELINE

PRE-1833 Incas explore the upper reaches of the mountain, possibly reaching the summit.

1833 German Paul Gussfeldt attempts Aconcagua.

1896-97 First ascent of Aconcagua, by Swiss mountain guide Matthias Zurbriggen, was made under the leadership of Edward FitzGerald.

1934 First Argentine ascent, by Lieutenant Nicolas Plantamura.

1934 First ascent of the Polish Glacier, by Poles Konstanty Narkiewicz, Jodko Adam Karpinski, Jan K. Dorwaski, Stefan Osiecki, Victor Ostrowski, and Stefan Daszynski.

1940 First female ascent, by Frenchwoman Adriana Bance.

1953 First winter ascent, by Argentineans E. Huerta, H. Vasalla, and F.A. Godoy.

1954 First South Face ascent, by French Pierre Lesueur, Adrien Daory, Edmund Denis, Lucien Berardini, Guy Poulte, and the chief René Ferlet.

1981 First South Face solo climb completed, by Frenchman Ivan Girardini.

1985-86 Spaniard Fernando Garrido spends sixty-six days on the summit.

2002 Mountain guide Gabriel Cabrera makes six ascents in one season.

2008 Eleven-year-old American Jordan Romero becomes the youngest climber to summit.

alpinist named Paul Gussfeldt made an unsuccessful attempt. The first successful climb didn't come until 1896–97 when a team under the leadership of Edward FitzGerald placed one climber on top of the peak, the renowned Swiss mountain guide Matthias Zurbriggen.

The Great South Face later fell to a French team led by René Ferlet in 1954, four years after French climbers summited the first 26,000-foot (8000 m) peak: Annapurna. The South Face rises 8000 feet (2440 m) above Plaza Francia, base camp for the South Face.

Today, around four thousand climbers from all over the world attempt Aconcagua each year. Most of those climb one of two relatively nontechnical routes through the Vacas and Horcones Valleys. The number of climbers reaching the summit is increasing each year.

CLIMBING CHALLENGES

Aconcagua is a relatively safe mountain compared to Mount Everest and Denali, but climbers should still be aware of some hazards. Many climbers underestimate the seriousness of Aconcagua because of its limited technical difficulty and ease of access. This apathy can get people into trouble in the form of altitude illness from rushing the climb or accidents due to not being prepared. It's imperative to ascend slowly, be aware of the signs and symptoms of altitude illnesses, hydrate, and not be afraid to alter the schedule due to altitude problems or sickness.

Another significant hazard on Aconcagua is rockfall in the Canaletta, a long, broad gully leading to the summit, which is often kicked loose by climbers from above. Some years the rock is glued together with snow, but on drier years rockfall hazard is significant. Be very careful not to knock rocks down on others below you, and always be aware of falling objects and who is above you. Wait to the side of the Canaletta if there's a lot of rockfall.

River crossings used to be one of the most dangerous parts of climbing Aconcagua, but with new bridges, the hazard is much less. However, sometimes the bridges wash out, making for very tricky wading. The Vacas

A mule skull at the entrance to the Relinchos Valley

River crossing to access the Relinchos Valley and Plaza Argentina can be quite treacherous in years with lots of snowmelt. Ski poles and river booties are essential for a safe river crossing. If you are unsure of your ability to cross, simply ask your mule driver for a ride across on the mules and consider giving them a tip.

" ACONCAGUA'S SOUTH FACE

The South Face of Aconcagua is among the biggest of the world's big walls; its towering 9000 feet are made up of dreadfully rotten rock, collapsing ice cliffs, and steep, plunging slopes of snow and ice. It seems an environment designed to repel anyone with any sense of self-preservation. Still, for all these unappealing traits, the force of the nature of Aconcagua's South Face beckons to all climbers to test their skills.

The legend of the South Face fascinated me for years. After a long but extremely successful guiding season on the Normal Route on the opposite side of the mountain, it came to me that it was time to ask Aconcagua's permission to scale its more daunting side.

I needed a partner. Damian, my twin brother, still had guiding responsibilities elsewhere. Second in line was Horacio Cunety, who had more than a decade of experience on this mountain: without any reservations, he jumped into this crazy but fulfilling idea of climbing the South Face.

High-altitude sickness would not be an issue, since we had climbed the mountain four times already that season. Feeling strong and confident, we decided to climb fast and light, carrying only the minimum necessary: supplies for two days of climbing—although the normal time is five days.

As we left Puente del Inca in the morning, the weather was fantastic. We set off full of energy as we hiked toward the route, when suddenly the immensity of the South Face was before us, its terrain appearing like the surface of the moon. Unavoidable doubts haunted us; we felt preyed upon by the face's constant, overwhelming presence. It seemed almost impossible to look anywhere else; our eyes were constantly drawn to the avalanches sweeping the face as we searched it for clues, wondering, worrying. The knowledge that we'd soon be up there, enclosed by the vertical world, brought immediacy and a cold reality to our expedition.

Familiarity however, is a wonderful salve: we know this mountain well; we have thirty years of combined experience; we have studied every feature a thousand times. We felt more comfortable as we got closer and closer. We wasted no time, starting to climb right away, and when darkness engulfed us, we were surrounded by towers of less than desirable rock. We advanced quickly to the base of the towers, where we made a cozy bivy.

After a good sleep, we started climbing again at 4:00 AM under the glow of our headlamps. A mist descended on us, but we were in a mystical place and we moved in perfect harmony, not needing to think, not needing to say anything: we knew what to do. By late afternoon, we had reached the base of the Superior Glacier. After a few minutes searching for a perfect bivy spot, we settled for an uninviting crevasse where, in desperate need of hydration, we quickly started to melt snow.

Sunrise brought us to the base of the dreadful serac. Searching for a safe passage was a hard and stressful undertaking; every side seemed crazy until we finally managed to find a perfect tunnel. Some ingenious digging brought us to the surface of Superior Glacier, where my eyes feasted upon the savage beauty of this mountain.

By the end of the day, we had reached the halfway point on the French Pillar, at 19,500 feet (5944 m). Under darkness, we started the long and exhausting process of digging on the ridge crest to create a platform scarcely big enough to accommodate half of me, let alone the two of us.

Dehydration and sore muscles were the norm by morning. It was cold and windy, but the rocks were the best we had seen so far. Still, the mighty South Face was not giving up. Every foot we gained was through hard work, but despite the difficulties, we were moving well. At one belay, I discovered under some snow, much to my surprise, climbing artifacts from the first ascent by the French Expedition in 1954. So many years ago. In that moment I was struck by thoughts of that historic ascent, of those amazing climbers.

Finally we reached the summit ridge ourselves; the South Face had given us its permission. By late afternoon, Horacio and I stood atop the roof of the Americas; the South Face had brought me humility, trust, and teamwork.

WILLIE BENEGAS
ACONCAGUA TRAVERSE SPEED RECORD-HOLDER,
FIFTY-PLUS ACONCAGUA SUMMITS, AND TEN-TIME EVEREST SUMMITER

PLANNING AN EXPEDITION

Planning for the climb must begin six to twelve months before the trip date in order to train for the climb, secure the appropriate gear, find a guide service or local logistics provider, and organize flights. A typical Aconcagua expedition is three weeks door-to-door, with most of that time spent on the mountain living in a tent. There are no teahouses as you find en route to Mount Everest, lodges as on the Marangu Route of Mount Kilimanjaro, or chairlifts as on Mounts Kosciuszko and Elbrus. Beyond mule support during the trek to base camp, climbers are on their own to ferry heavy loads to higher camps and brave the elements. Most teams spend fourteen to eighteen days on the mountain to allow ample time to acclimatize and double-carry from camp to camp.

GUIDED TRIP VERSUS INDEPENDENT CLIMB

Although the altitude is borderline extreme, Aconcagua is one of the Seven Summits that is reasonable for climbers to tackle on their own. Climbers attempting Aconcagua without a guide service should have previous experience climbing at altitude and must understand the effects of altitude on the body before venturing on the peak. Also, independent climbers need to be familiar with camping and carrying heavy loads for days at a time.

Overall, the climbing on the most common routes on Aconcagua is not technically difficult, and the logistics are manageable. Hotels, transportation, and mule services can be secured easily without the help of a guide service, and there are no special regulations requiring people to climb with a guide service. Almost half of the people attempting Aconcagua climb independently, although far fewer independent climbers reach the top because they lack the benefit of a guide's expertise. Climbing independently on Aconcagua means nailing down the logistical details six months or more in advance and adhering to a strict physical conditioning regimen.

There are still many good reasons to consider using a guide service. As mentioned above, there is a greater chance of success with the experience and expertise of a guide on your side. Guides with a lot of experience at altitude can recognize altitude symptoms and are trained in what to do should a climber get sick from altitude illness. This is a huge safety concern, considering summit day reaches nearly 23,000 feet (7000 m), the highest point outside of the Himalayas. Also, guide services have contacts with local outfitters and can arrange all the logistics for you, greatly facilitating the process. As with guide services on most of the Seven Summits, they range from basic to extravagant, and you usually get what you pay for. Unless climbers have a good deal of experience at moderate altitudes and have climbed independently several times before, I strongly recommend using a reputable guide service.

Afternoon clouds build in the valley below Polacos Camp 1.

CLIMBING SEASONS AND WEATHER

The Austral summer is the time to climb Aconcagua. December is a good time to climb, but January and February have the best weather. Almost half of all ascents occur in the month of January. Less than 10 percent of climbers choose months before or after these three.

Aconcagua is known for its clear skies and consistent weather. It is a high-mountain desert environment, which means hot midday sun and clear, cold nights. Major storms are infrequent, although snow dumps of a foot or more are common at least once a climbing season. Overall, the weather is much better and more consistent than on Denali or Mount Elbrus and most similar to that of Vinson Massif.

Aconcagua is notorious for the Viento Blanco, or "White Wind," which can scour the mountain for days or weeks at a time. The highest winds I've ever experienced were in 2005 at Camp Cholera, high camp on the Plaza Argentina–False Polish route, which sits at 19,500 feet (5944 m). The night following our summit bid, we were hammered by gusts of 100 miles per hour (160 kph). We were glued to the side of the tent for hours to protect the battered tent walls, to no avail. Eventually the tent poles began to break one by one before we abandoned the effort, collapsed the tent, and dragged its entire contents into a more protected tent nearby. The storm eventually abated enough for us to pack up and bolt down lower.

Generally, major storms arrive from the northwest off the Pacific Ocean, which is the prevailing weather trend. Mule services can alert you to major storms over their VHF radio channels. Thermal activity producing clouds and snow in the afternoon is very common and usually benign, dissipating throughout the night. Thunder and lightning storms can be seen to the southeast of the mountain toward Mendoza in the afternoons due to this weather pattern.

DOCUMENTS

Argentinean visas are free, and it's not necessary to purchase one in advance. There have been rumors of Argentina beginning to charge a reciprocal visa fee determined by a climber's home country as Chile does. Double-check visa requirements for your country before you go. Airlines hand out embarkation paperwork on the flight to Argentina.

Permits are required to climb Aconcagua, and climbers must arrive in person with their passports to fill out the requisite paperwork and secure the permits. There is no selection process for the permits; anyone who shows up and pays the fee will be granted a permit, although it may be necessary to gain prior approval for climbers under eighteen years of age. Minors may need to provide additional legal documentation or have a legal guardian climbing with them. Permits are for individuals, not groups, so be sure to get a permit for each individual in the group! Permits must be presented to park officials at several points during the climb, so it's very important not to lose or destroy permits after purchase. Climbing permits are valid for twenty days after entering the park.

Permit prices have risen significantly since 2005 and will probably continue to do so since there is such a great demand to climb Aconcagua. There are three permitted climbing seasons on Aconcagua: low, medium, and high—all with different permit prices. There are different (higher) rates for foreign climbers than for Argentineans. The high season is the most expensive. As of 2012, the foreign-climber prices for low season, November 15–30 and February 21–March 15, was 1200 Argentine pesos; for midseason, December 1–12 and February 1–20, 2200 Argentine pesos; and for high season, December 13–January 31, 3000 Argentine pesos.

The location of the Aconcagua permit office has changed several times over the last decade. For several years it has been located in Mendoza on Avenida San Martin just south of the Sarmiento walking plaza (Pasco Sarmiento), on the third floor of the Mendoza visitors center. Check the Aconcagua Provincial Park website in Resources at the end of this book for updated information about office location and permit fees. Maps may be bought at the permitting office, at a map stand immediately across the street from the permit office, or at Los Penitentes.

ACONCAGUA PROVINCIAL PARK RANGERS AND DOCTORS

Rangers have been in Aconcagua Provincial Park since 1990, but over the last decade their presence has risen dramatically to deal with increased numbers of climbers, human waste, and medical concerns. They have created a comprehensive system to facilitate climbing and maintain environmental standards. During the climbing season, park rangers are stationed at six locations, the biggest two being Plaza de Mulas and Plaza Argentina. Other smaller stations include Confluencia, the entrances to Horcones and Vacas Valleys, Pampa de Leñas campsite, and Nido de Cóndores. They monitor VHF frequency 142.800 MHZ during the season in case of emergency.

At Plaza de Mulas and Plaza Argentina, there are medical stations with a doctor on standby. These doctors check climbers for altitude-related issues before they head up the mountain. Park fees cover a rescue cost only if a doctor representing Aconcagua Provincial Park checks your condition and signs off on your permit. All climbers should check in both with park rangers and with the doctor at their respective base camps before ascending higher on the mountain. Medical facilities are staffed from December 15 to January 31 in Plaza Argentina and from November 15 to March 15 in Plaza de Mulas.

COSTS

Local currency is the Argentinean peso ($); as of 2012 the exchange rate is 3–5 Argentinean pesos to $1US but it can be volatile. To change currency, look for a local

With the Gran Acarreo behind him, a climber approaches the Canaletta.

FAST FACT

About 3 miles (6 km) west of Los Penitentes is a cemetery, called "the climber's cemetery" in English, where many notable Andean and Aconcagua climbers were put to rest. If you have extra time, it's worth a visit.

currency exchange service, called *casa de cambio*. Cambio Santiago on Avenida San Martin in the heart of town is the biggest and safest exchange house and usually has the best rate. Major credit cards are accepted throughout Argentina. There are a few ATMs in Mendoza. Many businesses in Argentina will accept American dollars, although Argentinean pesos are preferred. Argentina is less expensive than the United States or Europe.

Climbers have the benefit of mule support during the trek into base camp, making it possible to bring luxury food items and fresh food for those days. Pack perishables and breakables tightly in coolers to protect them. Wrap anything made of glass in thick newspaper or Styrofoam. Be careful there is nothing sharp sticking out of the gear bags that could irritate or injure the mules. Meals are available for purchase at base camp. Bring US$500 to US$1000 in small bills for incidentals, such as gifts, sodas, Internet access, beer, food, and tips for mule services staff.

- Permit: $300–$700
- Lodging: $200–$800
- Food: $300
- Transportation: $100–$200
- Mule service: $400
- Guide service: $3000–$5000

CONDITIONING

Climbing Aconcagua is a long and serious expedition. Ability to take care of yourself in cold and windy conditions, multiday camping, cramponing, and self-arrest are all important skills for Aconcagua. Loads are quite heavy on Aconcagua despite double-carrying: 40–70 pounds (18–32 kg). You will need the requisite fitness to handle these loads for multiple days at a time. Most climbers are affected by minor to severe acute mountain sickness at some point during the climb, despite a slow climbing progression. Prior exposure to moderate or extreme altitudes is beneficial. For more specific information regarding conditioning for Aconcagua, please see "Fitness" in Part I.

IMMUNIZATIONS

Diphtheria-tetanus (DPT) and hepatitis A and B vaccines are the most important for Argentina. It's important to be up-to-date on the rest. Consult your physician and double-check your immunization record.

COMMUNICATIONS

The most important forms of communication for Aconcagua are a satellite phone for outside communication and VHF and UHF radios for communication on the mountain. The park rangers and mule services generally use VHF frequencies and monitor them continuously, but UHF radios are an effective means of communication within a group.

GETTING THERE AND GETTING AROUND

The route to Aconcagua leads through Mendoza, Argentina, a quaint and hospitable town that climbers must visit to secure a climbing permit. To reach Mendoza, most Aconcagua climbers coming from Asia or North America fly Lan Chile through Santiago, Chile; those coming from Europe or Africa fly Aerolineas Argentinas via Buenos Aires, Argentina. Both cities are major South American airline hubs that make for an enjoyable stopover before or after the climb. There are several flights in and out of Mendoza to Santiago and Buenos Aires each day. It's important to book your flights well in advance. Taxis from Mendoza's airport into the city center are easy to get, safe, and cheap. It is about a twenty-minute trip.

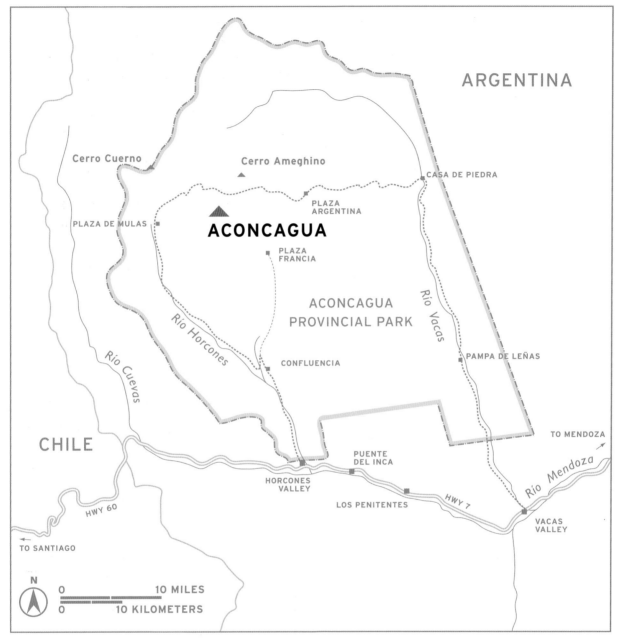

Aconcagua environs and approaches

Mendoza is a beautiful city of one million people at 2460 feet (750 m) above sea level at the center of the Argentinean wine industry. Mendoza is an excellent staging point for Aconcagua expeditions, offering all the amenities needed for a comfortable stay. It is one of the safer cities in South America (although it is still plagued by petty theft).

There are plenty of large grocery stores in Mendoza to shop for expedition food. The largest one is Jumbo, located on the outskirts of the city. (Every cab driver knows where it is.) The food selection is excellent, albeit a bit different from other continents. If you have specific food that you can't do without, such as specialty climbing food like energy bars, electrolyte replacement drinks, or power gels, then bring it from home. Otherwise, you should be able to find most things in Mendoza, thus minimizing baggage fees.

Argentina doesn't allow import of meats, cheeses, nuts, or fruit. Although enforcement of this law used to be somewhat lax, they are beginning to crack down. If you bring these items into the country, you should expect to have them taken.

Siesta is a part of Argentina's daily routine, as it is throughout the rest of South America. Stores are typically open from 9:00 AM to 1:00 PM and 4:00 or 5:00 PM to 8:00 PM, with siesta in between. This can take some getting used to for climbers not familiar with Latin culture. Once you do get used to it, though, you'll probably enjoy it.

GROUND TRANSPORTATION

From Mendoza, climbers must catch a three-hour transport for the 150 miles (240 km) to the small ski resort of Los Penitentes, high in the Andes on Highway 7. If you

Sunrise illuminates the route above Camp Berlin.

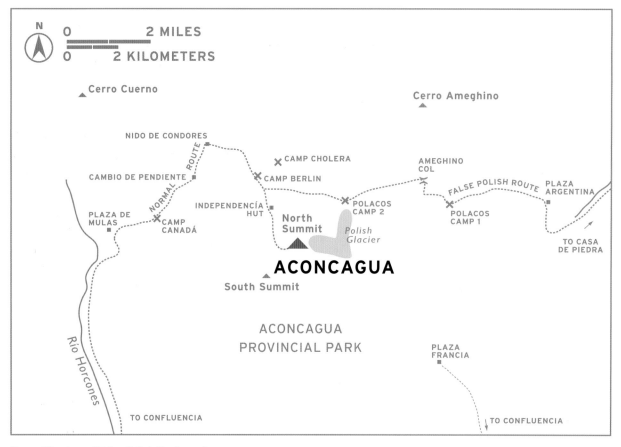

Normal Route and False Polish Route on Aconcagua

have hired a climbing guide service, they will arrange your transportation to and from Aconcagua. Independent climbers have several options. Mule services have connections with transportation companies and can arrange a ride for you, and private companies can be hired. (See Resources at the back of this book.) Public buses are the cheapest way to reach Los Penitentes. They are clean and travel frequently to Santiago from Mendoza, passing through Los Penitentes. They will drop climbers at Los Penitentes on request.

From the stopping-off point of Los Penitentes, mule services usually offer transportation to the trailhead. If you're not using a mule service, you'll need to arrange your own transportation: a short lift to either the trailhead for the Normal Route (Horcones Valley approach) or the Vacas Valley trailhead (Plaza Argentina approach).

The Horcones Valley is roughly 15 miles (25 km) to the west of Los Penitentes; the Vacas Valley begins about 10 miles (18 km) to the east.

From either valley entrance, it's about a three-day approach hike, usually supported by mules, to the respective base camps where the climb begins.

GATEWAY SETTLEMENTS

Los Penitentes is a three-hour drive west from Mendoza sitting on Highway 7, the major east-west highway connecting Argentina and Chile. Los Penitentes, at roughly 8500 feet (2580 m) in the Andes, consists of several hotels, restaurants, and a small ski area. It is a ski resort in the winter and a hub for Aconcagua climbers and mountain bikers in the summer. Most teams spend a night at Hotel Ayelen in Los Penitentes before beginning their trek to base camp. Hotel Ayelen is moderately priced with reasonable accommodations located about halfway between the start of the Vacas Valley and Horcones Valley approaches. Several mule services are based out of Los Penitentes, making it a convenient place to organize gear and make mule loads.

OTHER ACTIVITIES: WINE TOURING

Mendoza is located in the heart of the Argentine wine industry, so it's possible to arrange a wine-tasting tour after your climb. There are many options for wine tours and most hotels can connect you with transportation and route information. If you are climbing in February, be sure you check out the "Vendemia" or wine festival. You'll find wine tour services, which also offer a traditional Argentinean Asado (grilled meats) experience, in Resources.

CLIMBING ACONCAGUA

Aconcagua is a technically easy climb at near-extreme altitudes. Aconcagua has two main routes of similar difficulty: the Horcones Valley "normal" route to the west, and the False Polish (*Falso Polacos*) Vacas Valley route to the east. Both routes start from Highway 7, the highway from Mendoza to Santiago. More than 90 percent of people climbing Aconcagua use these two routes. The mighty South Face hosts some of the world's best climbers and most difficult big-mountain routes.

For more than twenty years, Aconcagua Provincial Park has stationed rangers (*guardaparques*) on the mountain to facilitate climbing and protect the natural habitat. Their main posts are at Plaza de Mulas, Plaza Argentina, Confluencia Camp, Nido de Cóndores Camp, and Pampa de Leñas; their radio frequency is 142.800 MHZ FM.

Climbers have the benefit of mule support during the multiday trek in to base camp, making it possible to bring luxury food items and fresh food for those days. Mules stay with the climbers on their three-day approach to base camp, allowing climbers to day hike with light packs. This service must be hired well in advance of the trip start date. These mule services are headquartered just outside the park entrances for both approaches, near Los Penitentes, allowing these services to easily send mules to support climbers in both valleys. Muleteers, or *arrieros*, drive the mules and facilitate the trek in. All mule companies charge roughly the same, ranging from $250 to $400 for round-trip mule support. Guided trips work with specific mule services, and this price is included in the trip package. Mules carry gear from the trailhead to base camp and back out again at the end of the expedition.

After base camp, it's up to climbers to ferry their loads up the mountain. Mules are tough on gear, so make sure duffels are packed tightly and fragile items are well protected. Make sure nothing sharp is sticking out of the mule gear bags that could irritate or injure the mules.

ROUTES

There are two main approaches that climbers take to the mountain; both require a three-day approach and share the same summit day but are different in character.

NORMAL ROUTE VIA HORCONES VALLEY

The Normal Route, the Horcones Valley approach, begins from the south and climbs the western flank of the mountain. This route, ascended by the majority of Aconcagua climbers, is the easiest to climb and navigate, and it is the shortest. The Normal Route takes seven to ten days of climbing above base camp.

FALSE POLISH ROUTE VIA VACAS VALLEY

The other route described in this guide was pioneered later and begins to the south, ascending the east side of the mountain. This route, which follows the Vacas Valley approach to Plaza Argentina, is generally called the *Falso Polaco*, or "False Polish," Route; it is longer, less crowded, and more scenic, and it has slightly more objective and navigation hazards. The False Polish Route takes nine to eleven days of climbing above base camp.

Combining the False Polish Route with a traverse of the mountain allows you to see the other side of the

Arrieros help transport gear into base camp.

mountain and also save a day on the descent by traveling the shorter Horcones Valley on the way out.

ACCLIMATIZATION

Aconcagua's largest difficulty lies in its summit altitude. More people die or fall ill from altitude issues than from anything else on this mountain. Due to Aconcagua's technically easy reputation and its hospitable climate, climbers underestimate how dangerous the high-altitude aspect of the mountain can be. It's crucial to allow sufficient time for your body to acclimatize to the altitude throughout the climb. Many begin feeling symptoms of acute mountain sickness at Los Penitentes even before reaching the approach hike to the mountain. Allow at least a week to climb the mountain above base camp; more days might be needed, depending on your response to altitude. If symptoms of altitude sickness occur, slow the rate of ascent and even consider descending if necessary.

Do your homework regarding altitude illness and acclimatization before heading to Aconcagua, and if climbing with a guide, listen to their recommendations. It never hurts to be on the conservative side of altitude illness.

WATER, SANITATION, AND GARBAGE

Aconcagua used to have a reputation for being a dirty mountain when regulations for using toilets and packing off human waste and trash were lax. Over the last decade, Aconcagua Provincial Park has set strict regulations in place, backed by potential fines, and has allocated significant resources to cleaning up the mountain. This change in tactics has done a lot to improve sanitation and the mountain's reputation.

Rangers have established pit toilets to collect and properly dispose of human waste at the major camps on both approaches. Upon arrival at base camp, climbers are required to check in with the park service and obtain garbage and human waste bags to use during the climb.

The rangers write individual climbers' permit numbers on their garbage and human waste bags, which must be accounted for at the end of the expedition. It is mandatory to haul all waste off the mountain. Human refuse gets dropped in the park ranger bin, to be flown off at the end of the expedition. Climbers will be fined if they don't turn in their bags, accounting for their waste, at the end of the climb.

Water is piped to camps from streams close by. It's prudent to treat this water, as with any water on Aconcagua. Iodine or chlorine tablets work great. Filters clog easily from the prodigious amounts of glacial silt and sediment in the muddy rivers.

THE CLIMB: NORMAL ROUTE VIA HORCONES VALLEY

Horcones Valley, on the western side of Aconcagua, is the most popular ascent route, called the Normal Route. Most early expeditions approached from this valley, and it later became popular for independent teams and commercial services. It's a shorter and more straightforward climb than the Vacas Valley's False Polish ascent. The trek to base camp, Plaza de Mulas, through the Horcones Valley, takes three days covering 18 miles (29 km) and more than 5000 feet (1500 m) of vertical gain. The Horcones Valley is awe-inspiring for many reasons, including its grandeur, surrounding mountains, and impressive geology; however, the trekking route is flat.

The Normal Route above base camp can be a bit monotonous, since it mainly consists of walking up well-worn paths zigzagging across a nearly 8900-foot (2700 m) scree slope. What it lacks in diversity of terrain it makes up in directness, however, and that's specifically why many climbers choose this route. It's straightforward, relatively safe, and short. Climbing consists of walking up low-angle scree and snow slopes to several well-designated camps along the route. The climb typically takes seven to ten days.

SAMPLE CLIMBING ITINERARY:
ACONCAGUA'S NORMAL ROUTE VIA HORCONES VALLEY

Day	Location	Start Elevation	End Elevation	Elevation Gain	Distance
1	Fly to Mendoza		2460 ft (750 m)		
2	Sightsee in Mendoza				
3	Drive to Los Penitentes	2460 ft (750 m)	8465 ft (2580 m)	6005 ft (1830 m)	150 miles (240 km)
4	Drive to Horcones Valley entrance	8465 ft (2580 m)	9350 ft (2850 m)	885 ft (270 m)	15 miles (25 km)
	Trek to Confluencia	9350 ft (2850 m)	10,892 ft (3320 m)	1542 ft (470 m)	6 miles (10 km)
5	Acclimatization hike				
6	Trek to Plaza de Mulas	10,892 ft (3320 m)	14,009 ft (4270 m)	3117 ft (950 m)	12 miles (19 km)
7	Rest day				
8	Carry to Camp Canadá	14,009 ft (4270 m)	16,667 ft (5080 m)	2658 ft (810 m)	3 miles (5 km)
9	Move to Camp Canadá	14,009 ft (4270 m)	16,667 ft (5080 m)	2658 ft (810 m)	1.5 miles (2.5 km)
10	Carry to Nido de Cóndores	16,667 ft (5080 m)	18,340 ft (5590 m)	1673 ft (510 m)	4 miles (6.4 km)
11	Move to Nido de Cóndores	16,667 ft (5080 m)	18,340 ft (5590 m)	1673 ft (510 m)	2 miles (3.2 km)
12	Carry to Camp Berlin	18,340 ft (5590 m)	19,455 ft (5930 m)	1115 ft (340 m)	2 miles (3.2 km)
13	Climb to Camp Berlin	18,340 ft (5590 m)	19,455 ft (5930 m)	1115 ft (340 m)	1 mile (1.6 km)
14	Climb to summit	19,455 ft (5930 m)	22,841 ft (6962 m)	3386 ft (1032 m)	3 miles (5 km)
	Descend to Camp Berlin	22,841 ft (6962 m)	19,455 ft (5930 m)	−3386 ft (−1032 m)	3 miles (5 km)
15	Contingency				
16	Contingency				
17	Descend to Plaza de Mulas	19,455 ft (5930 m)	14,009 ft (4270 m)	−5446 ft (−1660 m)	4.5 miles (7.3 km)
18	Trek to Horcones Valley entrance	14,009 ft (4270 m)	9350 ft (2850 m)	−4659 ft (−1420 m)	18 miles (29 km)
19	Drive to Mendoza	9350 ft (2850 m)	2460 ft (750 m)	−6890 ft (−2100 m)	165 miles (265 km)
20	Fly home				

HORCONES VALLEY ENTRANCE TO CONFLUENCIA

The first day of the trek to base camp, starting at 9350 feet (2850 m) and ending at 10,892 feet (3320 m), is a three- to five-hour hike to Confluencia camp. After checking in with the *guardaparques* (park rangers) at the Horcones Valley park entrance, continue up the access road to an obvious bridge in the center of the valley. Here the route switches from the west to the east side of the Horcones River and continues on mule paths for another two hours of rolling terrain to camp, 6 miles (10 km). It may be necessary to wait several hours this first day for the mules to reach camp since the mules have to travel a long distance to the trailhead before being

This well-used camp on the False Polish Route makes for a social climbing atmosphere.

loaded with your gear. Mule services have accommodations in Confluencia camp where you can get out of the sun and dust while waiting for the mules.

Confluencia is a large camp and the only established camp before Plaza de Mulas. Climbers using this route spend at least one rest day here to acclimatize before moving up. The location of Confluencia has changed several times over the last decade, but it seems to be well established now at its current location slightly downvalley of the *confluencia*, the confluence of two rivers, one coming from Plaza de Mulas and the other coming from Plaza Francia and the South Face. Confluencia has dining tents, prepared meals, and other amenities.

CONFLUENCIA TO PLAZA DE MULAS

Beyond Confluencia, the route descends to the Horcones River, crosses a metal bridge, and continues up a broad, flat, seemingly endless valley. It's approximately 12 miles (19 km) from Confluencia to Plaza de Mulas. Most of the trek consists of gradual walking on a rough riverbed underneath the hot sun. The last few miles of trail begin to undulate over debris and alluvial fans before climbing steeply up a terminal moraine the last mile into camp. Remember to check in with the park service as you enter camp and with the park medical station before beginning the climb.

Plaza de Mulas sits at 14,009 feet (4270 m) near the head of the Horcones Valley below the majestic-looking Cerro Cuerno. This is the largest camp on Aconcagua, with as many as four hundred people at one time during the high season. This camp has all the amenities that Plaza Argentina has on the opposite side of the mountain, and more: hot showers, Internet access, steaks, beer, pizza, coke, even an art gallery! Across the valley from camp at the same altitude is Hotel Refugio, where some climbers opt to stay. It's a twenty-minute walk from camp, and lodging is bunk style in unheated rooms.

PLAZA DE MULAS TO CAMP CANADÁ

From Plaza de Mulas the climb of the Normal Route begins! The route ascends a steep slope directly above camp and then disappears from view onto the slightly more moderate terrain above. Climbing on the Normal Route consists mainly of loose scree trail with occasional stretches of firm trail on 20- to 30-degree slopes. Switchbacks aid climbers to wind their way up the looser sections.

The first camp on the Normal Route is Camp Canadá, located above a rock buttress at 16,667 feet (5080 m). The climb to Camp Canadá ascends almost 2700 feet (810 m) over 1.5 miles (2.5 km) and takes three to five hours. This small camp with space for about twenty tents has a stream flowing just north of camp later in the day when there's more snowmelt. There are great views of Cerro Cuerno and base camp from here.

CAMP CANADÁ TO NIDO DE CÓNDORES

The climb above Camp Canadá continues up loose scree for another 800 feet (244 m) before relaxing in steepness at a primitive camp called *Cambio de Pendiente* or "Change of Pitch." Not many climbers use this camp, preferring to proceed up another 873 feet (266 m) to

> **GUIDE TIP**
>
> Look for the most braided parts of the river to cross. This will spread out the force of the water. Use ski poles for balance and make a train of people holding on to one another to break the current if necessary.

a well-established camp called Nido de Cóndores, or "Condor's Nest." The climb above Cambio de Pendiente is more gradual on firm ground until reaching Nido de Cóndores. There can be consolidated snow on this stretch, making crampons helpful. The climb from Camp Canadá to Nido de Cóndores consists of 1673 feet (510 m) of altitude gain over 2 miles (3.2 km) of terrain and takes three to five hours.

Nido de Cóndores sits on a plateau at 18,340 feet (5590 m) just below the lower terminus of the Gran Acarreo, a wide, steep scree slope leading to the summit. Most of the summit day's route can be viewed from this camp, providing a good idea of what type of climbing lies ahead.

Nido de Cóndores is fairly well protected from the wind and is quite expansive with plenty of room for tents. Drinking water is melted from snow around and above camp; be sure to treat or boil the water. Historically, this camp wasn't very clean, but with new regulations in place regarding waste management, it has improved significantly. Climbers spend one to four rest days here before moving to high camp, either Camp Berlin or Camp Cholera.

NIDO DE CÓNDORES TO CAMP BERLIN

The climbing above Nido begins gradually but quickly steepens as it enters a broad gully leading to high camp. The route ascends obvious switchbacks the entire way to Camp Berlin. The slope consists of firm trail, loose scree, and often consolidated snow. The climb to high camp takes from three to five hours ascending 1115 feet (340 m) over 1 mile (1.6 km).

Camp Berlin is the traditional high camp, sitting just climbers' right of the ascent route. Camp Berlin consists of two small wooden "huts" surrounded by several spaces for tenting. Snow accumulation around camp is used for drinking water. This camp sits at 19,455 feet (5930 m), which is just below the height of nearby Camp Cholera, often used as the high camp for the False Polish Route (see route map for the False Polish Route).

Camp Cholera sits directly above the ascent route from Nido de Cóndores at 19,504 feet (5945 m) and is accessed by a small, steep rock ramp leading to an obvious low point in the ridge. This camp started becoming popular a decade ago and is often crowded. It is much larger than Camp Berlin though. This camp is used not only by climbers from the Normal Route but also those from the False Polish Route via Plaza Argentina. Access to the summit is just as easy from Camp Cholera as it is from Camp Berlin.

CAMP BERLIN TO THE SUMMIT

From Camp Berlin to the summit takes seven to nine hours up and half that to descend. The route climbs nearly 3400 feet (1032 m) and covers approximately 3 miles (5 km). Extremely cold conditions feel even colder due to the lack of oxygen at these extreme altitudes. Ambient temperatures can often reach -30 degrees Fahrenheit (-34°C) on summit day, and most climbers wear thick down parkas, insulated pants, and at least a plastic double boot if not an Everest-type triple boot.

The route to the summit from either camp leads straight up the scree slope above, converging after thirty minutes' hiking up moderate terrain. The route then traverses up rock benches and through rock spires where it begins to level out on a broad bench at about 20,505 feet (6250 m) and one and a half hours of climbing. Some teams climbing the False Polish Route put in a higher camp here to shorten summit day. This is where the

A team beginning their trek in the Vacas Valley

False Polish Route and the Normal Route converge. This camp is roughly one-third of the way to the summit.

After half an hour, the climb steepens on scree and snow ascending behind rock towers to Independencia Hut at just shy of 21,003 feet (6402 m). Independencia Hut is a small, dirty, abandoned structure offering little shelter but makes a good spot for a break.

Above Independencia Hut, the route climbs steeply for 200 feet (62 m) to a ridge. There will invariably be a strong wind beyond this ridge and for the next several hours across what's known as the Gran Acarreo. The wind, combined with cold morning temperatures, can be a recipe for frostbite. Be sure to cover all exposed skin and put on goggles and heavy mitts. The traverse across the Gran Acarreo to the start of the Canaletta (summit couloir) is about two hours and ascends 700 feet (213 m). The rest of the climb can be either snow or scree, depending on the year. If snow, this traverse is exposed and a slip could result in a serious fall if you cannot self-arrest.

At the base of the Canaletta, a big cave offers a nice break spot. Take a good rest here before tackling the steeper, more strenuous terrain above. Ascend the Canaletta on 30- to 40-degree snow and scree on the right side for 1000 feet (305 m). The route traverses left just below the summit ridge for 500 feet (152 m) before cresting the summit pyramid. Along the summit ridge, climbers can peer down the mighty South Face 9000 feet (2743 m) to Plaza Francia.

The summit is a flat area about half the size of a football field with a cross marking the highest point in the Americas. It is truly a remarkable view from this vantage point. Thermals start to build in the early afternoon, and the summit is typically enveloped in cumulus clouds by 1:00 PM.

Plan on the descent to high camp (Camp Berlin) taking four to five hours. It is easy to miss the turn off the Normal Route back to Camp Cholera if using that camp (Camp 3). Make a mental note of where the intersection is and mark it with a GPS coordinate to avoid descending the wrong route.

DESCENT

The Normal Route is the only logical choice for descent. Traversing to the other side of the mountain would lengthen the descent and complicate logistics. Descend to high camp for a night, and then from high camp to Plaza de Mulas and rest a day before beginning the trek out.

THE CLIMB: FALSE POLISH ROUTE VIA VACAS VALLEY

The False Polish Route is not quite as popular as the Normal Route yet still receives a lot of traffic. It's a picturesque and varied route that follows the broad and expansive Vacas Valley to the intersection with the much smaller Relinchos Valley heading west. The Relinchos Valley opens up to Plaza Argentina, which sits on a bench just below the upper slopes of the mountain. The climbing above Plaza Argentina consists of rolling and varied terrain traversing much of the east flank of Aconcagua. The route intersects Aconcagua and its smaller brother, Cerro Ameghino, and offers excellent views of the upper South Face and the Polish Glacier. This route generally takes twenty-one days door-to-door, with thirteen to seventeen of those days spent on the mountain, either on the approach trek or on the climb.

Climbers are supported by mules for the first three days to Plaza Argentina, just like the trek to Plaza de Mulas on the west side of the mountain. There is one moderate river crossing below base camp on this route, which the mules can help climbers cross. Plan on several rest days on this route to allow the body ample time to acclimatize. Overall, the trek and the climb are on technically easy terrain even though days can be long and arduous, especially above base camp. Typical weather consists of blue skies and warm temperatures, with clouds building in the afternoon. Wind on Aconcagua can be strong and persistent.

The trek from the Punta de Vacas park entrance through Pampa de Leñas and Casa de Piedra camps to Plaza Argentina, base camp for the False Polish Route, begins in a broad valley ten minutes (by car) east of Los Penitentes. It takes three days to trek to base camp.

Climbers must check in at the head of Vacas Valley with park rangers before starting the hike. The first two days of the trek to Plaza Argentina are relatively short, consisting of less than 10 miles (16 km) of hiking per day and gaining roughly 2900 feet (875 m) in total. Both days follow the open Vacas Valley on well-worn trails on rolling terrain. The final day to Plaza Argentina is the longest, covering 10 miles (16 km) and gaining more than 3000 feet (970 m) through a steep, tight valley before opening up into a broad plateau.

SAMPLE CLIMBING ITINERARY: ACONCAGUA'S FALSE POLISH ROUTE VIA VACAS VALLEY

Day	Location	Start Elevation	End Elevation	Elevation Gain	Distance
1	Fly to Mendoza		2460 ft (750 m)		
2	Sightsee in Mendoza				
3	Drive to Los Penitentes	2460 ft (750 m)	8465 ft (2580 m)	6005 ft (1830 m)	150 miles (240 km)
4	Drive to Vacas Valley entrance	8465 ft (2580 m)	7628 ft (2325 m)	−837 ft (−255 m)	10 miles (16 km)
	Trek to Pampa de Leñas	7628 ft (2325 m)	9379 ft (2860 m)	1751 ft (535 m)	7 miles (11 km)
5	Trek to Casa de Piedra	9379 ft (2860 m)	10,499 ft (3200 m)	1120 ft (340 m)	8.7 miles (14 km)
6	Trek to Plaza Argentina	10,499 ft (3200 m)	13,678 ft (4170 m)	3179 ft (970 m)	10 miles (16 km)
7	Rest day				
8	Carry to Camp 1	13,678 ft (4170 m)	16,273 ft (4960 m)	2595 ft (790 m)	6 miles (10 km)
9	Move to Camp 1	13,678 ft (4170 m)	16,273 ft (4960 m)	2595 ft (790 m)	3 miles (5 km)
10	Carry to Camp 2	16,273 ft (4960 m)	18,405 ft (5610 m)	2132 ft (650 m)	6 miles (10 km)
11	Rest day				
12	Move to Camp 2	16,273 ft (4960 m)	18,405 ft (5610 m)	2132 ft (650 m)	3 miles (5 km)
13	Rest day				
14	Climb to summit	18,405 ft (5610 m)	22,841 ft (6962 m)	4436 ft (1352 m)	3.75 miles (6 km)
	Descend to Camp 2	22,841 ft (6962 m)	18,405 ft (5610 m)	−4436 ft (−1352 m)	3.75 miles (6 km)
15	Contingency				
16	Contingency				
17	Descend to Plaza de Mulas	3,496 ft (1340 m)	14,009 ft (4270 m)	−4396 ft (−1340 m)	4.5 miles (7.3 km)
18	Trek to Horcones Valley entrance	14,009 ft (4270 m)	9350 ft (2850 m)	−4659 ft (−1420 m)	18 miles (29 km)
19	Drive to Mendoza	9350 ft (2850 m)	2460 ft (750 m)	−6890 ft (−2100 m)	165 miles (264 km)
20	Fly home				

The route above Plaza Argentina on Aconcagua changes slightly every year.

GUIDE TIP

The trek to base camp is dusty and windy. Wear a handkerchief or Buff over your mouth to keep the dust out of your lungs (and help prevent respiratory infections). A Buff can double as a thin face mask higher on the mountain, helping to prevent frostbite.

VACAS VALLEY ENTRANCE TO PAMPA DE LEÑAS

From the Punta de Vacas entrance at 7628 ft (2325 m), the Vacas Valley quickly constricts, and the route follows well-used trekking and mule trails along the west side of the Vacas River. The trail stays low in the valley for most of the day, with only slight undulations and a total altitude gain of 1751 feet (533 m). After about three hours of trekking, having covered most of the distance to camp, you'll climb a 300-foot (90 m) hill just left of the river and stay on top of a plateau for most of the rest of the hike. The total trek is about five hours at a moderate pace.

Pampa de Leñas camp lies at 9379 feet (2860 m), just below a large black rock face close to the river. You'll see the Argentinean flag flying above the park ranger's quarters and the check-in station. It's a moderately sized camp with a good water source and several pit toilets. There is ample room to camp on well-established tent spots away from the river.

PAMPA DE LEÑAS TO CASA DE PIEDRA

It gets very hot around midday lower on Aconcagua and then quite windy in the afternoon, so get an early start. The route travels 0.6 mile (1 km) up a flood plain on the west side of the river before crossing an obvious metal bridge. This bridge has changed locations several times and was not put in place until about a decade ago. Once across the bridge you will be on the east side of Vacas River for the rest of the day.

The trail winds through bushes on an alluvial fan before climbing a broad ravine and traversing over the top of a plateau. Then the route traverses rolling terrain, large alluvial fans, and braided river valleys for the rest of the day, following the right side of the river. Often the braided river changes course, altering the trail slightly. Keep an eye open for new trails and route markings.

Just before entering camp at Casa de Piedra, you will be treated to a remarkable view of Aconcagua's South Face and Polish Glacier. Take a few minutes to photograph the peak you'll spend the next few weeks climbing. This trek takes five to six hours.

Casa de Piedra ("Rock House") consists of a few primitive tent sites at 10,499 feet (3200 m) below the *casa*. The actual *casa* serves as accommodations for the muleteers. The camp is windswept in the afternoons. The *guardaparques* (park rangers) maintain a toilet, as they do at Pampa de Leñas, just above the *casa*. A short distance past the toilet is a freshwater source that climbers can use for cooking and drinking—but treat or boil it.

CASA DE PIEDRA TO PLAZA ARGENTINA

The following morning begins at the crack of dawn! The hike from Casa de Piedra to Plaza Argentina is long, taking seven to nine hours with roughly 3000 feet (970 m) of altitude gain. The muleteers need to start early to deliver your gear at camp and make the long trip out the same day.

This is the point where the route leaves the north-south-oriented Vacas Valley and turns west into the tighter, steeper Relinchos Valley. The first objective of

GUIDE TIP

The main rivers in each of the approach valleys are silty, making them less-than-ideal for drinking water collection. Silt clogs water filters quickly making them ineffective. Look for the frequent clearer side streams flowing into the main river and take advantage of them for drinking water.

the day is to cross the Vacas River. Most climbers bring neoprene water booties or Teva sandals, and shorts, for crossing the cold mountain stream. The river can be waist deep on big snow years but is usually no more than knee level. Once on the other side of the river, switch back to hiking boots and pants and hang your wet sandals on the outside of your pack to dry.

Once across the river, the trail climbs the north side of the tributary valley. After 0.6 mile (1 km) the trail intermittently leaves the river, leading to higher ground and exposed hiking above the cliffs. Use caution here. The loose, steep trail can be treacherous. The trail continues up the canyon for two more hours, ascending 1500 feet (457 m). The last pitch before exiting the small canyon and gaining the plateau climbs a long, steep dirt slope with switchbacks.

The hiking becomes easier on the wide plateau above the constricted Relinchos Valley. Water access is limited to one small, clear tributary about halfway up the canyon and the main stream at the beginning of the plateau. Cross this stream and hike up the south side of the river for the rest of the day. This is a smaller river crossing than the Vacas River at the start the day. The terrain is gradual and rolling the rest of the way.

Plaza Argentina sits at 13,678 feet (4170 m) on a broad shelf just east of Cerro Ameghino. Base camp is a small, bustling seasonal village erected each year by the mule services and guide services. During the high season, three hundred people or more may be in camp. There are dining tents, gear tents, meal services, Internet access, and a park service camp.

Once in Plaza Argentina, climbers must check in with the park rangers and get checked out by the high-altitude physician before ascending higher. This takes an hour and is a good time to find out current route and weather information.

PLAZA ARGENTINA TO CAMP 1

Climbers employ the "climb high, sleep low" climbing style above Plaza Argentina, which means for all camps above base camp, climbers will carry loads to camp before descending back down and then finally moving camp up the following day. The climb to Camp 1 takes from five to seven hours and half that time to descend.

The route leaves Plaza Argentina to the west up gradual switchbacks on easy terrain. It eventually enters a constricted valley created by rockfall debris on the left and the moraine of a glacier on the right. Proceed up this valley for one hour or about 600 feet (180 m) before entering a wide glacial cirque traveling on rock-covered glacier. The route traverses this glacier, winding around walls of ice and small glacial ponds for an hour. Then climb steeply up a scree slope at the head of the valley, up zigzags on a broad ramp. Eventually, climbers are forced to traverse right up either the snow or loose scree on either side of a small stream. No matter what the medium, it's an arduous push to the top and in to Camp 1.

Camp 1 sits at 16,273 feet (4960 m) on a flat shelf. The stream below camp used for drinking water is clearest in the morning, so stock up early on water for the day. Groups either set up a toilet tent away from the water source or use a portable toilet with bio-bags just over the roll to the east of camp. Remember, groups are required to remove all waste from the mountain. After climbing to Camp 1, climbers descend to base camp to spend the night before moving camp and the rest of their gear up to Camp 1 the following day.

CAMP 1 TO CAMP 2

From Camp 1 there is a great view of the climbing to come. The trail climbs the open slope above camp, starting to the north side of the valley and traversing back south to the center of the slope, before cresting to the Ameghino Col, the low pass between Cerro Ameghino and Aconcagua.

The route then climbs a steep slope on climber's left (south) out of the col and then traverses west, making a long ascent in to Camp 2 at approximately 18,405 feet (5610 m). The climb to Camp 2 is a strenuous five- to seven-hour push.

Camp 2 sits on a large, flat bench with room for thirty tents or more, offering little protection from the wind

> ## GUIDE TIP
>
> Many climbers experience altitude headaches during the descent from Aconcagua's summit because their bodies aren't working as hard as on the ascent; they're circulating less oxygen because they aren't breathing as forcefully. Remember to consciously throw in extra breaths on the way down to prevent headaches.

just above a steep slope and below the base of the Polish Glacier. Melt pools offer plentiful snowmelt as a water source for climbers later in the day when it's warm. There are impressive views of the Polish Glacier directly above camp and of the mountain chain to the north, including Cerro Zurbriggen, La Mano, and Mercedario. Most climbers opt for the longer and less technically challenging Falso Polaco, or False Polish, Route to the summit from this camp rather than challenging the steep, icy, and potentially lethal Polish Glacier.

CAMP 2 TO THE SUMMIT

Most climbers summit from Camp 2, although some opt to traverse to Camp Cholera at 19,504 feet (5945 m) to add a day of acclimatization and to shorten summit day. An early start (5:00 to 7:00 AM) is essential to make the summit and back to camp in daylight. The climb will take seven to eleven hours and ascend more than 4400 feet (1300 m) of altitude. This very long, cold day should not be underestimated. Aconcagua's summit day challenges even very experienced high-altitude climbers. Be aware of potential altitude illnesses throughout the day.

The False Polish Route traverses to the west of the Polish Glacier on a well-worn trail up moderately steep scree and snow slopes, joining the Normal Route at 20,505 feet (6250 m) after several hours of climbing. Thirty minutes after joining the Normal Route, the climb steepens on scree and snow, ascending behind rock towers to Independencia Hut at 21,003 feet (6402 m), which offers little shelter but makes a good spot for a break.

Above Independencia Hut the route climbs steeply for 200 feet (61 m) to a ridge, beyond which there invariably is a strong wind and across the Gran Acarreo. The wind and cold morning temperatures can lead to frostbite; be sure to cover all exposed skin and put on goggles and heavy mitts. The traverse across the Gran Acarreo to the start of the Canaletta (summit couloir) is about two hours and ascends 700 feet (213 m). The rest of the climb can be either snow or scree depending on the year. If snow, this traverse is exposed and a slip could result in a serious fall if you cannot self-arrest.

A big cave at the base of the Canaletta offers a nice break spot. Take a good rest here before tackling the steeper, more strenuous terrain above. Ascend the Canaletta on 30- to 40-degree snow and scree on the right side for 1000 feet (305 m). The route traverses left just below the summit ridge for 500 feet (152 m) before cresting the summit pyramid. Along the summit ridge, climbers can peer down the South Face 9000 feet (2743 m) to Plaza Francia.

The summit, a flat area about half the size of a football field with a cross marking the highest point in the Americas, has a truly remarkable view. Thermals build in the early afternoon, when the summit is typically enveloped in cumulus clouds.

The descent takes four to five hours. It is easy to miss the turn off the Normal Route back to Camp 2. Make a mental note of where the intersection is and mark it with a GPS coordinate to avoid descending the wrong route.

DESCENT VIA PLAZA DE MULAS

Once back at Camp 2, climbers can either traverse an hour west to Camp Cholera at 19,504 feet (5945 m) and descend via Plaza de Mulas and the Horcones Valley or descend the ascent route through Plaza Argentina. Descending to Plaza de Mulas is referred to as the Traverse, which has become very popular in the last decade. The Traverse shortens the hike out and lets climbers see a new valley. However, traversing climbers must arrange to order mules prior to descending to

Plaza de Mulas. A pair of light hiking boots or sneakers must be carried up and over the mountain for the hike out from Plaza de Mulas.

The descent to Plaza de Mulas from Camp Cholera is fairly obvious, consisting of loose scree for several thousand feet (see the Normal Route description for details). Most teams take six to nine hours to reach the park exit at Horcones Valley from Plaza de Mulas. Make sure to check out with the park service at the park exit.

ACONCAGUA GEAR LISTS

Keep in mind that you'll be carrying your own gear, possibly in inclement weather; bring only what you'll need.

TRAVEL, TREKKING, AND PERSONAL GEAR

- Passport (obtain visa upon arrival for most countries)
- Travel wallet, to store passport, money, and travel documents
- Pesos (for drinks, food, and tips for muleteers)
- 2 large waterproof duffel bags
- 1 small duffel bag for storing street and casual clothes
- 3 locks for duffel bags
- Day pack for travel and trekking
- Pack cover (make sure it fits your pack)
- 2 collapsible trekking poles
- Ten Essentials
- 2 pairs glacier glasses
- 2 pairs goggles: 1 clear, 1 dark
- 30+ SPF sweatproof sunscreen
- 2 headlamps and extra batteries
- Altitude watch
- Lightweight trekking boots
- Sneakers for camp and around town
- Sandals for wading rivers
- Casual and city clothes
- Trekking clothes
- Warm outer layer: jacket, hat, and gloves

- Waterproof, breathable rain shell
- Sleeping bag rated to -20˚F (-29˚C)
- 2 sleeping pads: 1 inflatable, 1 closed-cell foam
- 2–3 1-quart water bottles
- 2–3 water bottle jackets
- Water treatment (iodine or chlorine)
- 1-quart thermos
- Snacks and specialty climbing and comfort food
- Multitool (with pliers)
- Prescription medications
- Toilet paper
- A few small bottles of hand disinfectant
- 1-quart pee bottle
- Garbage bags to waterproof and to cache your gear
- Camera
- Several books (can trade with others at base camp)

CLIMBING GEAR

- Large internal-frame backpack (6000 cubic inches, 98 liters)
- Alpine ice ax
- 12-point crampons with a good fit
- Helmet

CLOTHING

Temperature extremes between the night and day are common so you'll be adding and shedding layers.

FOOTWEAR:

- Double climbing boots
- Gaiters and/or supergaiters
- 4 pairs climbing socks of varying weights

LOWER-BODY LAYERS:

- 2 pairs climbing pants of different weights, soft shell material
- Insulated pants for in camp and summit day (down or synthetic)
- 3 sets underlayers of different weights (synthetic or merino wool)

UPPER-BODY LAYERS:

- Heavy down parka with a hood
- 3 midweight pile layers, preferably with hoods
- 1 cotton T-shirt, for base camp
- 3 under-layer tops (synthetic or merino wool)

HEADGEAR AND HANDWEAR:

- 1–2 heavy ski hats
- Balaclava
- Face mask
- 2 Buffs
- Sun hat or baseball cap
- Heavy climbing gloves
- Heavy down mitts (must fit over base-layer gloves)
- Base-layer gloves for trekking and warm climbing
- Several pairs hand warmers

GROUP GEAR

- Big base-camp tent
- Tents
- Stoves and fuel (white gas)
- Cooking gear and utensils, including cutting boards
- Group food
- Coolers to pack food in
- Camp table and chairs
- Water bags, for collecting and transporting water
- Shovels

- Short rope (for rescue on summit day)
- 2 pickets (for rescue)
- First-aid kit
- Repair kit
- Satellite phone
- VHF and UHF radios
- Duffel bags, for mules

SUMMIT CHECKLIST

- Warm down parka
- Ski hat
- Balaclava
- Goggles
- Warm gloves and mittens as a backup
- Ice ax
- Crampons
- Ski pole
- Headlamp and extra headlamp batteries
- 1 extra headlamp per group
- Short, thin rope for short roping on final slopes
- Repair kit for crampons and pack straps
- Medical kit
- Plenty of food and water for 12+ hours of strenuous climbing
- Water bottle cover to keep your bottles from freezing
- Summit flags for pictures
- Camera

VINSON MASSIF

ALTITUDE
16,050 feet (4892 m)

DIFFICULTY RATINGS
Technical: 3
Physical: 3

SUMMIT GPS WAYPOINTS
S 78 31.088
W 85 37.585

ELEVATION GAIN
(base camp to summit)
9160 feet (2792 m)

DISTANCE
(base camp to summit)
11.8 miles (19 km)

TIME
(door-to-door)
16 days

SEASON
Mid-November–end of January

Climbers overlook
the sea of ice in
Antarctica.

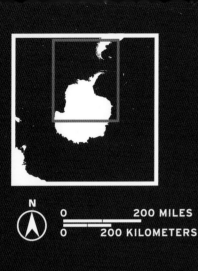

0   **200 MILES**

0   **200 KILOMETERS**

SANTIAGO

ARGENTINA

CHILE

BUENOS AIRES

PUNTA ARENAS

Strait of Magellan

Drake Passage

South Pacific Ocean

ANTARCTIC PENINSULA

Weddell Sea

VINSON MASSIF

South Atlantic Ocean

ELLSWORTH MOUNTAINS

Bonne Ice Shelf

WEST ANTARCTICA

Ross Sea

TRANS ANTARCTIC MOUNTAINS

ANTARCTICA

Ross Ice Shelf

SOUTH POLE

QUEEN MAUD MOUNTAINS

QUEEN MAUD LAND

Cape Adare

EAST ANTARCTICA

CHAPTER 7

VINSON MASSIF

ANTARCTICA'S HIGHEST SUMMIT

[ANTARCTICA] IS AS CLOSE AS YOU WILL EVER GET
TO ANOTHER PLANET WITHOUT LEAVING THIS ONE.

—PHIL ERSHLER, DIRECTOR, INTERNATIONAL MOUNTAIN GUIDES

Antarctica is truly the last frontier. This continent, a mass of rock and ice covering 5,405,400 square miles (14 million sq km) of area, including the South Pole, is larger than Europe. Antarctica has no government, no permanent population, is not ruled by any one country, and is the only continent without an indigenous population. The landmass is controlled under the Antarctic Treaty, signed in 1959 and in force as of 1962. Antarctica is a desert that mainly consists of ice. It also has the distinction of being the highest continent, as defined by overall average height of the surface, due to the thick ice layer covering all land except for the tallest mountain ranges. It, of course, is the coldest continent on Earth.

A curious penguin at one of the local penguin colonies near Punta Arenas (Photo by Jane Lee)

Vinson Massif, the tallest mountain on the continent, lies in western Antarctica just south of the Antarctic Peninsula in the Ellsworth Mountains. The expansive Ellsworth Range is divided into two subranges, both of which are mostly covered by glaciers. Vinson sits at 78 degrees south latitude, making it the Seven Summit mountain that is closest to a pole. The thinner atmosphere at such an extreme latitude makes Vinson "feel" several thousand feet higher due to the lower atmospheric pressure. Despite this polar effect, Vinson Massif is of only moderate altitude for the Seven Summits, being comparable to Mounts Kilimanjaro and

Elbrus. The difficulty of climbing Vinson, however, does not lie in its height but in its extreme environment; it is the coldest of the Seven Summits. Vinson, which lies in the Chilean-controlled section of the continent, is closer to Chile than any other country outside of the continent, and most travelers travel through Chile to access it.

All of these unique characteristics combine to create an incredible climbing experience for those with a true sense of adventure. Many of the Seven Summits can be logistically challenging, but not nearly to Vinson's degree. Logistics can be the largest obstacle to overcome for attaining this peak. However, the first few parties to ascend Vinson Massif had a lot more logistical obstacles than we have today. They had to secure a plane, typically from a government, which cost hundreds of thousands of dollars for the private charter. Even though there is more infrastructure in place today and commercial flights to Antarctica are much more common than they were thirty years ago, you are flying almost literally to the end of the earth, which presents lots of challenges.

Just getting to Punta Arenas, Chile, is quite a journey in itself, and here the adventure only begins. From Punta Arenas climbers must hire a special cargo plane equipped and certified to land on an ice runway, then hire a smaller passenger plane equipped with skis to deliver them to base camp, all in the harsh and unpredictable polar region. At this point, climbers will have been away from home for a week or more without even beginning the climb! Now they must ascend a physically and technically demanding mountain in one of the most rugged environments on Earth, followed by long and sometimes delay-ridden trip home. Some climbers say that the biggest challenge in climbing Vinson is being completely committed to being on the continent. Once the plane flies away, you are stuck there until another one arrives, which can sometimes be weeks. Climbers often find themselves at the whim of the weather when it's not safe to fly, and this gives them a helpless feeling, especially challenging for high-powered types who are used to pulling strings—but there simply isn't another feasible way off the continent.

NATURAL HISTORY

It is believed that Antarctica was originally part of Gondwana, the southernmost supercontinent encompassing the South American, African, and Australian landmasses after Pangaea broke up. During the Cambrian period, west Antarctica was in the Northern Hemisphere, while east Antarctica was on the equator. The weather must have been milder then than it is now!

West Antarctica resembles South America geologically in that it was created by tectonic uplift of seabed sediments during the Paleozoic and Mesozoic

ANTARCTIC FAST FACTS

- On July 21, 1983, the Soviet Station Vostok recorded a record low temperature of -128.6 degrees Fahrenheit (-89°C).
- Antarctica is the continent with the highest average height: 6100 feet (1860 m).
- Antarctica is the driest continent on Earth, getting less than 1 inch (2.5 cm) of rain per year in the interior. Some areas are said to have not received precipitation for two million years.
- The coldest month's average temperature is -40 degrees Fahrenheit to -90 degrees Fahrenheit (-40°C to -68°C); the warmest is -31 degrees Fahrenheit to 5 degrees Fahrenheit (-35°C to -15°C).
- Antarctica's ice sheet is the biggest body of freshwater on Earth, containing 68 percent of the world's freshwater and 90 percent of the world's ice.
- If the Antarctic ice sheet were to melt, it would raise Earth's oceans by 180 feet (55 m).
- At its thickest, Antarctica's ice sheet is 16,000 feet (4880 m).

periods. Eastern Antarctica was mainly formed during the Precambrian era, making this area much older. Some formations date to three billion years or more. East and west are pulling away from one another at the west Antarctic rift. Along this rift, the Trans Antarctic Mountains are one of the longest ranges in the world, extending for 2170 miles (3500 km).

What we know as the shape of Antarctica as a continent today is mainly ice covering two much smaller landmasses. It's suggested that the landmass would rise nearly a thousand feet (several hundred meters) in a relatively short time if the ice sheet weren't depressing it.

The Ellsworth Mountains, of which Vinson Massif is part, consists of two subranges: the Sentinel Range to

VINSON MASSIF TIMELINE

1935 American Lincoln Ellsworth (for whom the Ellsworth Range is named), makes the first Antarctic transcontinental flight.

1958-61 Ellsworth Mountains surveyed.

1959 Antarctic Treaty is signed by twelve countries.

1966 First ascent of Vinson Massif, by American team of Barry Corbet, John Evans, William Long, and Pete Schoening.

1983 Dick Bass climbs Vinson.

1985 Adventure Network International, later bought by Antarctic Logistics and Expeditions, begins operation.

1988 First solo ascent is made by American Vern Tejas.

1990 Pioneering pilot Giles Kershaw is killed in a gyrocopter crash on the Antarctic Peninsula.

1991 First solo ascent via a new route (Rudi's Runway) is completed by German Rudi Lang.

the north, including Vinson Massif on its southern end, and the Heritage range to the south. The rock of Vinson Massif and the surrounding area is mostly marine sedimentation pushed up by tectonic activity during the Cambrian to Precambrian eras, rock that is indicative of west Antarctica and the peninsula.

Vinson Massif itself is almost completely covered in glaciers. Due to the extreme conditions on the continent, and especially in the Ellsworth Range, there is very little flora or fauna. Most life is found on the coastline and peninsula in the west. The majority of plant life consists of liverworts, mosses, lichens, and bryophytes. There are a few flowering plants on the Antarctic Peninsula, such as *Colobanthus quitensis* and *Deschapsia antarctica*. I have never personally observed any plants or animals on or around Vinson Massif.

Marine mammals inhabiting the coastal regions of Antarctica include the famous emperor penguins, fur seals, and several other types of penguins such as the rockhopper, gentoo, and king. Beyond these larger marine mammals, Antarctica also hosts invertebrates such as mites, nematodes, and midges. There is essentially no obvious macroscopic life in the Vinson region.

CULTURAL AND POLITICAL BACKGROUND

No one country owns Antarctica and, since it is the only continent on Earth without a native human population, many countries have worked together to establish guidelines for the area. A series of international treaties have been enacted to determine how Antarctica is controlled. The Antarctic Treaty System ratified in 1962, originally signed by twelve countries and now signed by more than fifty, established the continent as a scientific preserve and banned military activity.

The Madrid Protocol, which is part of the 1962 treaty, dictates environmental guidelines for the protection of Antarctica. Tour companies operating on the continent must obey the Madrid Protocol measures. Climbing on Vinson Massif is directly affected by the Madrid Protocol in many ways, including removing all human waste and garbage from the mountain, among other efforts to preserve the fragile polar desert environment.

CLIMBING HISTORY

Vinson was the last of the Seven Summits to be climbed, and for good reason. Antarctica is the remotest continent on Earth and logistically difficult to reach. The American Lincoln Ellsworth was the first to see the Ellsworth Mountains, in 1935 on his legendary first

Climbers on Vinson's
summit ridge

transcontinental flight. It wasn't until 1957 that Vinson Massif itself was first seen, by US Navy pilots on a reconnaissance mission. Vinson Massif was named after a supporter of Antarctic exploration and a chairman of the US House Armed Services Committee, Carl Vinson.

Not until 1966 did Antarctica receive its first expedition that was dedicated solely to climbing, the American Antarctic Mountaineering Expedition, which consisted of several notable climbers. Barry Corbet, John Evans, William Long, and Pete Schoening achieved their goal of climbing the highest mountain on the continent on their first attempt. After making the seventh ascent of Vinson Massif, Giles Kershaw, Pat Morrow, and Martyn Williams started Adventure Network International, the first commercial outfitter offering service to the Sentinel Range in 1985. This began the modern era of climbing on the continent's highest peak. To date, Vinson has received roughly two thousand ascents, which is approximately half of the number that have climbed Mount Everest.

CLIMBING CHALLENGES

The biggest hazard climbers deal with on Vinson is the cold. Climbers venturing to Antarctica must be able to take care of themselves in extremely cold conditions. Frostbite and hypothermia can cause serious issues if climbers fail to diligently prevent them. The remoteness of climbing in Antarctica increases the seriousness of any injury, whether it's due to the cold or not.

The route has a minimal amount of technical terrain, but proficiency in cramponing, self-arresting, fixed-line ascension, crevasse rescue, and fixed-line descent are a must. Prior time spent at altitude is also important. Many climbers describe Vinson as a mini-Denali climb. Like Denali, Vinson requires carrying heavy loads.

Open crevasses both from Base Camp to Camp 1 and from Camp 2 to the summit are a real concern. In poor weather, the time required to rescue a climber from a crevasse can quickly lead to hypothermia or frostbite. In a whiteout it's difficult to see where the crevasses lie, making travel treacherous. Be sure to mark route waypoints during the climb, and mark any crevasses with wands. These waypoints will come in handy in a whiteout.

Antarctic Logistics and Expeditions (ALE), a company that offers flights to Vinson Massif, as well as other destinations in Antarctica, fixes ropes at the beginning of each climbing season on a steep ridge leading from Camp 1 to Camp 2. It's smart to inspect the ropes each time you use them and inform ALE if they need maintenance. Be careful not to kick or drop anything on climbers below, and alert teammates if objects fall from above.

PLANNING AN EXPEDITION

Vinson Massif is a serious climb, one that requires sound cold-weather management skills, a commitment of three weeks or more, and patience. Vinson should be reserved as one of the later climbs in a Seven Summits bid due to its seriousness, time commitment, and cost. There is rarely an ascent of Vinson Massif that goes off without a hitch due to its extreme locale. A climb without delays would take two weeks door-to-door; however, most expeditions take three to four weeks due to delays. These delays, often caused by poor flying conditions either in Chile or in Antarctica, can occupy half of the duration of the expedition.

Almost all climbers use a reputable guide service to guide them up Vinson due to the tight restrictions put in place by the concession holder, ALE. A guide service will have experience planning this trip and will help to guide you through the process. Because of the extreme conditions of the trip and the price tag, climbers should begin planning a climb of Vinson as early as possible, often a year or more in advance.

ANTARCTICA WAS THE LAST TRUE LAND FRONTIER ON EARTH.

— RICK RIDGEWAY, FROM *SEVEN SUMMITS* BY DICK BASS, RICK RIDGEWAY, AND FRANK WELLS (1988)

DAMIEN GILDEA

Since 2001, Australian Damien Gildea has been leading mountaineering expeditions to Antarctica, climbing mainly in the Sentinel Range on and around Vinson Massif. He has climbed many of the continent's highest peaks while putting up numerous first ascents. A main priority of Damien's exploration has been the precise surveying of Antarctic peaks. In 2007 he published a new topographical map of Vinson Massif and the Sentinel Range. He has also skied 700 miles (1130 km) to the South Pole in 2000–2001. Some of Damien's other publications include *Antarctic Mountaineering Chronology*, *Mountaineering in Antarctica: Climbing in the Frozen South*, and articles published in climbing journals.

Beyond securing funds for the expedition, training for the climb, and purchasing plane tickets, climbers who haven't previously climbed in polar-like conditions, such as on Denali or in the Himalayas, must acquire the appropriate gear. These specialty items are sometimes hard to find, especially for climbers living outside of the United States and Europe, where most of this specialized gear is produced. These extreme-weather items aren't cheap, adding a major cost to the overall price of the trip.

Also, the limited number of spots available on the flights to Vinson Massif can fill up six months or more in advance. Visas are relatively easy to secure and can be picked up upon arrival in both Chile and Antarctica for climbers of nearly all nationalities.

GUIDED TRIP VERSUS INDEPENDENT CLIMB

Essentially everyone who climbs Vinson Massif will find that they are using ALE for climbing logistics. ALE has a contract to work in Antarctica under a special set of rules and has a virtual monopoly on Vinson climbing logistics. Reputable guide services leading expeditions to Antarctica use ALE for flights to and from the continent as well as to Vinson Base Camp. In turn, ALE is confident that these guide services will climb safely, follow mandated environmental protection guidelines, and screen potential clients based on their climbing resumés

to ensure that they are prepared for an attempt on the mountain. For safety reasons ALE is very selective about who it allows to climb unguided. Unless you have an overwhelmingly extensive climbing and polar exploration resumé, plan on hiring a guide service to lead you on a Vinson expedition.

ALE has been organizing flights, on- and off-continent infrastructure, and safety personnel for adventures and climbing expeditions on Antarctica since 2003, when it purchased Adventure Network International. The first few teams to climb the mountain hired their own planes at a great cost. The infrastructure that ALE now has in place has greatly simplified the logistics in climbing Vinson Massif but comes at a significant cost. Each climbing season, ALE hires a Russian Ilyushin 76 (IL76) cargo plane and a full Russian crew to run fuel, equipment, and loads of adventurers back and forth from the ice. ALE also has a base camp at Union Glacier, where the IL76 lands, and staff on hand at Vinson Base Camp to facilitate climbing and aid in rescues. They also offer flights to the South Pole and the coast.

This service isn't cheap: as of 2012, the cost for a seat on the ALE plane was well in excess of $20,000. There currently are no other reasonable options for flying to Vinson.

CLIMBING SEASONS AND WEATHER

Antarctica, being the coldest place on Earth, sees climbing only in the Austral summer. ALE operates

Climbers eat well during flight delays at Union Glacier. (Photo by Jane Lee)

their logistics business from the middle of November through the end of January. It is nearly impossible to get to Vinson Massif at any other time of the year.

Weather throughout Antarctica is quite stable. Being a desert, it obviously has very little precipitation. Wind activity is the major weather issue. Warmer air cools over the South Pole and flows north toward the coast, causing katabatic wind events. Antarctica can be as windy as almost any place on Earth, with occasional windstorms reaching to 100 miles per hour (160 kmh) or more. (The record wind speed was in 1972 when winds reached 199 miles per hour [327 kmh].)

The Ellsworth Mountains disrupt the natural flow of wind from the pole to the outskirts of the continent, funneling it up the broad mountain slopes, creating higher winds and an even more difficult environment for life to survive in. ALE now offers weather updates for climbers, but due to the dearth of weather stations on the continent, it's not overly useful. Be careful not to get stuck at Vinson's exposed high camp when a windstorm hits.

DOCUMENTS

Advance visas for Chile aren't necessary for citizens of most countries (China may be an exception). Tourist cards are required and can be bought in Santiago, Chile, before clearing customs at a reciprocal price for your country of origin. The most expensive in 2012 is the United States, at about $100. Tourist cards are good for ninety days and must be surrendered when leaving the country. A valid passport with at least six months left on it before expiry after the date of travel is required for entry into Chile. Inspectors in Chile prohibit meats, cheeses, and fruits from entering their country and now seize all of these items, including cooked meats. It is possible to find all of these items in Punta Arenas.

No advance visas are necessary for Antarctica. Please check current visa information for Antarctica before traveling to Chile. The flight to Antarctica is international, which requires passing through security and customs with a valid passport. Security will confiscate knives, so remember to pack them in your duffels.

COSTS

The Chilean peso ($) is the currency you'll use en route from Chile to Antarctica; as of 2012, the exchange rate is 500 Chilean pesos to $1US.

- Guided expedition (including flight from Chile to Antarctica, and from Union Glacier to Vinson Base Camp, which run $20,000-plus): $33,000-plus
- Potential delay expenses: up to $1000

CONDITIONING

Many compare a climb of Vinson Massif to a small version of Denali, except with colder weather. Climbers attempting Vinson must be very capable of taking care of themselves in extremely cold conditions. Also, climbers need to be in "Denali" shape. The ability to carry up to 70 pounds (32 kg) divided between a pack and a sled in harsh conditions for several days in a row is a necessity. The duration of the expedition is shorter and the

> **GUIDE TIP**
>
> Antarctic Logistics and Expeditions often supplies a small paper map of Vinson Massif and surrounding peaks to climbers at their briefing. This is a great resource with helpful information and statistics and it is a section of cartographer and adventurer Damien Gildea's larger map of the Sentinel Range. Talk to an ALE representative to purchase this map. Other maps of the continent can be bought via the Internet or from several bookstores in Punta Arenas, Chile.

> **GUIDE TIP**
>
> Cold management is crucial in Antarctica. Have your warm mitts, face mask, winter hat, and down parka handy in your pack in case of sudden weather changes. A quick change into warmer gear can save you from getting frostbite and/or hypothermia and allow you to be more comfortable while climbing.

altitude is lower than on a climb of Denali, so Vinson is not viewed as being as difficult. However, it is physically more difficult than any of the other Seven Summits except, perhaps, Mount Everest.

For more specifics on conditioning for the Seven Summits, please see part I.

IMMUNIZATIONS

No vaccines are required to travel via Chile or Argentina, but hepatitis A and B, typhoid, and rabies are recommended. Also, no vaccines are required in Antarctica, but hepatitis A and B, typhoid, and meningococcal vaccines are recommended. Other routine vaccinations are prudent, including measles, mumps, and rubella (MMR); diphtheria-tetanus (DPT); and poliovirus.

COMMUNICATIONS

Most teams bring a satellite phone on Vinson climbs to communicate with ALE staff both at Vinson Base Camp and Union Glacier, as well as with others off the continent. The other common mode of communication is VHF radios. Much of the route is not line of sight, making UHF talk-about radios less useful. ALE uses both satellite phones and VHF radios to communicate with climbers.

GETTING THERE AND GETTING AROUND

All Vinson Massif expeditions begin from Punta Arenas, Chile. Most climbers fly through the major South American cities of Santiago, Chile, or Buenos Aires,

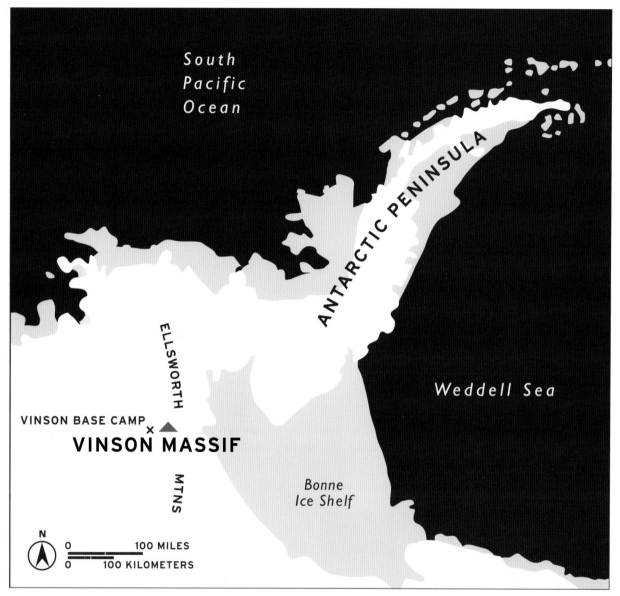

South
Pacific
Ocean

ANTARCTIC PENINSULA

ELLSWORTH

Weddell Sea

VINSON BASE CAMP
× ▲
VINSON MASSIF

MTNS

Bonne
Ice Shelf

N

| 0 | 100 MILES |
| 0 | 100 KILOMETERS |

Vinson Massif environs

Argentina, to reach Punta Arenas. Both of these urban centers offer tourism opportunities and make for nice extended layovers to relax on the beaches and experience the culture. Both cities have a well-established wine region nearby.

Lan Chile airline offers several flights a day from Santiago to Punta Arenas, the southernmost city of its size in Chile (Ushuaia in Argentina is slightly farther south). Over the centuries, Punta Arenas, which lies on the Strait of Magellan, has thrived on adventure and exploration.

Guide services will arrange transportation for you from the airport into town, but ground transportation is also relatively easy to secure on your own, as taxis and private vehicles regularly travel between the airport and town. Once you arrive at your hotel, your guides will

An Ilyushin 76 on an ice runway in Antarctica (Photo by Jane Lee)

contact ALE. If you are climbing without a guide service, you will need to hire a transport company and also contact ALE in Punta Arenas (see Resources).

Punta Arenas is a fairly modern tourist hub that offers nice lodging and amenities. Despite the constant battering of fierce Austral winds, it's an enjoyable place to spend a few days. There are plenty of hotels, eateries, Internet cafés, and bars; several large supermarkets and gear shops supply just about everything climbers might need for an expedition.

AIR TRAVEL TO ANTARCTICA

The morning before your flight from Punta Arenas to Antarctica, ALE holds a mandatory briefing. Here they discuss all of the aspects of a Vinson climb, from safety concerns to logistics before and after arriving in Antarctica. After this meeting, you are given a time to weigh your gear before handing it off to ALE representatives to load the plane for the next morning's flight. Each climber is allowed 114 pounds (52 kg) of gear, all inclusive. Once ALE takes this gear, you won't be able to access it even if there are delays, so keep with you important medications or other smaller items that you may need.

Vinson Base Camp is plagued by low-lying fog that can prevent flights from getting in and out, so delays in Punta Arenas, at Union Glacier, and at Vinson Base Camp can be part of the equation. Be patient. ALE has an interest in getting you where you need to go and will fly if it's safe.

> ## GUIDE TIP
>
> Before you start climbing, be sure you've prepared a "ditch loop," or sling, that you can use to clip your pack to while climbing on steep terrain so you don't lose it. Dropping your pack on the fixed lines or the summit ridge could mean the end of your trip and could seriously injure someone below.

It takes four to five hours to fly from Punta Arenas to Antarctica; this direct flight is on a Russian Ilyushin 76 (IL76) cargo plane. Lunch and drinks are provided on the flight. Items essential to bring for the flight from Punta Arenas to Union Glacier are your passport and Chilean embarkation card (which you fill out on arrival in Chile), a down parka, down pants, sunscreen, face protection, winter hat, cold-weather boots, and warm gloves. Be prepared for arctic conditions upon arrival at Union Glacier, where it can be -40 degrees Fahrenheit (-40˚C) and windy.

GATEWAY SETTLEMENTS

In 2009 ALE moved its blue-ice landing strip in Antarctica from Patriot Hills to Union Glacier, about 20 miles (32 km) to the west toward Vinson Massif, eliminating some of the notorious Vinson flight delays. Usually climbers spend a night at Union Glacier before flying on to Vinson Base Camp, depending on the weather, but delays can leave climbers stranded at Union Glacier for several days or more.

Union Glacier, a remote outpost in the interior of Antarctica, serves as the center for ALE's intra-continent operations. It lies on a flat expanse of glacier close to mountains, offering skiing and climbing opportunities. There are WeatherPort (semipermanent) tents with tables and chairs, cookstoves, a weather station, toilet systems, and staff camp tents. The IL76 lands on the ice close to the Union Glacier camp. Climbers camp in their own tents but are welcome to relax in ALE's heated tents.

DOMESTIC FLIGHTS

The last leg of the journey is from Union Glacier to Vinson Base Camp. From Union Glacier, it takes forty-five minutes to reach Vinson Base Camp by Twin Otters equipped with skis. The flight traverses stunning glaciers and mountainous terrain en route to the runway at Branscomb Glacier and Vinson Massif.

Flights into and out of Vinson Base Camp can be as finicky as those to and from Union Glacier. The Twin Otters cannot land at base camp in low-visibility conditions, which are quite frequent at base camp. Patience is a virtue. Delays are just part of climbing in Antarctica, and they can last for days at a time.

ALE keeps a semipermanent camp at Vinson Base Camp for the climbing season. Several personnel stay at base camp to educate climbers about Leave No Trace practices and to aid in rescues. Vinson's summit is almost visible from base camp.

OTHER ACTIVITIES: SKIING

Skiing Vinson is becoming more popular because of its speed and efficiency, especially on descent, and because more climbers are taking to skiing the Seven Summits. Conditions for skiing in Antarctica are rarely ideal due to the minimal amount of snowfall; don't expect knee-deep powder! Skiing often consists of windblown sastrugi, wind crusts, or icy conditions. Skiing is also an effective way for teams to mitigate crevasse risk since skis spread out a person's body weight over the surface. Attempting to ski Vinson is recommended only for very experienced skiers due to the extreme environment and difficult snow conditions.

CLIMBING VINSON MASSIF

Few climbers have had the opportunity to climb in Antarctica's unique environment. Still, exploration throughout the continent and the Ellsworth Range has increased steadily over the last several decades. A climb of Vinson without delays takes a week, including rest days once at Vinson Base Camp.

MAPPING ANTARCTICA'S MOUNTAINS

Antarctic climbers got lucky with Vinson Massif. It's not impossibly steep like the rock towers in Queen Maud Land, nor is it lashed by terrible wet storms as the Antarctic Peninsula is. The continent's highest point is mostly a friendly giant, but one that's just sharp enough around the edges to keep us alert. On a good day we cruise over Vinson, smiling and soaking up endless views under the sun, only our crampons crunching the stillness. On a bad day we struggle across ice on our knees and hunker in tents stomped down by giant winds, whimpering for homes too far away.

Initially I was drawn to Antarctica's Sentinel Range because it seemed so impressive yet so unknown. For a decade these high peaks were always on my mind, forming my plans, my dreams, my work. I navigated this personal geography by a series of annual questions—questions that could be answered only by climbing: to discover the true height of Mount Shinn, the real topography of the Vinson and Craddock massifs; to explore the scattered lower peaks, often seen but rarely touched; to venture onto the long, rocky ridges and the western faces of the chiseled northern Sentinels. Reaching a summit, I always found myself looking beyond, only to see the next question that needed to be climbed. It was a formidable combination, this science and adventure, exciting yet useful, serious but fun. Sometimes we were alpinists and chose the best lines; sometimes we were scientists and chose the easiest or the safest. Sometimes they came together as one.

So often, we were the continent's highest campers, all alone on a summit or high camp, shouting into the wind, hoping the GPS unit wouldn't slip off a tiny outcrop. Twisted into a cramped tent high on Mount Gardner, shivering as if we could drag the sun around east to warm us, we wondered how an hour could last so long. Pushing sleepless across the night to enchain the subpeaks of the Vinson Plateau, we could find no place to wait out the coming storm. Picking our way unroped up and down virgin ground on Mount Epperly, Mount Anderson, and others, we pushed our minds beyond our bodies. As we listened to the storm shred the tent around us, huddled fully dressed for escape, we had nowhere to run. We were climbing for mountains of data, all to improve everybody's knowledge of Antarctica's highest peaks. Our work refined the height order of Antarctica's highest mountains, something achieved decades earlier on every other continent. We climbed dozens of new routes and first and second ascents, all to place a GPS coordinate where it needed to be, to make one map for everyone.

The first ascent of Vinson in 1966 was an exemplar of all that is best in human Antarctica: a group of people coming together with a common aim, with assistance from all quarters. They cooperated to get a job done and then worked to excel beyond that to achieve something extraordinary, both on and off the mountain. We tried to do the same, I hope we succeeded. I hope you do too.

DAMIEN GILDEA
CARTOGRAPHER, AUSTRALIAN ALPINIST,
AUTHOR OF *MOUNTAINEERING IN ANTARCTICA: CLIMBING IN THE FROZEN SOUTH*

ROUTES

Many routes have been climbed on Vinson, although the majority of ascents are on the "main route." This route, used by all commercial expeditions, ascends gradual glaciated terrain, steeper fixed lines, and a sporty summit ridge. The climbing is never more than moderately difficult, although it's physically demanding.

ACCLIMATIZATION

Climbers double-carry loads to the two camps above base camp and sleep low. This technique allows teams

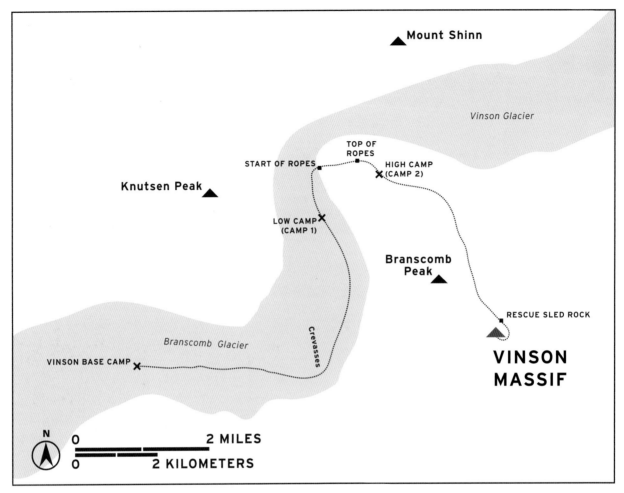

Vinson Massif climbing route

to ferry the large amount of equipment required to climb the peak while providing climbers extra time to acclimate. Weather on Vinson Massif can be as cold and windy as anywhere in the world, and getting caught in a storm at High Camp can turn desperate quickly if you are not prepared.

WATER, SANITATION, AND GARBAGE

ALE, which operates its service with a concession under the guidelines of the Antarctic Treaty, adheres to strict practices to maintain health and a pristine environment for all who use it. Any waste that is left on the continent remains visible for a long time due to the lack of snowfall. Following environmental standards is crucial

to making sure that Vinson Massif will continue to be a beautiful and clean mountain for climbers to enjoy for many years to come and that climbers will be allowed to enjoy the mountain well into the future.

Climbers melt snow as a water source. It's important to be aware of where you collect this snow; obviously, avoid collection from near the latrines. Due to the strict environmental regulations, melted snow water shouldn't need to be treated before you drink it. There is plenty of snow and ice at all of the camps, so finding snow to melt is never a problem.

Below are some of the most important waste management guidelines for climbers to follow while in Antarctica. All of these are also general Leave No Trace–minimal impact principles that should be followed anytime you are in the backcountry:

- Collect all food waste and garbage in garbage bags.
- Collect all human refuse in supplied latrines or your

personal toilet bags. Pee in designated pee locations.

- Pour "gray water" (water from cooking) into designated pee areas.
- Leave nothing on the mountain, including wands, broken gear, garbage, etc.

SAMPLE CLIMBING ITINERARY: VINSON MASSIF'S MAIN ROUTE

Day	Location	Start Elevation	End Elevation	Elevation Gain	Distance
1	Fly to Santiago				
2	Fly to Punta Arenas				
3	Mandatory meeting in Punta Arenas				
4	Fly to Union Glacier	0 ft (0 m)	2633 ft (803 m)	2633 ft (803 m)	
5	Fly to Vinson Base Camp	2633 ft (803 m)	6890 ft (2100 m)	4257 ft (1297 m)	62 miles (100 km)
6	Carry from Base Camp to Low Camp	6890 ft (2100 m)	9022 ft (2750 m)	2132 ft (650 m)	11.2 miles (18 km)
7	Climb to Low Camp	6890 ft (2100 m)	9022 ft (2750 m)	2132 ft (650 m)	5.6 miles (9 km)
8	Carry to High Camp	9022 ft (2750 m)	12,139 ft (3700 m)	3117 ft (950 m)	3.6 miles (6 km)
9	Rest day				
10	Climb to High Camp	9022 ft (2750 m)	12,139 ft (3700 m)	3117 ft (950 m)	1.8 miles (3 km)
11	Climb to summit	12,139 ft (3700 m)	16,050 ft (4892 m)	3911 ft (1192 m)	4.4 miles (7 km)
	Descend to High Camp	16,050 ft (4892 m)	12,139 ft (3700 m)	−3911 ft (−1192 m)	4.4 miles (7 km)
12	Descend to Vinson Base Camp	12,139 ft (3700 m)	6890 ft (2100 m)	−5249 ft (−1600 m)	7.4 miles (12 km)
13	Fly to Union Glacier	6890 ft (2100 m)	2633 ft (803 m)	−4257 ft (−1300 m)	62 miles (100 km)
14	Fly to Punta Arenas	2633 ft (803 m)	0 ft (0 m)		
15	Fly to Santiago and home				

THE CLIMB

Because Antarctica has so little precipitation and thus little snow accumulation, there is rarely a need for snowshoes on this climb. The High Camp (Camp 2) is a brutal place in a storm, similar to high camp on Denali or the South Col on Mount Everest. Bring three to five days' worth of food to High Camp to allow for a few extra tent days if a storm hits or for rest days if needed. ALE maintains rescue caches at Low Camp (Camp 1), High Camp, and near the summit.

Note: Since the declination on Vinson Massif averages 41°14'E, I give all of the route description in terms of true north rather than magnetic north (reference the Omega Foundation, 2007, and map by Damien Gildea and Camile Rada).

A "clamshell" tent at Union Glacier (Photo by Jane Lee)

Amundsen

VINSON BASE CAMP TO LOW CAMP (CAMP 1)

Teams carry part of their gear 5.6 miles (9 km) to Low Camp the first day, making a cache, before returning to Vinson Base Camp to sleep low, and then they move camp up to Low Camp the following day. The route to Low Camp climbs gradually up the center of the Branscomb Glacier, traveling east and then due north.

Begin by traversing toward Vinson's summit, traveling east for two hours before eventually turning north (left) through a few ice rolls and a small broken section to Low Camp. The broken section just after the turn can be icy and crevassed. The ascent takes five to seven hours and the return about half that.

Low Camp lies on a compression zone in a large basin at the base of broad summit ridges leading to the summit. There are few crevasses in this area, but high winds are common. Solid snow-block walls can protect your tents from gusts and drifting snow. Winds have reached 100 miles per hour (160 kph) at Low Camp.

LOW CAMP TO HIGH CAMP (CAMP 2)

The route from Low Camp to High Camp climbs fixed ropes heading east up the obvious, broad face and ridge above Low Camp for four to five hours, gaining 3117 feet (950 m). The total distance is 3.6 miles (6 km). This push from Low Camp to High Camp is also done by carrying and caching a load the first day, returning to sleep lower at Low Camp, and then moving to High Camp the following day.

Climb the glacier heading northeast for half an hour, gaining a few hundred feet to the base of the climbing ropes before ascending fixed lines climbing east up 30- to 40-degree snow slopes up the ridge. The fixed lines are on firm snow slopes and make for good cramponing. ALE staff resets these ropes at the start of every climbing year and maintains them throughout the climbing season. The fixed line runs for 3940 feet (1200 m) before topping out on a plateau an hour below High Camp. There is only one good resting point during the fixed-line climbing about 1970 feet (600 m) from the base of the ridge. Be considerate; work with other climbing groups to make the rest spot available to everyone.

From the top of the fixed lines, the route hugs a rock ridge heading toward Branscomb Peak to the southeast, crests a small rock and ice hill, then drops a few feet into camp. High Camp sits on the edge of the glacial plateau in a relatively protected nook below rocky buttresses and Branscomb Peak. From High Camp, most of the summit day's route is visible to the south.

HIGH CAMP TO THE SUMMIT

Some groups head for the summit the day after arriving at High Camp, weather permitting, while others take a day to further acclimate. Summit day covers a lot of terrain over ten to fourteen hours of climbing and descending back to High Camp.

The summit route follows the broad, gradual glacier below the summit pyramid, heading south. Most of the day consists of relaxed glacier hiking, but the final slopes of the summit pyramid are steeper and more exposed. Crevasse danger is minimal throughout the day.

Summit day is often windy with little protection from terrain features. High winds combined with extreme temperatures this high up on Vinson can be dangerous.

Ambient air temperatures typically range from 0 degrees Fahrenheit to -40 degrees Fahrenheit (-18˚C to -40˚C) throughout summit day, and winds of 10 to 30 miles per hour (15 to 50 kph) are common.

The summit route is very open with few landmarks and in a whiteout can be very confusing. Make sure to enter route waypoints into your GPS before the climb to help with navigation in case of low-visibility conditions.

Once you are at the summit pyramid, there are two ways to tackle the final slopes. To the west of the summit pyramid, a slightly shorter route of three hours ascends an open, 30- to 40-degree snow and ice slope, gains a rock ridge, and then traverses east to the top. Most teams, however, choose to traverse east for three and a half hours around the back of the summit pyramid, ascending more gradual snow slopes to the eastern summit ridge. On the ridge, the last hour consists of rolling, moderately exposed climbing leading to the true summit. This latter route is more gradual and less exposed, overall a safer option.

DESCENT

The summit is only halfway! Storms tend to roll in later in the day, so make sure you reserve strength for the descent. After spending a night at High Camp after summit day, most teams try to make the entire trip back to base camp in one push, collecting their cached goods at Low Camp en route.

VINSON MASSIF GEAR LISTS

Vinson Massif is the most remote of the Seven Summits; triple-check your gear!

TRAVEL GEAR

- Passport (valid for at least six months after expedition)
- Travel wallet
- Cash
- 2 large duffel bags
- 1 small duffel bag for sled haul
- 3 locks for duffel bags

Descending to High
Camp after a long
summit day
(Photo by Jane Lee)

- Small backpack for overhead bins
- Casual clothes for walking around town

CLIMBING GEAR
- Large internal-frame pack (6000-plus cubic inches, 98-plus liters), with a ditch loop, jumar rigged for fixed-line ascension, and a sled haul loop
- Alpine ice ax
- 12-point crampons that fit well
- Climbing harness with detachable leg loops and belay loop
- 2 locking carabiners
- 4 nonlocking carabiners
- 3 slings
- Ascender
- 2 prusik loops

CLOTHING
Bring only the best cold weather clothing—and make sure you know how it works.

FOOTWEAR:
- Triple boots or double boots with overboot (warmest boots possible)
- 3 pairs climbing socks of different weights
- Camp booties (down or synthetic)

LOWER-BODY LAYERS:

- Heavyweight insulated pants (down or synthetic)
- Waterproof, breathable rain shell with a full zipper
- 1 pair heavyweight climbing pants
- 2 pairs underlayers of different weights (synthetic or merino wool)

UPPER-BODY LAYERS:

- Waterproof, breathable rain shell
- Heaviest weight down parka with hood
- 3 soft-shell synthetic pile layers: "puff" jacket and fleece
- 2 sets underlayers of different weights (synthetic or merino wool)

HEADGEAR AND HANDWEAR:

- Warm ski hat
- Face mask
- 2 Buffs
- 1 pair light pile gloves
- 1 pair heavy climbing gloves
- Down overmitt (must fit over light gloves or climbing gloves)

PERSONAL GEAR

- Ten Essentials
- No need for a headlamp! Twenty-four hours of sunlight November through January.
- 30-plus SPF sweatproof sunscreen
- Adjustable ski poles for hiking
- Down sleeping bag rated to -40°F (-41°C)
- 2 sleeping pads: 1 closed-cell, 1 inflatable
- 2 pairs glacier glasses
- Goggles with dark lenses
- 2 1-quart water bottles
- 2 water bottle jackets
- 1-quart thermos
- Cup, bowl, and spoon

- Snack food for 12–14 days
- Multitool (with pliers)
- Toiletries
- Personal wipes
- Toilet paper
- 1-quart pee bottle
- 3 large garbage bags for caching gear
- 3 stuff sacks
- Camera
- Extra batteries

GROUP GEAR

- 4-season tents
- Cooktent
- Cookstoves, fuel, pots, etc.
- Food for 12–14 days
- 25 wands
- Sleds (provided by ALE)
- Ropes
- Pickets
- VHF radios
- Satellite phone

SUMMIT CHECKLIST

- All warm clothes
- Face mask
- Goggles
- GPS device
- Wands
- Crampons
- Pickets
- Ice ax
- Rescue gear: sleeping bag and pad, stove, cookpot, fuel, and bivy sack
- Thermos
- Water
- Food
- First-aid and repair kits

MOUNT ELBRUS

ALTITUDE
18,510 feet (5642 m)

DIFFICULTY RATINGS
Technical: 2
Physical: 2-3

SUMMIT GPS WAYPOINTS
N 43 21.129
E 42 26.010

ELEVATION GAIN
(base camp to summit)
5715 feet (1742 m)

DISTANCE
(base camp to summit)
5.6 miles (9 km)

TIME
(door-to-door)
15 days

SEASON
June-August

Ascending the
final steps to
the top of Europe

CHAPTER 8

MOUNT ELBRUS

EUROPE'S HIGHEST SUMMIT

WE WERE BOTH ON VERY PRIVATE JOURNEYS,
LOOKING FOR OUR INNER SELVES, BUT THE
PLEASURE AND SATISFACTION OF CLIMBING WERE
BEST SHARED.

—JOSEP PUJANTE, ON CLIMBING MOUNT ELBRUS, FROM *SEVEN SUMMITS*
  BY STEVE BELL (2000)

Mount Elbrus, the highest summit of Europe, rises 18,510 feet (5642 m) above sea level in the Caucasus Mountains, a range 700 miles (1125 km) in length, sandwiched between the Caspian and Black Seas. To the north of the Caucasus lie forest and steppe; to the south, a drier, desertlike environment. The Caucasus Range includes the fourteen highest mountains in Europe. Mount Elbrus is tucked deep within the Caucasus Range in the southwestern corner of Russia, close to its border with Georgia. It has two prominent summits: the east (18,442 ft, 5621 m) and the west (18,510 ft, 5642 m), with the main climbing route ascending to the col between the two.

The single chairlift carries climbers, skiers, and tourists to the barrel huts on the slopes of Mount Elbrus.

Mount Elbrus has more than twenty-two glaciers covering 53 square miles (138 sq km) of terrain with ice that can be hundreds of yards (meters) thick. The glaciers' meltwater feeds three major rivers in the region: the Baksan, Kuban, and Malka. This inactive volcano is a ski resort in the winter and tourist viewpoint in the summer. A cable car to the top of the ski area on Mount Elbrus was completed in 1976, providing access for skiers, climbers, and tourists to enjoy the upper reaches of the mountain. This flood of people to the mountain continues today, with literally thousands riding the cable car on clear summer days for views of the Caucasus and to play in the year-round snow. The Russian ski team trains on the glaciers throughout the summer months and has a training facility in the valley. Similar European ranges, such as the Alps, are overrun by climbers, skiers, and trekkers, but the Caucasus (other than Mount Elbrus) remains relatively untouched, which gives them a wild, frontier feel.

NATURAL HISTORY

Mount Elbrus is an inactive volcano that last erupted about two thousand years ago. It has a typical volcanic shape with broad slopes and two defined conical summits draped in glaciers. Mount Elbrus dominates the landscape, although many other impressive peaks rise to the south and west. At 43 degrees north latitude, the Caucasus has very pronounced seasons and weather fluctuations.

The mountain is surrounded by alpine pastures, coniferous forests, and fertile valleys to the north, east, and south; Elbrus is adjacent to the rest of the Caucasus Range to the west. The forests below it are similar to those at the same latitude in the far western United States and throughout western Europe. These forests are replete with deer and bears, among other animals. Ranchers graze their cows low in the valleys, and fields of sunflowers add color to the valley floor in the summer months.

CULTURAL AND POLITICAL BACKGROUND

Though Mount Elbrus is located in the Russian Federation, its region has a different demographic than that of Moscow and St. Petersburg to the north. The proximity of Georgia, North and South Ossetia, Azerbaijan, Chechnya, and Armenia creates a melting pot of ethnicities. The different ethnic groups often have strong feelings about each other and the Russians farther north, making for a tumultuous history.

Since the fall of the Soviet Union in 1991, the Russian Federation is now a republic in the Commonwealth of Independent States. The political situation in this part of Russia has become more volatile in the past two decades. Although conflicts rarely reach into the Baksan River valley of Mount Elbrus, it is always prudent to be aware of current events prior to traveling there. Terrorist incidents have closed the region to climbing in the past.

The local Kabardino-Balkarian people are hearty, with a unique way of life and traditions. They are mostly ranchers or tradespeople. Food in the region is a mix of typical Russian dishes and local specialties; if you like heavy, flavorful food, it's some of the best in the world. After a week of this menu, my guided groups are always desperate for a salad, however.

CLIMBING HISTORY

The east summit of Mount Elbrus was the first to be climbed. A Karchay guide native to the region, named Killar Khashirov, led the ascent for the Imperial Russian Army's scientific expedition in July 1829. This is generally considered to be the first ascent of the east peak, although some say it wasn't reached until much later, in 1868. The first ascent of the west (true) summit came in July 1874, by a team of Englishmen led by F. Crauford Grove and a Swiss guide, Peter Knubel. The British took interest in the Caucasus Mountains and for years returned to make first ascents on several of the highest peaks in the range.

There was little climbing activity on Mount Elbrus until the late 1920s, when Germans and Austrians put up several first ascents. The peak played a role in World War II when the Wehrmacht occupied the area from mid-1942 to January 1943. The Mir Station museum, at the top of the ski area tram that delivers people to the upper slopes of Mount Elbrus, depicts the military presence and battles on the slopes of Elbrus.

Until the collapse of the Soviet Union, international climbing parties in Russia were very limited. Since then, the number of climbers has skyrocketed despite the frustrating red tape and corruption sometimes encountered here.

Mount Elbrus was the first of the Seven Summits attempted together by pioneers Dick Bass and Frank Wells in 1981, and for good reason. Although it's an arduous climb with potentially brutal weather, it makes a good stepping stone to bigger climbs such as Denali and Aconcagua. A climb on Mount Elbrus is a good indicator of how your body will respond to more extreme altitudes, and it will give you an idea of your fitness. Among the Seven Summits, Elbrus is a good place to start your adventure because of its minimal technical difficulties and moderate altitude.

MOUNT ELBRUS FAST FACTS

- Mount Elbrus is considered an inactive volcano.
- In the 1990s, Land Rover brought a car to the top of the east summit of Mount Elbrus for an advertisement. Locals say it is still there (although I've never seen it personally).
- Mount Elbrus was one of the first of the Seven Summits to be climbed.
- Mount Elbrus lies in Russia, close to the borders of Georgia and Armenia.
- Mount Elbrus was the first peak of the Seven Summits to be climbed together by Dick Bass and Frank Wells.

CLIMBING CHALLENGES

Mount Elbrus is an arduous climb with serious weather. Although it isn't very technically demanding, its summit day of roughly 5700 feet (1700 m) elevation gain is one of the longest and most demanding on the Seven Summits circuit. However, one of the most difficult parts of the climb can be just getting there. Several modes of travel and a significant amount of travel time are needed for climbers coming from continents other than Europe. Without command of the Russian language or familiarity with Russian culture, traveling there can be vexing. Climbing with a guide service greatly mitigates these obstacles.

The often-lengthy visa process requires a special invitation from a Russian company. Climbers must submit their passport and paperwork or personally visit a Russian embassy.

Because of ethnic conflicts in the area, military presence is ubiquitous and checkpoints are frequent throughout the region. Some checkpoints are organized by the military, but most are routine police stops.

The lack of infrastructure in the region and the military presence make the Caucasus more challenging to explore than ranges such as the Alps, but increasing numbers of climbers are venturing into the Caucasus each year. Most of this traffic is concentrated on Mount Elbrus, mainly on Elbrus's southern flank. Many climbers underestimate Mount Elbrus because of its reputation as a nontechnical climb of moderate altitude, but apathy can get climbers into trouble.

You should also be aware of several objective hazards during a climb of Mount Elbrus. The most common are weather changes and navigation problems, and the two are often closely related. Storms arise quickly on Mount Elbrus. The glaciers are expansive with few features, making it easy to get off route. Once off route, dangers include crevasses, cliffs, and avalanche slopes. During most seasons, however, plenty of highly visible route markers well placed by local guides (for the annual race to the summit) are obvious in good weather. Just below the route on the traverse to the col are several large crevasses. It's important to stay on the worn trail to avoid these. A length of rope can double as a short-roping tool on the steep pitch above the col as well. Bring a screw and a picket on the climb for emergency anchors.

Solid avalanche assessment skills are important for this climb. If there's new snow and/or high winds, be aware of potential hazards on the route. Exercise particular caution on the slopes above the traverse to the col and above the col en route to the west plateau.

MOUNT ELBRUS TIMELINE

JULY 1829 First ascent of the east peak of Mount Elbrus by an Imperial Russian Army team is led by local guide Killar Khashirov.

JULY 1874 First ascent of the west (true) summit by an English team is led by F. Crauford Grove and Swiss guide Peter Knubel.

LATE 1920s Austrians and Germans make several first ascents.

MID-1942–JANUARY 1943 Elbrus region is occupied by the German Wehrmacht.

1976 A cable car from the base of the mountain to more than 12,000 feet (3660 m) is completed, greatly facilitating climbing, skiing, and exploration on the mountain.

A team resting below
Pastokov Rocks on an
acclimatization hike

THE UNEXPECTED CHALLENGE OF MOUNT ELBRUS

Climbing the Seven Summits was often an experience in creative problem-solving. Mount Elbrus in Russia was my last expedition, and by this point, I had been to the Himalayas several times, snuck through a sudden political strike in Punta Arenas, Chile, and survived a snowstorm on Aconcagua. With Elbrus being one of the "easier" climbs, I anticipated a stress-free conclusion to the Seven Summits.

As it turned out, just getting to Elbrus was virtually impossible. Beginning in February 2011, Elbrus was closed and entry into the Baksan Valley, where the mountain is situated, was restricted. The official reason blamed the presence of terrorist cells that had bombed a cable car line and attacked a tourist bus. This development seemed pretty plausible, with the region being close to Georgia and Ossetia, states that share no lost love for Russia.

I wanted to climb in July, but Elbrus had been closed for months. Guiding companies were canceling their trips to the mountain, and getting a visa was difficult. Also, upon arrival in Russia, you need to request and fill out an additional tourist registration at the hotel, then have it stamped and signed by the hotel staff. Given the fact that it's a crucial document, it's bewildering that unless you specifically ask for it, no one will voluntarily inform you of the necessary procedure before you check out. Of the Seven Summits, Russia definitely required a little more work navigating administrative details.

With the trip getting increasingly complicated, I had to jettison my original plan of climbing with a friend in favor of hiring a local guide. I was fortunate that my guide spoke English, because it seems that very few people in Russia do, even in cosmopolitan Moscow unless you stay on the main tourist drags. However, until I met my guide in Mineralnye Vody, I was on my own. Traveling alone in Russia with two giant duffel bags in tow and trying to get around on public transport was a painful exercise. Add to that the fact that my domestic flight to Mineralnye Vody was canceled with no prior announcement until passengers were due to check in. Even then, the announcements were made only in Russian so I didn't understand them. I eventually deduced from the frustrated passengers walking away that I probably wasn't going to be flying that day.

When I finally arrived in Mineralnye Vody, I wasn't prepared for how heavily patrolled the road leading into the Baksan Valley was. There was minimal information available online, and the situation on the ground was drastically different from the outdated information circulating on the Internet. At the first roadblock, we were ordered out of the car and surrounded by eight burly Russian Army guards, complete with tattoos and Kalishnakovs. We were eventually allowed through.

From the valley, most climbers ride the cable car to the upper station on the lower slopes of Elbrus before arriving at the barrel huts after a brief climb. This option was closed to us as the cable car was in disrepair, so we hiked up instead. The climb up to the summit of Elbrus the next morning was an extremely rushed affair since the border guards wanted us out of the valley as soon as possible due to the unrest in the area, but we summited in good weather and descended safely the same day. Elbrus rounded out my Seven Summits on the Fourth of July. Elbrus definitely wasn't the easiest trip because Russia can be a difficult place to travel, but it was a great adventure, a beautiful climb—and I came home with a great story.

JANE LEE

FIRST SOUTHEAST ASIAN (SINGAPOREAN) WOMAN TO CLIMB THE SEVEN SUMMITS,
LEADER OF THE 2009 SINGAPOREAN WOMEN'S EVEREST TEAM

Climbing above
Pastokov Rocks

PLANNING AN EXPEDITION

More than some of the Seven Summits, planning an ascent of Mount Elbrus must begin well in advance of the trip start date. The complicated visa process requires at least several weeks to complete, and climbers should allow extra time in case of complications throughout this process. Also, during high season make sure to book the mountain huts at least a month in advance of your climb.

Most who climb Mount Elbrus spend time in Moscow or St. Petersburg, or both, before or after the climb.

Most teams allow two weeks for a Mount Elbrus expedition: a week for the climb of Mount Elbrus, plus another week for touring Moscow and St. Petersburg and for travel time. Hotel reservations and sightseeing tours need to be arranged well in advance. It's difficult to get more than a taste of these two great historical cities in this amount of time, so consider extending your trip if you can.

Russia has a great variety of food for the climb in supermarkets, both in the larger cities and in the town of Mineralnye Vody and the Baksan Valley. However, if there are specific items you are used to eating on climbs, bring them from home. Gel packs, trail bars, and other specialty items are not readily available in Russia.

GUIDED TRIP VERSUS INDEPENDENT CLIMB

Most climbers use a guide service for climbs of Mount Elbrus because of the protracted visa process (see "Documents" below) and logistical challenges of the climb. However, if you are willing to put in the time and effort to organize your own climb, once on the mountain it is reasonable for experienced climbers to ascend on their own, assuming they have a strong background in cramponing and routefinding techniques such as GPS use. It is important for independent climbers to allow sufficient time for acclimatization.

CLIMBING SEASONS AND WEATHER

The main climbing season is from June through August, with July being the busiest month. Several parties traditionally make the ascent on New Year's Day, when weather permits. Permanent snow line is around 11,000 feet

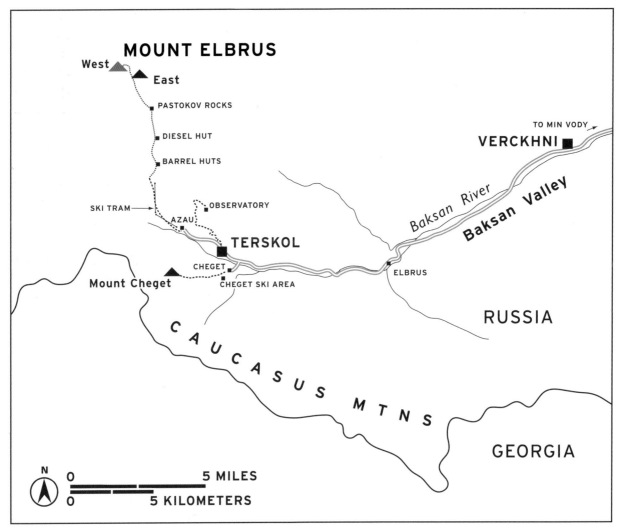

Mount Elbrus environs

PRIUTT HUT

In the 1930s, the Russians built an impressive structure called the Priutt Hut at roughly 13,500 feet (4115 m) that became the main lodging on the mountain for some time. The Priutt Hut slept nearly two hundred people and helped open up climbing to the masses. In 1998, a fire started in the kitchen and the hut quickly caught fire, burning to the ground. Most of the people in the hut made it to safety, but one climber died and several others were injured by jumping off the three-story building trying to escape the blaze. The Priutt Hut was never rebuilt; several other smaller huts were erected to fill the void. Accommodations have been an issue on Elbrus since the fire because of the increasing number of climbers. There is currently no plan to build a new, large single structure like the old Priutt Hut.

(3350 m), and above this the temperature is rarely above freezing at night. Temperatures can reach 90 degrees Fahrenheit (34°C) during a sunny day. The best time to ski Mount Elbrus is in June when there's more snow.

It's hard to predict the weather on Mount Elbrus. Afternoon clouds and thunderstorms are common. These storms dissipate through the night unless they're the front end of a larger system, which can sometimes linger for weeks. The larger storms are usually a result of sea-effect moisture from the Caspian Sea. Mount Elbrus has more dynamic weather than the rest of the range because of its height. Even on good days, the summit of Elbrus is often scoured by winds and buffeted in clouds.

Despite the seemingly benign atmosphere created by the athletes and tourists who throng the Mount Elbrus area on nice days, the peak is a potentially dangerous place with fierce weather. On average, fifteen to thirty people die here each year.

DOCUMENTS

One of the most difficult parts of climbing Mount Elbrus is obtaining a visa. This can be a frustrating process, especially if you're trying to do it on your own—usually guide services have a representative take care of this.

To visit Russia, you must first obtain a letter of invitation from a business in Russia. Guide services submit this from their business contacts, or a local tour operator can provide it for you.

Once you have obtained the invitation letter, apply for a visa by completing the paperwork from the consulate, paying the visa fee (usually $100 for a six-workday turnaround), and submitting your passport and passport photos. Be sure your passport has open pages and is valid for at least another six months after the planned dates of travel.

Once you have secured a visa, double-check that your visa dates are the same as your actual travel dates, if not a little longer, so your trip doesn't inadvertently get cut short. Make sure to keep your passport, visa, and immigration card with you at all times while traveling in Russia.

Once you are in the Elbrus region, register in the area by handing your passport and documentation to your guides or the hotel staff. It usually takes a few hours to register, and your passport is necessary.

COSTS

Local currency is the Russian ruble; as of 2012 the exchange rate is about 31 rubles to $1US. There are a few ATMs in Terskol and Cheget that work erratically; rubles are generally the only currency accepted.

- Visa: $80
- Guide service: $3000–$5000
- Hotels (five–six nights in Moscow or St. Petersburg, plus five–six nights in Terskol or Azau): $1000

A paraglider
prepares to launch
off the summit of
Mount Elbrus.

- Food (two weeks; restaurants and mountain food): $500
- Domestic flights: $400 (including overweight-baggage fees)
- Ground transportation: $300
- Mountain huts (two–three nights): $100

CONDITIONING

Mount Elbrus is an arduous climb demanding excellent fitness. Summit day consists of 5700 vertical feet (1700 m) and more than twelve hours of climbing, with short breaks, to reach the summit and descend. The typical climber's pack weighs 20–40 pounds (9–18 kg). Day hikes and multiday hikes of long distances at least once a week for five to ten hours at a stretch are the best way to train for a Mount Elbrus climb. Beyond this, cardio training at a higher heart rate is important. A routine of five or six days of training per week is appropriate for several months leading up to the expedition.

IMMUNIZATIONS

Currently, there are no mandatory immunizations for travel in Russia, although a few are recommended. Check with your local travel clinic for updated information. Hepatitis A and tetanus vaccines are a good idea for travel to any international destination, including Russia. Check your immunization records to make sure you're up to date, and leave plenty of time to get any boosters before your departure date.

COMMUNICATIONS

Most teams bring a satellite phone and several UHF talk-about radios with them on the mountain. There is cell phone coverage much of the way up Mount Elbrus as well, if you have a local SIM card or a phone that ties into the local cellular networks.

GETTING THERE AND GETTING AROUND

Due to the remote location of Mount Elbrus, getting there can be challenging. Most people fly through either Moscow or St. Petersburg and spend time sightseeing there. Some commercial guide services arrange for their groups to fly in through one of these cities and out through the other to take advantage of the cultural opportunities of each. Moscow, Russia's capital, is the home of Red Square, the Kremlin, cathedrals, palaces, museums, Gorky Park, and several universities. St. Petersburg, known as Leningrad in the days of the USSR, is an industrial center that also contains the Winter Palace and other museums including the world-class Hermitage.

DOMESTIC FLIGHTS

To get to Mount Elbrus from either of these major Russian cities, climbers take a domestic flight to the small town of Mineralnye Vody (nicknamed Min Vody), which means "mineral water." Climbers flying into Moscow need to catch a local bus or taxi in order to change airports to make the domestic flight to Mineralnye Vody. St. Petersburg uses one airport for both international and domestic flights, although they have separate terminals.

Russian domestic terminals are rustic, and planes are cramped. There's little room on the plane for carry-ons, and overhead bins are just a shelf like those on a bus. Fees for overweight baggage are high (roughly $1.35 per pound, $3 per kg) and the internal allotment of baggage weight is minimal. The excess baggage fees are paid in rubles at check-in time, before you receive your ticket from the flight representative.

GROUND TRANSPORTATION

Once you're in Min Vody, it's possible to hire a taxi just outside the terminal exit that will take you to the base of the mountain. If you have hired a local company or an international guide service, you will be met upon exiting the baggage claim area. Either way, it's a three-hour ride from Min Vody through smaller towns and beautiful countryside to get to the Baksan Valley and the base of Mount Elbrus where the climb begins.

GATEWAY SETTLEMENTS

Several small towns are scattered around the base of Mount Elbrus. Azau, the highest town, at the terminus of the Baksan Valley, consists of a few small hotels and the ski tram buildings. There's a small market in Azau with local handicrafts and souvenirs and vendors selling the local barbecue specialty, *shaslik*. Terskol, a bigger town lower in the valley, has grocery stores, hotels, housing, and an ATM. The town of Cheget sits downvalley from Terskol in a side valley. Cheget, roughly the same size as Terskol, has several hotels, shops, and its own ski area, on Mount Cheget.

OTHER ACTIVITIES: SKIING

Skiing Mount Elbrus is gaining popularity, and for good reason—Mount Elbrus is virtually perfect for skiing. Skiing makes for a quick and easy descent, especially if conditions are right. Several international guide services now offer ski mountaineering options. Almost the entire climbing route from the barrel huts at the top of the chairlift to the summit is good terrain for moderate to advanced skiers. There are several hazards that you need to be aware of, however: avalanche slopes, crevasses below the marked route on the traverse to the col, and patches of ice. The only slope reserved for experts

Night falls on Elbrus and the barrel huts.

GUIDE TIP

Look for the steps of climbers ahead of you. It's much harder to kick your own staircase than to use one that's already in place. As you start up, take a moment to look for these tracks and save yourself some energy.

or for a ski belay is the pitch from the summit plateau, on the west summit, to the col. This 35- to 40-degree pitch can be quite icy. Keep your crampons and ice ax handy in case you decide not to ski this steeper pitch on the descent.

CLIMBING MOUNT ELBRUS

Climbers generally tackle Mount Elbrus in two stages. The first stage consists of acclimatization based out of one of the small towns at the base of the mountain in the Baksan Valley. Climbers acclimatize by hiking in the valley or taking the tram up to the mountain for day hikes. The second stage consists of acclimatization hikes on the mountain while sleeping in mountain huts prior to the summit bid. These requisite acclimatization days allow climbers to succeed on the massive 5700-foot (1700 m) summit day.

The overwhelming majority of climbers ascend Elbrus via the ski area on the southwestern side of the mountain. Here, a whole industry is based around climbers and skiers exploring the mountain, providing a solid infrastructure for climbing not found anywhere else on the mountain. This ascent route, consisting of mainly low-angle cramponing with a short steeper pitch of 40 degrees or less, is not technically difficult.

Accommodations in Terskol in the Baksan Valley offer everything needed for a comfortable stay: good restaurants, clean rooms, hot showers, food stores, and gift markets. Once on the mountain, climbers must provide their own food and melt their own water with their own cooking supplies. On the mountain, accommodations providing beds, rudimentary toilets, and kitchen

facilities are more rustic than in the valley. Few climbers sleep in tents, opting to use one of many mountain huts. From the huts, a well-used trail meanders up the glacier toward the summit on gradual terrain.

ROUTES

Mount Elbrus has several climbing routes, but the Baksan Valley approach is the normal route, described in this chapter. Most other routes get only a few ascents per year, making up a tiny fraction of the overall number of climbs.

Some climbers avoid the tram by taking the Kiukurtliu Route to the west of the ski area. This leads over glaciated terrain to gain the northwest spur, where you climb up moderate terrain to the summit plateau. Once acclimatized, this route takes about a day more than the normal route due to the heavy loads.

ACCLIMATIZATION

Driving to 7000 feet (2135 m) and taking the tram to more than 12,000 feet (3660 m) makes for an exceptionally easy approach to start a Mount Elbrus climb, one that often gets climbers into trouble because they don't take adequate time to acclimatize. A conservative approach to climbing Mount Elbrus consists of five to seven days of acclimatization before attempting a summit bid.

Spend three days acclimatizing in the Baksan Valley before heading up to stay at the mountain huts. Options for acclimatization hikes around the Baksan Valley before heading up Mount Elbrus include walking up to an observatory just south of Mount Elbrus on a steep dirt road leaving from Terskol. This ascent takes approximately three hours (2000 ft, 610 m), passing a picturesque waterfall after two hours; plan on another one to one and a half hours back down. On a clear day, this hike offers excellent views of the Caucasus Range.

Another option is to hike or take the chairlift up Cheget ski area and then hike to a high mountain lake to the west. It takes two hours to hike to the top of the lift and another hour to reach the lake. This beautiful alpine

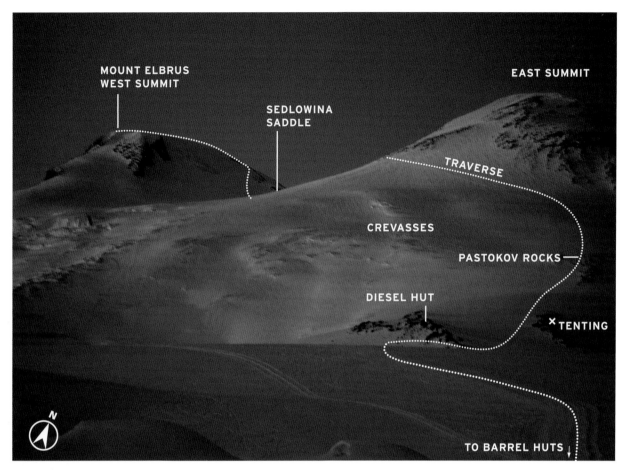

Elbrus Normal Route

hike has excellent views of Mount Cheget and the southern Caucasus Mountains.

Climbers can also take the tram up Mount Elbrus ski resort to its terminus and hike around that area. The tram rises 5000 feet (1525 m) in two stages, starting at 8000 feet (2439 m) in the valley and ending at 12,000 feet (3658 m) at the foot of the glacier. Tickets can be purchased upon arrival at the base station. You need to show these tickets to the tram staff both on the way up and the way down. From the top of the tram, a short single chairlift ride leads to the glacier, or you can hike for thirty minutes on a rough dirt access road.

The "barrel huts" used by many climbers for mountain accommodations are located at the top of the single chairlift above the tram at roughly 13,000 feet (4000 m).

This series of rustic, oversized barrels propped off the ground have been turned into cabins sleeping four to six (see "The Climb" below). Once at the barrel huts, climbers take at least a day, and sometimes as many as three, to acclimatize before making a summit attempt.

There is realistically only one acclimatization hike to do at this point to kill a day or two: up to the top of the gully just below Pastokov Rocks, a rock outcropping that penetrates the glacier in the middle of the ascent route. Follow the glacier up the main corridor past the mountain huts for four hours (2500 ft, 760 m), and you'll reach Pastokov Rocks. From here, the ascent starts to get a bit steeper and more crevassed, making this a good place to turn around for a day hike. The terrain above the barrel huts and below Pastokov Rocks is excellent for skiing, which makes for great acclimatization day trips for skiers.

WATER, SANITATION, AND GARBAGE

Water purification is important on Mount Elbrus, since the only water source is the snow, which can be dirty due to the great numbers of climbers; be sure to use only clean snow away from huts and camping areas. After melting the snow, use purifying tablets or a filter instead of boiling the water, to save valuable fuel.

Toilets are rudimentary everywhere on the mountain, often consisting of old wooden structures suspended over collection barrels or a cliff. This lack of sanitary facilities is a real issue on Mount Elbrus, one that doesn't seem to be getting addressed. Climbers can stay healthy by using copious amounts of hand sanitizer after using these facilities and before handling food.

Trash cans are provided in most huts, but climbers must carry all their trash off the mountain and dispose of it in the Baksan Valley below.

THE CLIMB

Most climbers take the gondola and single chairlift when they head up Mount Elbrus for the climb. Access roads up the ski area lead to the starting point, but

The author on the summit plateau of the west summit with the east summit in the distance

they're not enjoyable to hike. They are dusty, with loose gravel, and you may find yourself confronting a three-ton dump truck charging down a narrow road. Some people ascend the broken glaciers to the west of the ski area connecting the dirt road with the glacier tongues higher, but it makes for an awkward hike.

At the toe of the glacier marking the starting point for the climb are the barrel huts, which are open to the public. A reservation is needed, and the price is around $30 per night per person. The barrels are dusty and

rustic, as are most of the accommodations on Mount Elbrus. Propane gas tanks and stoves are also available for guests.

Some groups make their summit bid from one of several higher huts to shorten the length of the summit day. This guidebook bases the climbing itinerary on starting from the barrel huts, however. The higher huts sit just above 13,780 feet (4200 m), about 1000 feet (300 m) above the barrel huts. Reservations are also needed for these upper huts to guarantee space.

SAMPLE CLIMBING ITINERARY: MOUNT ELBRUS'S NORMAL ROUTE

Day	Location	Start Elevation	End Elevation	Elevation Gain	Distance
1	Fly to St. Petersburg				
2	Sightsee in St. Petersburg				
3	Fly to Min Vody; drive to Terskol		6943 ft (2116 m)		
4	Acclimatization hike to observatory	6943 ft (2116 m)	10,180 ft (3103 m)	3237 ft (987 m)	8 miles (13 km)
5	Acclimatization hike to top of gully below Pastokov Rocks	6943 ft (2116 m)	13,993 ft (4265 m)	7050 ft (2149 m)	3.75 miles (6 km)
6	Ascend to barrel huts; acclimatization hike to top of gully below Pastokov Rocks	6943 ft (2116 m)	13,993 ft (4265 m)	7050 ft (2149 m)	3.75 miles (6 km)
7	Acclimatization hike to Pastokov Rocks; return to huts	12,795 ft (3900 m)	15,355 ft (4680 m)	2560 ft (780 m)	5 miles (8 km)
8	Climb to summit	12,795 ft (3900 m)	18,510 ft (5642 m)	5715 ft (1742 m)	5.6 miles (9 km)
	Descend to barrel huts	18,510 ft (5642 m)	12,795 ft (3900 m)	-5715 ft (-1742 m)	5.6 miles (9 km)
9	Contingency				
10	Contingency				
11	Descend to Terskol	12,795 ft (3900 m)	6943 ft (2116 m)	-5852 ft (-1784 m)	3 miles (5 km)
12	Sightsee in Terskol				
13	Fly to Moscow				
14	Sightsee in Moscow				
13	Fly home				

Descending from
Elbrus's west summit
in fresh snow
(Photo by Jane Lee)

BARREL HUTS TO THE SUMMIT AND BACK

Once climbers have acclimatized to the altitude through several hikes on the mountain, it's time for summit day, weather permitting. The summit day is completed in one push from your mountain hut to the summit and back the same day.

Summit day begins early—around 3:00 AM, to leave plenty of time for ascent and descent in light during the "heat" of the day. The route from the barrel huts climbs straight up the moderately angled glacier following the snow groomer track toward the unmistakable east and west summits of the mountain. An outcropping of rocks in the middle of the glacier, called Pastokov Rocks, is the most obvious landmark in this glaciated terrain above the huts, and it takes three hours to reach from the barrel huts. The rocks sit alongside and at the top of a steeper snow pitch directly below the east peak. Although this is technically glacier travel, I have never seen crevasses forming below Pastokov Rocks on or near the ascent route, although they may form to the north and south.

Above Pastokov Rocks, the slope steepens 10 degrees while continuing up snow. From Pastokov Rocks, it takes three to four hours to reach Sedlowina Saddle between the east and west summits. Climb directly above Pastokov Rocks for an hour heading northeast before beginning a gradual and natural traverse to the left (north) for 1 mile (1.6 km) to the obvious low point between the two peaks. This traverse continues for another two or three hours and roughly 2500 feet (760 m).

The pitch directly above the saddle heading north en route to the summit is the steepest of the climb, at 35–40 degrees for almost 750 feet (230 m). Crampons and an ice ax are needed even in good snow conditions. Climb directly above to the north for 300 feet (100 m), then traverse northeast, angling upward to a broad ridge and a low point on the summit plateau.

Once on the plateau it's half an hour of easy, flat walking to the west to a small summit cone 0.6 mile (1 km) from gaining the plateau. This plateau is usually wind-scoured névé, which makes for good cramponing and easy walking despite the high altitude. Climbers gain only 150 feet (46 m) of elevation on the plateau before the final 100-foot (30 m) climb up the summit cone to the true summit.

The descent route, which is the same as the ascent, goes quickly. If someone is unstable, employ short-roping techniques or running protection on the steeper pitch down toward the col. Climbers average seven to nine hours on the ascent and four to five hours to descend.

MOUNT ELBRUS GEAR LISTS

Excess-weight baggage fees are high so pack light—but don't skimp on the avalanche gear.

TRAVEL GEAR
- Passport with valid visa
- Travel wallet
- Cash
- 2 large duffel bags
- 2 locks for duffel bags
- Small day pack to use as carry-on

CLIMBING GEAR
- Large internal-frame pack
- Alpine ice ax
- 12-point crampons
- Climbing harness
- 2 locking carabiners
- 2 regular carabiners

SKI EXPEDITION GEAR
- Skis and bindings with touring mode
- Ski poles
- Alpine touring or telemark boots
- Climbing skins
- Ski crampons
- Avalanche transceiver
- Avalanche probe
- Collapsible shovel
- Day pack

CLOTHING
Bring clothing that can accommodate a variety of weather conditions.

FOOTWEAR:
- Double climbing boots
- Lightweight hiking shoes
- 2 pairs thick climbing socks

LOWER-BODY LAYERS:
- Shell pants with full-length leg zippers
- Gaiters
- Climbing pants
- Lightweight hiking pants
- 1 pair synthetic under layer

UPPER-BODY LAYERS:
- Shell parka
- Light- to medium-weight insulated parka (down or synthetic)
- Soft shell jacket
- Lightweight hiking shirts
- 2 pairs synthetic underlayers

HEADGEAR AND HANDGEAR:
- Warm ski hat
- Bandana or Buff
- Baseball cap
- Ski gloves
- Liner gloves
- Warm mittens

PERSONAL GEAR
- Ten Essentials
- Sleeping bag rated to 0˚F (-18˚C)
- Inflatable sleeping pad
- Ski goggles
- Wrist-watch altimeter
- Adjustable ski poles
- 2 wide-mouth 1-quart water bottles
- Insulated bottle covers
- Insulated mug with lid
- Bowl and spoon
- Personal medications
- Lightweight toilet articles
- 1-quart pee bottle
- Toilet paper
- Small bottle of hand sanitizer
- 3 large plastic garbage bags
- Camera and film

GROUP GEAR
- Medical kit
- Short rope for summit day
- Repair kit
- Extra headlamp, batteries, etc.
- Satellite phone

SUMMIT CHECKLIST
- Ice ax
- Crampons
- Headlamp and extra batteries
- 1 extra headlamp per group
- Short, thin rope for short-roping on final slopes
- Warm down parka
- Balaclava
- Ski hat
- Warm gloves and mittens as a backup
- Goggles
- Medical kit
- Plenty of food and water for 12 or more hours of strenuous climbing
- Water bottle cover to keep your bottles from freezing
- Repair kit for crampons and pack straps
- Summit flags for pictures
- Camera

MOUNT KOSCIUSZKO

ALTITUDE
7310 feet (2228 m)

DIFFICULTY RATINGS
Technical: 1
Physical: 2

SUMMIT GPS WAYPOINTS
S 36 27.250
E 148 16.196

ELEVATION GAIN
(base camp to summit)
Via Charlotte's Pass 1273 feet (388 m)
Via Thredbo Ski Resort 991 feet (302 m)

DISTANCE
(base camp to summit)
Via Charlotte's Pass 5.6 miles (9 km)
Via Thredbo Ski Resort 8 miles (13 km)

TIME
(door-to-door)
10 days

SEASON
December–February best
March–April and October–November OK

The final snow slope
above Rawson Pass
to the summit of
Kosciuszko

N

0   100 MILES

0   100 KILOMETERS

SYDNEY

NEW SOUTH WALES

AUSTRALIA

CANBERRA

COOMA

RANGE

MOUNT KOSCIUSZKO

THREDBO

BEGA

VICTORIA

GREAT DIVIDING

MELBOURNE

Tasman Sea

Indian Ocean

TASMANIA

CHAPTER 9

MOUNT KOSCIUSZKO

AUSTRALIA'S HIGHEST SUMMIT

AND DOWN BY KOSCIUSKO, WHERE THE PINE-CLAD RIDGES RAISE
THEIR TORN AND RUGGED BATTLEMENTS ON HIGH,
WHERE THE AIR IS CLEAR AS CRYSTAL, AND THE WHITE STARS FAIRLY BLAZE
AT MIDNIGHT IN THE COLD AND FROSTY SKY

—ANDREW BARTON PATERSON, FROM "THE MAN FROM SNOWY RIVER"

Mount Kosciuszko, or "Kozzie" as Australians call it, crowns the weathered Snowy Mountains of New South Wales, Australia. The Snowy Mountains are part of the Great Dividing Range that straddles Victoria and New South Wales. These mountains lie 120 miles (192 km) from the east coast of Australia. Kosciuszko is about a six-hour drive from Australia's two largest cities: Sydney to the north and Melbourne to the south. It's approximately 100 miles (160 km) southwest of Australia's capital city, Canberra.

An easy trail leads all the way to the summit, once the snow has melted.

The Snowy Mountains, also known as the Australian Alps, consist of rolling high country sparsely populated by stands of snow gum trees. Though they are Australia's highest mountain range, they have no glaciers. The lower lands surrounding the mountains are characterized by rolling, picturesque farming and ranching land.

Kosciuszko National Park, which includes the Snowy Mountains, covers 1,704,300 acres (690,000 hectares). The Snowy Mountains get more snow than anywhere else in Australia, providing a setting for a small ski industry. Several resorts, including Thredbo, Perisher Valley, and Blue Cow Mountain, offer skiers moderate terrain and decent snow throughout the winter months.

A DREAM OF KOSCIUSZKO

I will never forget the moment I stood on the summit of Kozzie. I was nineteen years old with a dream, a dream that seemed almost unreal or unachievable: a dream to climb the highest peak on every continent.

At the time, I had put together my sponsorship proposals and had been knocking on doors of large organizations for more than twelve months. I was desperately trying to find the funding to make my dream come true. Sadly, funding efforts in mountaineering are sometimes harder to achieve than the climbs themselves.

I remember sitting alone on top of Kosciuszko's stone monument at sunset. The wind was blowing fiercely in my face. I was surrounded by fast-moving clouds that blocked the beautiful setting sun behind them. Call me crazy, but in that moment, I asked the mountain if my dream would ever come true. As I finished the sentence, the most amazing thing happened. A cloud broke apart as it peeled off the summit, and a beam of bright sunlight shone through, lighting up all the other clouds that surrounded the summit in hues of orange, red, and pink.

I smiled to myself. In that moment, I knew the answer to my question.

Three years later, at the age of twenty-two, I sat on top of that stone monument again. This time the weather was perfect. I watched the sunset and thanked the mountain for an amazing journey! The dream was no longer a dream—it was reality.

Australia has no glaciated mountains, thus it does not provide amazing mountaineering challenges. It does, however, provide beautiful hiking and some great ski touring. It is well worth your while to visit this beautiful area known as the Snowy Mountains.

Australians have pride in telling it like it is, so the name of the area makes sense. It is the largest mountain range in Australia, and in winter (usually beginning in June and continuing until October) the snow settles. Thus the area is called the Snowy Mountains. Simple as the name may be, the mountains and surrounding area are beautiful and worth spending a couple of days to enjoy the environment.

As in any mountain range, the weather can change quickly. I have been on the summit in a storm with more than 44 mile per hour (70 kph) winds, zero visibility, and temperatures of 5 degrees Fahrenheit (-15˚C). An unprepared climber can certainly get caught out. Saying that, anyone with a good level of fitness should be able to walk up the peak in both summer and winter. If you are a skier, the winter season provides great backcountry touring.

In the summer months, a raised mesh walkway protects the vegetation. In winter this walkway is normally covered with snow and the route marked with poles. Many thousands of people climb to the summit each year. Most of the parties do this in summer. No matter what the season, happy climbing!

REX PEMBERTON
YOUNGEST AUSTRALIAN TO CLIMB EVEREST,
WING SUIT PILOT, VIDEOGRAPHER, AND SEVEN SUMMITER

NATURAL HISTORY

The Great Dividing Range is a very old and weathered mountain chain. The Snowy Mountains are part of this old mountain chain, dating to 800 million years old when the landmass was underwater. The geology of Australia is quite involved. The landmass consists of sedimentary rock intruded by granites around 200 million years ago, then covered over by successive layers of lava. These layers have lifted up and folded while rounding from weather and time. The Kosciuszko Plateau is

MOUNT KOSCIUSZKO TIMELINE

PRE-1840 The Monaro, people indigenous to the Mount Kosciuszko area, explore the mountain and most likely summit the peak.

1840 Polish explorer Paul Edmund Strzelecki makes the first ascent by a Westerner and gives the mountain its name: Mount Kosciuszko.

1900s The Great Snowy Mountains, specifically the Mount Kosciuszko area, becomes a center for the Australian ski industry with resorts such as Perisher and Thredbo.

1976 Officials close the road leading to Rawson Pass due to environmental concerns.

largely dominated by intrusive granites and residual sedimentary formations.

The national park contains different ecosystems at different altitudes. The high alpine areas consist mainly of heaths, feldmarks, herb fields, and bogs; the heath and herb fields reveal their tough beauty when, in the summer months, the flowers bloom. The eucalypt woodlands down low are composed of eucalyptus trees, alpine ash, mountain gum trees, and snow gum stands in between. Snow gum trees are very eye-catching due to their colored exfoliating bark and twisted trunks.

Animal life is scarce above tree line near the summit of Kosciuszko. Some of the hardy species that survive there include the rare black-and-yellow-striped Corrobree frog, which can be heard throughout the summer in the wet sphagnum bogs en route to Kosciuszko. This frog and the Bogong moth were harvested by indigenous populations; both endemic species are endangered. The mountain pygmy opossum, which lives only above 3500 feet (1100 m), was thought to be extinct until it reappeared in 1966.

Below tree line the forests are filled with kangaroos, wallabies, platypuses, and wombats; among the many birds species are the vibrant crimson rosellas, emus, and cockatoos.

CULTURAL AND POLITICAL BACKGROUND

The Mount Kosciuszko region of Australia was inhabited for more than 40,000 years by indigenous peoples, most recently by the Monaro tribe, before European settlement in the late 1700s. Now the region is part of southern New South Wales, an Australian state that also includes the country's capital city of Canberra and its largest city, Sydney. The region today consists of small towns and ranches in the lowlands and mainly uninhabited forests and alpine terrain in the highlands.

Although originally visited by the Dutch, Australia was claimed by the British in 1770. Australia cut most of its constitutional ties with the United Kingdom in 1942 when it adopted the Statute of Westminster 1931. Australia is officially known as the Commonwealth of Australia.

Australia is a wealthy nation with a high standard of living. Politically the country is a federal parliamentary democracy and a constitutional monarchy with two parliamentary chambers, the upper house or the Senate, and the lower house or the House of Representatives.

CLIMBING HISTORY

Most people believe the first ascent of Kosciuszko belongs to local aboriginal people who inhabited this area for thousands of years before European settlers arrived. The local people are the Monaro, a name that you encounter frequently in this part of Australia. The Monaro used to harvest the Bogong moth that gathered on the upper flanks of the mountain.

It wasn't until 1840 that a Polish explorer named Paul Edmund Strzelecki made the first ascent of the mountain by a Westerner. He named the mountain in honor of the famous Polish freedom fighter, Tadeusz Kościuszko, because of the mountain's resemblance to the hill above his tomb.

MOUNT KOSCIUSZKO FAST FACTS

- Mount Kosciuszko was originally thought to be lower than its neighbor, Mount Townsend.
- The mountain lies in the southeast corner of Australia.
- Mount Kosciuszko is the shortest and easiest of the Seven Summits to climb.
- In the winter, cross-country ski trails traverse the slopes just below the mountain.
- The track-road that leads from Charlotte's Pass to Rawson Pass used to be open to vehicle traffic.

CLIMBING CHALLENGES

Mount Kosciuszko is the easiest climb of the Seven Summits. This day hike takes only six to eight hours round trip and usually offers no technical climbing. The trail from either Charlotte's Pass or the top of Thredbo Resort is an easy hike even for novices. Climbing from the base of Thredbo Resort adds distance, vertical gain, and a bit of routefinding. Knowing how to use a GPS receiver in bad weather and routefinding ability can be important in the shoulder seasons.

The main hazards that may be encountered in the Snowy Mountains are whiteouts, cold injuries, and sunburn. Use a GPS and make sure to input route coordinates before beginning the hike. In poor visibility it's easy to get lost in the rolling, open terrain of the Snowy Mountains. It is always smart to bring a medical kit on a hike in the backcountry. During the summer, the sun reflecting off the snow can be very intense. Cover all exposed skin and use lots of sunscreen.

PLANNING AN EXPEDITION

For experienced world travelers, planning an expedition to climb Mount Kosciuszko is relatively easy. If you are climbing in the summer when the weather is good, the biggest challenges lie in booking plane tickets, hotel reservations, and rental cars. Since no guide or logistics services are needed, the planning process is quite straightforward. It's advisable to start organizing flights, gear, and other arrangements at least a month before your departure. Flights, hotels, and rental cars can sell out well in advance during the high season.

Of course, even though Mount Kosciuszko is the easiest of the Seven Summits, climbers should be in good shape to ensure success on the peak. Training for the climb should begin several months in advance, and climbers must be very familiar with their equipment.

Most climbers spend four to five days in Australia to climb Mount Kosciuszko. The first and last days are spent flying and driving to and from Canberra or Cooma and Jindabyne. An extra day or two should be added to the itinerary for weather days. The climb lies in Kosciuszko National Park, which charges an entrance fee of $16Aus per vehicle per day.

Many people bring their families and friends with them to Australia and combine the climb with several days of sightseeing in one of the major cities or relaxing on the famous Australian beaches. Traveling from far away can add several days to each end of the trip.

GUIDED TRIP VERSUS INDEPENDENT CLIMB

Climbing Kosciuszko is straightforward, so very few people use a guide. If you don't know the area, however, and the conditions are bad, then you may want to capitalize on local expertise. I list a few outfitters in Resources at the end of the book.

CLIMBING SEASONS AND WEATHER

The weather in the Snowy Mountains can be quite unpredictable. It can be calm and sunny or raining with gale-force winds, even on the same day. Above tree line, winds can be fierce and gusty. It's important to include a few extra days when planning a trip to Kosciuszko in case of bad weather.

TADEUSZ KOŚCIUSZKO

Mount Kosciuszko was named by Paul Strzelecki, who made the first recorded ascent of the mountain, in honor of Polish freedom fighter Tadeusz Kościuszko. Strzelecki felt that the area was quite similar to the highlands of Krakow, Poland, that overlook the tomb of Kościuszko. Kościuszko, born in 1746, moved to the United States and became a brigadier general in the Continental Army for his effort in the Revolutionary War. He was granted citizenship before returning to Poland and became a close confidant of Thomas Jefferson. He continued his military service upon returning to Poland and was the supreme commander of the National Armed Forces in the "Kościuszko Uprising" against Imperial Russia in 1794. He was wounded, captured, and imprisoned in the Russian Prince's Palace. He was released after the war and died of typhoid fever in Switzerland in 1817.

The best time to climb is the Austral summer (December, January, and February), because of the warmth and lack of snow. Winters (May through September) can be brutal, with frequent whiteout conditions. The shoulder seasons (October–November and March–April) also make for reasonable hiking. Even at the height of summer, climbers need to be prepared for cold winds, snow, and whiteouts.

DOCUMENTS

Australian visas must be secured in advance, but this process doesn't take long or cost anything for residents of most countries. Please check for current requirements for your country for Australian visas.

COSTS

The currency is the Australian dollar, and it is usually below the value of the American dollar by 5 to 20 percent.

- Domestic flights: $200–$400
- Rental car: $300–$500
- Hotels: $300–$600
- Food: $200

CONDITIONING

Climbing Mount Kosciuszko consists of at least several hours of sustained day hiking with an 8- to 25-pound (4–11 kg) pack on easy terrain. Although those attempting it don't need to be in world-class shape, it's important to be fit to be successful. Prior to the climb, stick to a regimented training program of four or more days per week. Hiking with a pack is the best way to train, but strength training and cross training are very helpful. For more detailed information about training for a Kosciuszko climb, please see "Fitness" in chapter 1.

IMMUNIZATIONS

Proof of yellow fever vaccination is required for climbers traveling from countries with risk of yellow fever transmission. Otherwise, recommended vaccinations include measles, mumps, and rubella (MMR); diptheria-tetanus (DPT); and rabies. Make sure your vaccinations are current, and get boosters well in advance of the trip date if needed.

COMMUNICATIONS

Communications on Kozzie are not a huge issue unless you are traveling in poor conditions in the winter. In the Austral summer, when the majority of people climb Kozzie, special devices for communications should not be needed. Some cell phones have coverage on the mountain. UHF radios can be handy for use within a climbing group, and a satellite phone is always a useful item to bring.

OTHER ACTIVITIES: FISHING, CAMPING, HIKING, AND SURFING

For climbers who have extra time, the Jindabyne and coastal areas offer lots of recreational options. Fly-fishing on the Thredbo and surrounding rivers for moderate-sized brown trout makes a great day excursion. The national park has many overnight trekking and camping opportunities. A well-maintained trail system traverses the range, offering campsites and a network of back-country huts. Many of these trails are open to mountain bikers too.

The Pacific Ocean, only a few hours' drive from Jindabyne, offers surfing, vacation towns, and sunny beaches. Climbers often bring their spouses along to combine the hike with a beach vacation.

GETTING THERE AND GETTING AROUND

The climb of Mount Kosciuszko begins with a flight to either Sydney or Melbourne, the two main hubs in Australia. Sydney and Melbourne are both major financial and cultural hubs, being the two largest cities in Australia. Sydney, however, is usually considered more of a tourist destination due to its picturesque cityscape, excellent beaches, and central location.

DOMESTIC FLIGHTS

From either Melbourne or Sydney, your next step is to fly to either Canberra (daily flights are around $200), or from Sydney to Cooma (there are flights every few days).

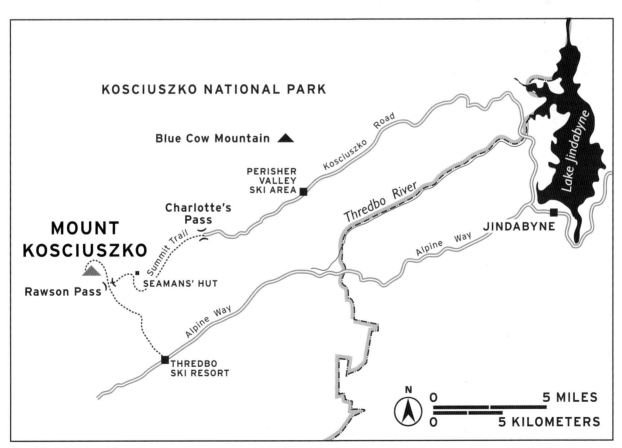

Mount Kosciuszko environs

Snow gum trees line the trail at the start of the Charlotte's Pass route.

GROUND TRANSPORTATION

Some climbers elect to rent a car from Melbourne or Sydney, more often Sydney, and drive to the mountain. I don't recommend this unless you want to spend some time experiencing the Australian countryside. Sydney can be difficult to navigate, and because of the dense traffic it's tough to get used to driving on the other side of the road if you're not used to it. It is a long drive that will cost you as much in gas as a roundtrip air ticket to Canberra.

From Canberra, the mountain is a two-and-a-half-hour drive; from Cooma, a small town of eight thousand people, the mountain is only an hour west.

Car rentals in Australia are reasonable and are realistically the only way of getting to the mountain in the summer months. A midsized car will run $500 to $600 for four days with insurance. Car rentals require a valid driver's license.

GATEWAY SETTLEMENTS

The last town below Kosciuszko is Jindabyne, the mountain sport capital of Australia. Many skiers, hikers, and outdoor enthusiasts live in Jindabyne because of its proximity to the mountains. The town, which lies on a large lake, offers good food and a variety of places to stay. There are a few mountain shops in town where climbers can find last-minute gear. The warm and welcoming people of the town of Jindabyne, Thredbo Ski Resort, and surrounding ranches help make any stay in the area a pleasant one.

CLIMBING MOUNT KOSCIUSZKO

A great way to experience the Australian countryside and the Great Snowy Mountains is to climb Mount Kosciuszko. It's also an excellent excuse to finally get to Australia and experience its unique culture and environment and explore some of the cities. Most Seven Summits climbers seem to either begin or end their campaigns with this peak because of its ease. Kozzie is a great introduction to the Seven Summits and an opportunity to work up to bigger climbs; it can also be a great way to finish by celebrating on an easier peak with friends and family, as Dick Bass did.

Often the most challenging part of the climb is just getting there. Unless you are from "down under," it's quite an expedition to get to the continent and to make your way to the mountain itself. Kosciuszko is climbed in a day from the valley floor, whether via the Thredbo Ski Resort or Charlotte's Pass approach. Regardless of the approach, it is a several-hour trek up gradual terrain for several hours of walking on well-marked trail through open tundra.

Although not a difficult climb, Kosciuszko offers breathtaking views and fabulous trekking. It traverses a harsh and rugged, open landscape where many fragile plant and animal species live. In the winter, the land is snow covered and windswept, while in the summer, school groups saunter up the metal-grate walkways on warm days en route to the top of the continent. As with any alpine environment, the weather can turn bad quickly and jeopardize safety and security. In the shoulder seasons and winter, snow will blanket the route. In summer, weather is often stable and warm, but storms can hit any time of year, making it difficult or impossible to climb.

ROUTES

From Jindabyne there are two options for climbing Mount Kosciuszko: Charlotte's Pass or the Thredbo Ski Resort. The hikes start from different parallel valleys intersecting just below the summit at Rawson Pass.

VIA CHARLOTTE'S PASS

The Charlotte's Pass route gets less traffic because the start is a bit more remote, but it offers similar hiking to the Thredbo ascent. It's a slightly longer hike that gains more altitude than hiking from the top of the Thredbo chairlift but not as much as hiking from the bottom of the chair.

VIA THREDBO SKI RESORT

The shortest approach is from Thredbo Ski Resort by taking the chairlift to the top station. The advantages of climbing from the Thredbo side are the accommodations right at the base and the ability to take the chairlift partway up. Climbing up the steep ski resort almost doubles the trip in time and altitude gain. Once at the top of the ski area the ascent is only slightly more steep and rolling than the Charlotte's Pass approach. The biggest challenges are bad weather and navigation up the final summit pyramid in low visibility conditions.

ACCLIMATIZATION

With a summit altitude of just over 7300 feet (2200 m), acclimatization is not a concern on Kozzie. A single summit-day climb should be sufficient.

WATER, SANITATION, AND GARBAGE

Once you are on the climb, there are no toilets or water sources. Climbers need to fill their water bottles and use the trailhead facilities before beginning the trek. There are also no garbage deposits, so carry your waste off the mountain.

THE CLIMB: VIA CHARLOTTE'S PASS

The Charlotte's Pass approach offers the most gradual climb on a well-marked dirt track. The Charlotte's Pass route is 11.6 miles (18.7 km) round trip and gains about 1300 feet (400 m). From Jindabyne drive on the Kosciuszko Alpine Way, which leads approximately

Mount Kosciuszko climbing route via Thredbo Ski Resort

18 miles (30 km) directly to Charlotte's Pass; near the top it is called Kosciuszko Road. Charlotte's Pass and a small parking lot that marks the beginning of the hike lie at the terminus of the road just past the Perisher Valley ski area and several miles beyond the park entrance.

SAMPLE CLIMBING ITINERARY: MOUNT KOSCIUSZKO VIA CHARLOTTE'S PASS

Day	Location	Start Elevation	End Elevation	Elevation Gain	Distance
1	Fly to Sydney or Melbourne				
2	Fly to Canberra				
3	Drive to Jindabyne and trailhead		6040 ft (1841 m)		
4	Climb to Rawson Pass	6040 ft (1841 m)	6940 ft (2115 m)	900 feet (274 m)	4.3 miles (7 km)
	Climb to summit	6940 ft (2115 m)	7310 ft (2228 m)	370 feet (114 m)	1.25 miles (2 km)
	Descend to the trailhead	7310 ft (2228 m)	6040 ft (1841 m)	−1270 ft (−387 m)	5.6 miles (9 km)
5	Contingency				
6	Contingency				
7	Drive to Canberra; fly to Sydney or Melbourne				
8	Sightsee in Sydney or Melbourne				
9	Fly home				

CHARLOTTE'S PASS TO THE SUMMIT AND BACK

The route from Charlotte's Pass climbs gradually up an old dirt road through open high-alpine terrain. At the beginning of the trek, the road is lined with stands of snow gum trees that give way to shrubs and rockier terrain higher up. The dirt road itself is well maintained and makes for easy walking. The pitch is made for driving, so it's never steep and maintains a gradual grade toward Rawson Pass, climbing 900 feet (274 m) in 4.3 miles (7 km). The total ascent is 5.6 miles (9 km) and gains about 1300 feet (400 m).

The trail to the mountain leaves the parking lot to the left (south), following the obvious dirt road traveling southwest on the left side of the valley. The road is marked by tall wood poles that stick through the deep snow in the winter. The road used to continue to the summit and was open for vehicle traffic until 1976, when it was closed for environmental and safety concerns. It's an unremarkable trail, gaining altitude gradually as it meanders up.

Follow the road up the valley, crossing the Snowy River at 3 miles (5 km) and passing Seaman's Hut in another half mile (kilometer). Another 1.25 miles (2 km) of hiking brings you to Rawson Pass and the intersection with the Thredbo ski area ascent route. A sign clearly marks the route to the summit and to Thredbo here.

Turn right and continue on a well-maintained trail or, when there's enough snow on the ground, climb the slopes directly above Rawson Pass to the summit. From Rawson Pass, another 373 feet (114 m) gets you to the top. Crampons are usually not necessary, but this section can be snowy and icy in the morning.

Just below the summit is a plaque about the mountain and its history; a large concrete post marks the true summit. The top is a large, flat area strewn with rocks and boulders.

To descend, return the way you came.

THE CLIMB: VIA THREDBO SKI RESORT

Climbing from the top of the Thredbo Ski Resort is 8 miles (13 km) round trip and gains almost 1000 feet (300 m) vertical; ascending from the bottom of the chairlift gains another 2000 vertical feet (700 m) and adds another 3 miles (5 km).

From Jindabyne, the drive to Thredbo travels the same direction as if heading to Charlotte's Pass. At the second roundabout a few miles north of town, signs point to a left turn to head to Thredbo on the Alpine Way traveling southwest. This road quickly begins to climb through the snow gum forests with the Thredbo River to the right (north). Travel approximately 18 miles (30 km) up Alpine Way until you see a large sign on your right for Thredbo ski area. Before you reach the ski resort, you'll enter the park and be required to pay an entrance fee.

> ## GUIDE TIP
> If you plan to take the chairlift both up and down from Thredbo Ski Resort, arrive early. The lift runs from 9:00 AM to 4:00 PM, and if you miss the last chair, you'll be forced to walk back down to the valley.

SAMPLE CLIMBING ITINERARY: MOUNT KOSCIUSZKO VIA THREDBO SKI RESORT

Day	Location	Start Elevation	End Elevation	Elevation Gain	Distance
1	Fly to Sydney or Melbourne				
2	Fly to Canberra				
3	Drive to Jindabyne and Thredbo ski area		4488 ft (1368 m)		
4	Take chairlift to top station	4488 ft (1368 m)	6319 ft (1927 m)	1834 ft (559 m)	1.25 miles (2 km)
	Climb to Route Point #1	6319 ft (1927 m)	6736 ft (2053 m)	417 ft (126 m)	2.5 miles (4 km)
	Climb to Rawson Pass	6736 ft (2053 m)	6940 ft (2115 m)	204 ft (62 m)	4.3 miles (7 km)
	Climb to summit	6940 ft (2115 m)	7310 ft (2228 m)	370 feet (114 m)	1.25 miles (2 km)
	Descend to top of chairlift	7310 ft (2228 m)	6322 ft (1927 m)	-988 ft (-301 m)	8 miles (13 km)
5	Contingency				
6	Contingency				
7	Drive to Canberra; fly to Sydney or Melbourne				
8	Sightsee in Sydney or Melbourne				
9	Fly home				

A climber enjoying the view of the Snowy Mountains from the summit

THREDBO SKI RESORT TO THE SUMMIT AND BACK

The Thredbo Ski Resort route leads climbers over rolling terrain on steel-grated walkways. The climb traverses beautiful high alpine terrain punctuated by boulders and large rock pinnacles, streams, and snow patches. Above the ski area, it is often windy and cold, even in the height of summer. The route leaves the snow gum tree stands behind at the top of the ski area. The route follows a metal-grated trail rolling over the high Australian Plateau across heather and snowfields. The ascent is gradual, never climbing much over 10 degrees except for the summit pyramid, which is a bit more.

From the top of Thredbo Ski Resort's chairlift to the summit, the path rises nearly 1000 feet (300 m) in two to four hours of climbing over 8 miles (13 km). The route travels generally north to Rawson Pass, 6.8 miles (11 km) from the top of the Thredbo lift. The pass sits just below the summit; turn west for the final climb to the summit. The final rise to the summit takes thirty minutes and rises 370 feet (114 m) in 1.25 miles (2 km).

Climbing from the base of the ski area makes for a long day of trekking, with more than 2800 feet (860 m) of ascent and another 1.25 miles (2 km) of distance. There are access roads up the ski area, but most climbers ascend straight up ski trails to the top station. Climbing the ski area adds more than 1800 vertical feet (550 m) and several hours of climbing.

The trail from Charlotte's Pass winds through alpine meadows. (Photo by Jane Lee)

MOUNT KOSCIUSZKO GEAR LISTS

Gear and clothing for Kosciuszko should be appropriate for changing weather conditions.

TRAVEL AND PERSONAL GEAR

- Passport and visa
- Travel wallet
- Casual clothes for traveling
- Ten Essentials
- Day pack

CLOTHING

- Lightweight hiking boots
- 1 pair socks
- 1 pair lightweight pants
- 1 pile insulating layer
- Warm winter hat
- Top and bottom rain layers

SUMMIT CHECKLIST

- Day pack
- Warm layers
- Crampons (if there is snow)
- Dark glacier glasses (if there is snow)
- Warm winter hat
- Hiking poles
- Ski equipment (optional)
- GPS device
- Communication devices as needed
- Camera

GUIDE TIP

Bring light aluminum crampons in the shoulder seasons when there might be snow and ice.

CARSTENSZ PYRAMID

ALTITUDE
16,024 feet (4884 m)

DIFFICULTY RATINGS
Technical: 5
Physical: 3

SUMMIT GPS WAYPOINTS
S 4 04.733
E 137 09.572

ELEVATION GAIN
(base camp to summit)
3124 feet (952 m)

DISTANCE
helicopter approach:
1.5 miles (2 km) from base camp
to summit

trek from Sugapa:
50 miles (80 km) trek to base camp;
1.5 miles (2 km) from base camp
to summit

TIME
(door-to-door)
21 days

SEASON
Year-round

A rainy trek
out to Illaga
(Photo by
Jason Edwards)

VIETNAM

PHILIPPINES

MANILA

SAIGON

MALAYSIA

South Pacific Ocean

BORNEO

CELEBES

NEW GUINEA

CARSTENSZ PYRAMID

IRIAN JAYA

PAPUA NEW GUINEA

JAKARTA

INDONESIA

BALI

JAVA

DENPASAR

Arafura Sea

Indian Ocean

AUSTRALIA

N   0 ——————— 500 MILES
      0 ——————— 500 KILOMETERS

CHAPTER 10

CARSTENSZ PYRAMID

AUSTRALASIA'S HIGHEST SUMMIT

AFTER MIDDAY, WE ENTERED THE "HEART OF DARKNESS"—
THE JUNGLE—EVERY BIT AS GEOGRAPHY BOOKS DESCRIBED IT
WITH LONG, THIN TREE TRUNKS REACHING UP FOR THE SUN AND,
IN THE GLOOM BELOW, A TANGLE OF FERNS, CREEPERS, AND SPIKY
PALMS. IT BECAME APPARENT THAT JUNGLE TRAVELING IS QUITE
DIFFICULT, ESPECIALLY WHERE THERE WAS SO MUCH RAIN, MAKING
IT MUDDY AND SWAMPY IN PLACES AND DIFFICULT TO WALK
THROUGH THE TANGLE OF CREEPERS.

— DOUG SCOTT, QUOTED IN *SEVEN SUMMITS: THE QUEST TO REACH THE HIGHEST POINT
ON EVERY CONTINENT* BY STEVE BELL

Deep in the heart of the Sudirman Range in the western central highlands of Irian Jaya lies Carstensz Pyramid. Irian Jaya comprises the western side of the island of New Guinea; the eastern part is Papua New Guinea. Irian Jaya (formerly West New Guinea or Dutch New Guinea) is part of Indonesia, a large collection of islands in southern Southeast Asia northeast of Australia. The bare, rocky, and near-vertical slopes of Carstensz Pyramid rise above the lush jungle environment and small settlements that characterize the moderately large island of New Guinea. Carstensz Pyramid is also known as Puncak Jaya by Indonesians.

Carstensz looms over the smaller peaks in the mountain range at a height of 16,024 feet (4884 m). The mountain is part of the Lorentz National Forest, the largest protected area in Southeast Asia. It is surrounded to the south by settlements belonging to several native Indonesian tribes, including the Dani. These people live mainly in simple structures and maintain a more traditional and primitive way of life than any culture experienced on the other Seven Summits. The local culture is part of what makes a climb of Carstensz Pyramid such a unique and adventurous experience.

Carstensz is one of the least climbed of the Seven Summits because of its logistical challenges, the prohibitive expense required, and its dubious status on the

CARSTENSZ PYRAMID TIMELINE

1623 Dutch explorer Jan Carstensz sees the mountain.

1909 A Dutch expedition led by Hendrik Albert Lorentz makes a first attempt at climbing Carstensz Pyramid.

1962 First ascent of Carstensz Pyramid is led by New Zealander Philip Temple and includes Austrian Heinrich Harrer, Australian Russell Kippax, and Dutchman Albert Huizenga.

1970 Italian Reinhold Messner makes a first ascent on the east ridge.

1972 Britons R.J. Isherwood, Leo Murray, and Jack Baines establish a new route on Carstensz' north face.

Seven Summits list, although more climbers are beginning to attempt the peak as awareness of the mountain and region grow. Carstensz is a very remote mountain that lies in an exotic, undeveloped region of the world.

The two common methods for approaching Carstensz are either helicopter or trekking through the jungle. When helicopters are available to transport people to and from base camp, climber traffic goes up dramatically, but helicopter service is frequently unavailable. The helicopter service is notoriously unreliable and is sometimes inoperable because of contract disputes. Many climbers choose to trek to base camp because the helicopter is unavailable or they want to remove this variable from the expedition. Trekking to and from base camp typically adds eight or more days of difficult and dangerous forest-trudging to a Carstensz expedition, however. Local guides and porters for this trek are unreliable and volatile, raging rivers that must be crossed on frail wooden bridges create dangerous obstacles, and local tribes can be menacingly territorial. The trek itself

CARSTENSZ PYRAMID FAST FACTS

- Carstensz Pyramid sits in Irian Jaya, which is part of Indonesia.
- Carstensz Pyramid entails the most consistently steep and technical climbing of all the Seven Summits.
- Some native tribes in Papua still practice cannibalism.
- Patrick Morrow was the first person to finish the Seven Summits with the Carstensz variation.

Flowers brighten the rugged landscape on the trek in to base camp. (Photo by Eric Remza)

is across terrain that is more treacherous than that experienced almost anywhere else on the Seven Summits circuit. Those considering an attempt of Carstensz Pyramid need to be aware of the associated risks and feel comfortable with those risks, especially if choosing to trek to base camp, as it is a serious and hazardous trip. It's imperative to understand that rescue is very unlikely, if not impossible, and that the climb itself is very remote. Expeditions to Carstensz Pyramid need to be completely self sufficient.

Most teams approaching the mountain on foot begin their journey in Sugapa just under 50 miles (80 km) to the north of the mountain, although some begin in Illaga or another small outpost.

NATURAL HISTORY

The Sudirman Range, of which Carstensz Pyramid is a part, was uplifted in the late Miocene Melanesian orogeny due to colliding Pacific and Australian Plates. This collision thrust Liocene limestone from the seafloor to its present position high above sea level thus creating Carstensz Pyramid. The Sudirman Range is the western portion of the larger Maoke Mountains.

Part of Carstensz Pyramid and the Sudirman Range are blanketed in glaciers. These glaciers were much larger decades ago but have been receding quickly, as have those on Mount Kilimanjaro in Africa. Scientists say these glaciers are receding at 20 feet (6 m) per year and will be completely gone in the next four to six years.

A local porter carries a generator as he crosses one of many rivers on the trek to base camp. (Photo by Eric Remza)

THE DANI TRIBESPEOPLE

The Dani are a tribe that inhabits the region below Carstensz Pyramid. Those at all familiar with Carstensz or the Seven Summits have probably seen images of the colorful and confident Dani men wearing nothing more than a penis-gourd and ritual paint. If climbers choose to hike in to the mountain from Illaga, they will pass through Dani towns and have the opportunity to experience Dani culture. Porters are likely to be Dani.

It is sometimes said that Dani are cannibals, although this statement is false. They are believed to have had a history of cannibalism but not in recent times. Other tribes in the region do still practice cannibalism, however.

The Dani people live simply off the land. Their staple diet consists of sweet potatoes and some meats, such as birds, pigs, and other small animals. They live in small thatched-roof huts and burn wood for heat. Since the 1950s, Christian missionaries have had a presence in this area and have helped build an infrastructure of roads and landing strips.

Irian Jaya, whose environment is an equatorial rain forest, is home to a huge variety of endemic plant and animal species. Some notable examples of plants are the giant ferny trees, small flowering plants, and large parasitic plants hanging from larger trees; animals include marsupials, bats, anteaters, and rodents.

CULTURAL AND POLITICAL BACKGROUND

The region now called Irian Jaya was controlled by the Dutch until 1963, but it is now part of Indonesia. Indonesia declared independence in 1945 after going through periods of Dutch rule and Japanese occupation, though its independence wasn't acknowledged until December 1949. Indonesia changed the name of its territory in West New Guinea in 1973 from Dutch New Guinea to Irian Jaya; Irian is an acronym for Indonesian Republic in the struggle Against the Netherlands. The Republic of Indonesia is a unitary presidential republic and one of the most populous countries in the world.

Several native tribes, including the Dani, inhabit the lush forests below Carstensz Pyramid, calling the mountain Namangkawee, or "Mountain of the White Arrow"

in their native tongue of Amungka. The two other groups of people in the area are the Moni and Dauwa. The three tribes are usually at peace with one another but they do have periodic skirmishes among them. Like the Dani, Moni are sometimes hired as porters.

CLIMBING HISTORY

Climbing on Carstensz Pyramid has occurred only in recent times. The first person to spot Carstensz Pyramid is reported to be the Dutch navigator and explorer Jan Carstensz in 1623, for whom the mountain is named. He wrote about seeing snow and glaciers at the equator and was largely ridiculed for this absurdity as long as he lived. Little interest was taken in the mountain until three hundred years later when, in 1909, a Dutch expedition led by Hendrik Albert Lorentz made the first attempt to climb the isolated giant. The expedition, full of hardship, was ultimately unsuccessful but piqued interest in the region again.

In 1962 Philip Temple, an alpinist from New Zealand finally made the first ascent of Carstensz Pyramid, climbing the Normal Route with three European climbers. Temple had attempted to climb the mountain six months earlier but had been thwarted. Then he had

Nearing base camp on the north side of Carstensz Pyramid (Photo by Jason Edwards)

an opportunity to team up with Heinrich Harrer from Germany, of Eiger Nordwand fame, an Austrian named Russell Kippax, and a Dutch patrol officer with no climbing experience named Albert Huizenga. They reached the top of the Sudirman Range on February 13.

Almost a decade later, famed Italian climber and guide Reinhold Messner made an expedition to the mountain after a Nanga Parbat expedition in the Himalayas. Messner climbed Carstensz successfully and even managed to get his client to the top via a new route on the east ridge, claiming the second ascent of the mountain.

In 1972, a British team climbed a new route on the mighty north face, marking the third ascent. Since then, many new routes have been put up on this remote giant. This may be partially attributed to the excellent quality of the limestone rock.

Today the mountain may see hundreds of attempts a year, with most teams successfully reaching the top.

CLIMBING CHALLENGES

The most challenging part of climbing Carstensz is just getting there. This isn't to say that the climbing is easy, but the difficulty in getting to the mountain is even more challenging than the ascent itself. Flights within Southeast Asia are best organized by experienced local outfitting services, but these are few and far between, and many don't meet operational standards maintained in other parts of the world. These flights often don't go as planned, which is certainly true for the helicopter flight into base camp. Climbers trekking in to base camp can avoid some of these flight complications but may have issues with local porter disputes and terrain obstacles during the hike. Those climbing Carstensz are usually up for a challenge, however, and most of these obstacles can be surmounted with a little patience, good humor, and persistence.

The visas and permitting process for Carstensz can be difficult as well. It mainly relies on the use of liaisons who know the local customs, rules, and regulations. It is very difficult to secure all of the requisite permits without local assistance.

Climbers should begin planning and preparing at least six months in advance of the climb dates to try to ensure everything is in order.

Once at base camp, the climbing begins. Carstensz Pyramid often has lines fixed by guides, but the quality of the rope depends on how new it is. Independent climbers can't count on these lines and must be prepared to climb sustained fourth- and fifth-class rock, up to 5.8 (Yosemite Decimel System rating), to reach the top. Summit day is long and strenuous at moderate altitude, often in poor weather conditions. Independent climbers should be prepared for as many as twelve to sixteen hours of climbing as well as for rescue situations.

" CARSTENSZ: THE CLIMB IS ONLY PART OF THE FUN

Although Carstensz is a fairly routine summit quest of eight to twelve hours from base camp, with mild technical skills required, it is the journey to get there that makes it such a crown jewel of mountaineering. Porters will most likely be local Dani and Moni tribespeople, donning secondhand mountaineering gear for the trek and the customary penis gourd back in their villages. These tribes, removed by only a few generations from their cannibal days, still live in a relatively lawless society, and disputes are still commonly settled by bow and arrow. I can attest that it will be the only place where your climbing porter may defiantly wave a machete at you, wanting higher wages or a hot meal. Spoken English is completely nonexistent, and your only chance of verbal communication is whatever Indonesian they may have picked up in school or along the trail portering for other climbers.

Our trek between the mountain and Sugapa, where we were to meet a plane to return to Timika, was five or six days of pure adventure: incessant rain, fording raging rivers, traipsing through thigh-deep mud, eating local game such as aardvarks and guineapig-like creatures. In the middle of our trek out, a porter collapsed with abdominal pain and lost consciousness. We four Westerners in the group of about twenty were looked upon both as the source of blame and the closest thing to doctors available. In investigating the porter's abdomen, we discovered he had an arrowhead lodged in his midsection from a tribal skirmish weeks before he had signed on to work for our trip. He was apparently undeterred by his wound from the opportunity for a competitive wage. We found out that he was a Moni and that our other expedition porters were primarily Dani—two tribes not at peace with one another.

We had to cross into Moni tribal territory to get to Sugapa, and we soon learned that if the Moni porter died, we would be killed in revenge for him dying on our expedition. Our only choice, other than doing our best to keep him alive until we got to the Moni village, was returning to Carstensz and seeking help from the Grasberg gold and copper mine. This fiercely protected mining area rarely grants permission to climbers to pass through. Our Indonesian guide, Remy, had entered the mine zone once before with a climber who had a broken leg and ended up spending two

A climber battles
the mud. (Photo by
Wayne Morris)

weeks locked in a shipping container. Remy was insistent that returning to the mountain and looking to the mining company for assistance was a very bad option—and besides, we had no food or strength left to continue trekking for several additional days.

Our patient was stabilized and, in a state of semiconsciousness, he was carried by the rest of the porters on a makeshift stretcher through the most difficult of terrain. He arrived in his village still hanging in there, and we soon scurried farther along the trail to the safety of Dani tribal land. A day or so later, we arrived to new faces in the jungle and the village of Sanguama. Here we completed the second goal of our journey: we bought a local penis gourd, stripped to our birthday suits except for Wellington boots, and posed with the locals in their unique garb.

I am sure every visitor lucky enough to attempt Carstensz in their Seven Summits quest will be rewarded with similar remarkable adventures. There is not much else left I know of in this ever shrinking and modernizing world that equals this great mountaineering and travel odyssey.

JEFF STRITE
AMERICAN CLIMBER AND TRAVELER WHO HAS
TRAVELED EXTENSIVELY IN MORE THAN FIFTY COUNTRIES AND
HAS ALMOST COMPLETED THE SEVEN SUMMITS

PLANNING AN EXPEDITION

Planning an expedition to Carstensz Pyramid is complicated and must start well in advance of the beginning of the expedition. Climbing with a reputable guide service and their trusted liaisons will take a lot of the work out of this logistics-heavy expedition. As interest in the Seven Summits and climbing in remote areas of the world grows, so does the number of people attempting to climb Carstensz Pyramid. This rise in popularity means that there is an increasing number of outfitters who offer trips to Carstensz with a wider variety of options. There are relatively inexpensive local providers as well as high-end foreign companies. Planning an expedition can be almost as easy or as difficult as you want it to be— or your budget allows—depending on how adventurous and independent you want to be.

If you attempt to plan an expedition on your own, it's important to recognize that things work differently in Irian Jaya and it may be necessary to be adaptable when logistics go awry. Do your homework on logistics providers to make sure there are no surprises once you start the expedition. The helicopter service is not always available, and expeditions have been canceled before they even begin because of paperwork, permitting, or other issues. Such is the nature of this climb; it is part of what makes it such an adventure.

GUIDED TRIP VERSUS INDEPENDENT CLIMB

It's not unreasonable for experienced travelers and strong rock climbers to climb Carstensz on their own but the involved logistics process makes the organizational part of this trip more work than most of the Seven Summits. This process can be very time consuming and difficult to do completely on your own and almost

> **GUIDE TIP**
>
> Be prepared for rain! Bring an umbrella and two sets of rugged rain gear. It's common to wear through a set on the trek due to the rugged nature of the trip. Ponchos are great because they cover everything and allow air to flow, keeping you cooler but keep in mind that they can get snagged by trees on the trek.

Carstensz Pyramid environs

all independent climbers hire a local liaison for at least basic logistical support. Guide services that have local contacts to facilitate the process will take care of more of the organization for a fee.

If you want to climb Carstensz on your own, you should be competent in climbing 5.8 rock or harder on lead. If you're climbing with a guide service, guides will fix ropes on the harder pitches. Guided clients must be comfortable ascending fixed lines, climbing rock pitches on toprope, and rappeling. If you have no experience with these skills, complete a relevant climbing course prior to joining an expedition.

CLIMBING SEASONS AND WEATHER
Rain! It doesn't *always* rain on Carstensz Pyramid, but it does frequently, and storms can come on quite suddenly.

Climbers should be prepared to get wet and bring the appropriate gear. Be aware that a storm could roll in on summit day. Afternoon showers are common, but it can rain any time of day. It's wetter near the mountain because air masses passing over the mountain range dump their water content.

Carstensz is close to the equator, so there is not much seasonal variation throughout the course of the year. No one time is necessarily better to climb the mountain than another.

Temperature doesn't fluctuate much during the year either, with temperatures ranging from 70 to 85 degrees Fahrenheit (21˚C to 30˚C) during the day. Afternoons and evenings are cooler. Temperatures can dip down to 40 or 50 degrees Fahrenheit (4˚C to 10˚C) at night at base camp and quite a bit lower on the summit. It rarely snows at base camp but it is common on and near the summit.

DOCUMENTS

Several permits are needed to travel and climb in this region, the most important being from the Indonesian government's Indonesian Tourist office, the Indonesian Army, and the Indonesian Papua Police. These permits are difficult to obtain on your own but the process can be made easier with the help of a local service provider. There are sometimes hiccups with the visa process but usually, if climbers begin the process well in advance, it goes smoothly.

Visas can be bought upon entrance into Indonesia. Purchase them at the booth just prior to Customs in Denpasar, Bali, or wherever you enter the country. Customs officials may ask for an onward ticket when you arrive. Visas are good for up to two months. Climbers must have a passport that is valid for at least six months after the trip.

There are few good, detailed maps available for Carstensz Pyramid.

COSTS

Currency is the Indonesian rupiah; roughly 9100 rupiahs are equivalent to $1US.

- Guide service (includes helicopter fee): $15,000–$20,000
- Food: $200–$500
- Hotels: $300–$500
- Flights: $300–$500
- Permits: $100–$200
- Porters: $60/day

CONDITIONING

Climbers must be in excellent shape to climb Carstensz Pyramid. Although the amount of total climbing is not a lot compared to the total trip length, summit day is long, steep, and technically difficult, taking ten to sixteen hours round trip. Rock climbing, climbing steep hills with a moderate-weight pack (20–40 lbs, 9–18 kg), and

WORKING WITH DANI PORTERS

Dani porters often craft camp out of trees and tarps. They start a fire and help climbers to dry out, especially if there have been recent rains. Setting up camp will require two to three hours. Often Dani families, including children and spouses, will join in on the trek.

It's important for the porters to have a strong Dani leader. Without a strong single leader it can be a chaotic atmosphere in which progress becomes limited. Make sure you identify the leader at the start of the trip and underscore his authority with the other porters to facilitate the cooperative process.

A local tribesman trying on the climbing gear (Photo by Wayne Morris)

MADRID2016
CIUDAD CANDIDATA

GUIDE TIP

Bring several pairs of gloves for summit day. The rock is very coarse and can abrade your hands if they're not protected. Also, it's cold up high and may rain or snow. Once your gloves get wet, your hands will be very cold. It's nice to be able to pull on a new pair of dry, warm gloves.

strength training are all appropriate Carstensz-specific methods of training.

Making the trek into base camp significantly lengthens the expedition and makes it much more physical. Climbers who trek should be prepared to carry heavy packs for long periods of time for several days in a row over rough terrain. Balance training is also important for this climb, for crossing thin wooden bridges across quick-moving streams and for ascending steep, technical rock terrain on summit day. Please see "Conditioning" in chapter 1 for more information.

IMMUNIZATIONS

Although no immunizations are required for travel to this region, it's smart to be up-to-date on those listed in "Immunizations" in chapter 2. A few to consider strongly are tetanus-diphtheria and hepatitis A and B. Please consult your doctor, local travel clinic, or the Centers for Disease Control and Prevention (CDC) for more information.

COMMUNICATIONS

The most effective means of communication on Carstensz are satellite phones and either UHF or VHF radios. Satellite phones allow climbers to communicate with others off the mountain or internationally, while UHF and VHF allow communication between groups or within a group on Carstensz. There is no cell phone coverage on Carstensz Pyramid.

GETTING THERE AND GETTING AROUND

Most climbers fly first to Jakarta and then on to Bali, Indonesia, en route to Timika on Irian Jaya. Jakarta, Indonesia's largest city and its capital, is a large, sprawling urban center. Bali is a picturesque tropical-island paradise in the Indonesian archipelago closer to Irian Jaya, with Denpasar as its largest city.

DOMESTIC FLIGHTS

From Jakarta or Bali, climbers transfer to domestic flights to reach their final destination on Irian Jaya: Timika, if flying to base camp or driving and hiking through the often-closed mine, or Illaga, if trekking. To reach Timika, a town south of the mountain, often it's necessary to fly through Jayapura or Nabire.

Trekkers who begin in Sugapa will need to transfer from Denpesar or Jakarta through Nabire, Jayapura, or Timika on Irian Jaya, as well. These larger towns are the gateway to smaller, more remote outposts such as Sugapa. Expect some delays during this series of short "puddle-jumper" flights.

It's important to work with a guide service, travel agent, or outfitter who knows the trip to find the tickets you need. Make sure to book these tickets months in advance of the climb dates to make sure they're available.

FLYING BY HELICOPTER FROM TIMIKA

From Timika, climbers can take a helicopter to base camp; this is the shortest, most convenient, and most expensive option but delays can plague this option. Flying directly to nearly 13,000 ft (3963 m) can be a recipe for altitude illness for an unacclimatized climber. If you are flying to base camp consider acclimatizing on another mountain, such as an Indonesian volcano, beforehand, and bring high altitude medications in case of sickness.

GATEWAY SETTLEMENTS

There are many possible routes to reach the mountain and they take climbers through a variety of towns and

Ascending the fixed lines on Carstensz on summit day (Photo by Jason Edwards)

villages. Timika is a coastal town south of the mountain which is mainly based around the mining industry of the nearby Grasberg Mine, largest gold mine and third largest copper mine in the world. Due to its proximity to the mine, Timika boasts lodgings, restaurants, and markets. Jayapura and Nabire, larger coastal towns to the northeast and northwest of the mountain, and Sugapa, a small settlement that lies in the jungle northeast of Carstensz Pyramid, do not offer much in the way of services. In general, Irian Jaya is a remote and sparsely inhabited region.

GROUND "TRANSPORTATION"

Ground transportation isn't really an option due to the remoteness of Carstensz Pyramid. A dirt road leads from Timika to within a short distance of the south side of the mountain but this road is part of the Grasberg mining operation and is rarely open to climbers. The most common form of ground transportation in this region is jokingly referred to as "bus #11," otherwise known as walking.

TREKKING FROM SUGAPA

The majority of climbers trekking in to Carstensz Pyramid start from Sugapa. This approach takes five to seven days on the way in and typically a day less on the way out. The trail from Sugapa is heavily used, relatively easy to follow, passes through several villages, and offers somewhat established camping locations. The trail connects with that of another popular start destination, Illaga, just before New Zealand Pass and not far from Carstensz base camp.

Trekking in to Carstensz Pyramid is not an easy journey. From Sugapa, it's a trip of five to seven tough, long days that traverses rugged forested and alpine terrain and covers almost 50 miles (80 km) on primitive game and hiking trails. There are few set camps along the route, so teams typically go as far as they feel comfortable each day and spend the night at one of many primitive camps en route to the mountain. The trek crosses several small or moderately sized streams, depending on rainfall, and the going is often very muddy and dangerous in the jungle forests. After several days of trekking, climbers gain enough altitude to rise above tree line, where the trail becomes drier and less muddy and traverses more open country over rocky steps and through pastures.

Although there are many hazards on this route and the route from Illaga including river crossings and muddy slopes, the trail becomes the steepest and most exposed on the final day in before reaching base camp. Similar to the conditions encountered on Kilimanjaro's Barranco Wall, the terrain is sometimes steep and requires Class 3 to 4 climbing on rocky walls, though here you will be confronted with more climbing and slick mud. Given that you are typically climbing in Wellington boots, the climbing can be difficult and hazardous. There is another class 4 pitch of rock climbing just below New Zealand Pass as well as a few other short steep pitches requiring

Returning to Carstensz base camp after a successful summit (Photo by Jason Edwards)

technical downclimbing very close to Carstensz base camp. Some teams fix ropes on these pitches to protect against a fall and to aid climbing.

Note: It's common for villages to charge a fee for teams passing through. This fee may be increased if there are religious ceremonies in progress that may have been disturbed by the interruption or for camping near a town.

TREKKING FROM ILLAGA

Some climbers making the trek to the mountain decide to start in Illaga, another small village to the northeast of Carstensz which lies at roughly 6300 feet (1920 m). This is the route Heinrich Harrer helped pioneer in 1962. It is generally similar to the Sugapa approach in many respects but receives even less traffic making it feel very remote. At times the route is difficult to follow. Once you reach the intersection with the Sugapa route, the trail becomes more obvious and is much easier to find. After the small town of Pinapa, about an hour out of Illaga, there are no more villages. The approach from Illaga takes five to seven days on the way in and a day less on the way out.

THE GRASBERG MINE DRIVING/ HIKING APPROACH

The easiest approach to Carstensz Pyramid is through the Grasberg mine but this is rarely an option and you shouldn't consider it unless you have been given express consent from the officials at the mine itself. The mine lies just to the south of the mountain. A series of roads connects the town of Timika with the northernmost part of the mine within three hours walking from base camp. It is very rare for the mine officials to allow special access.

CLIMBING CARSTENSZ PYRAMID

Carstensz Pyramid is as wild a cultural experience as it is a steep and challenging climb. Although it's one of the lowest peaks on the Seven Summits list, it's the steepest and most technically demanding climb on the circuit. Summit day is long, requiring many hours of ascending

steep fixed lines (when ropes are fixed) or high-level lead rock climbing (when lines are not fixed). Climbers must be comfortable moving over exposed technical terrain to gain the summit.

Before summit day, the trek to base camp requires excellent fitness, patience, and an ability to suffer through miles of rough jungle terrain. A climb of Carstensz typically takes two weeks door-to-door excluding the trek to and from base camp, but will require three weeks including the trek. This time frame can vary greatly depending on potential delays. Climbers can subtract a week of trekking time if they plan to use the helicopter service, but they will have to add a few days of acclimatization at base camp. Base camp sits on a small lake surrounded by steep rock cliffs of the Sudirman Range. To summit from base camp and return is done in a day.

ROUTES

Whether trekking in from Sugapa or Illaga or flying in from Timika, most climbers ascend the Normal Route, also the first ascent route climbed originally by Temple, Harrer, Kippax, and Huizenga in February 1962. This is probably the most technical "Normal Route" of all the Seven Summits climbs. Almost everyone climbs the mighty north face, ascending near-vertical layers of rock, culminating in an exposed summit-ridge traverse. Other routes receive very little traffic. The climb is a serious challenge even to experienced mountaineers.

ACCLIMATIZATION

Climbers who fly in to base camp must add a few days of acclimatization at base camp before attempting the summit. Two to three days is usually sufficient to climb to the summit without any altitude issues. Those trekking to base camp will already be fairly acclimatized and usually just take one rest day at base camp before climbing.

WATER, SANITATION, AND GARBAGE

Climbers should treat all water along the trek and at base camp to ensure proper sanitation. Along the trek to base

Makeshift bridges provide the only way across hazardous rivers. (Photo by Wayne Morris)

Normal Route on Carstensz Pyramid (Photo by Eric Remza)

camp, climbers use primitive bathrooms in the jungle. At base camp, toilet tents are set up to collect human waste and dispose of it properly. As on any mountain, climbers should remove all garbage when they leave.

THE CLIMB

Base camp lies in a low area next to a picturesque lake surrounded by other small lakes and rock buttresses. Base camp, which lies at 12,400 feet (3780 m), has room for many tents. There are no permanent structures at base camp; all teams set up tents and camp during their stay. Drinking water is plentiful but should be treated. Toilets are erected well outside of camp to avoid contaminating the water supply.

Base camp, which sits at the base of the route, makes a great staging point for the climb. Weather can be erratic here, with periods of perfect, clear, sunny weather and torrential downpours. The route is almost always climbed round-trip in a day to avoid carrying extra gear up or getting caught in the rain. It's important you don't waste good weather.

Although most of the route is scrambling, there are several sections of roped climbing. The rock on Carstensz is very coarse, requiring climbers to wear gloves. Begin climbing early in the day to maximize the amount of daylight you have to get up and back down safely and to avoid afternoon rain showers. Most teams take seven to nine hours to ascend and about half that on the descent.

SAMPLE CLIMBING ITINERARY: CARSTENSZ PYRAMID'S NORMAL ROUTE (HELICOPTER APPROACH)

Day	Location	Start Elevation	End Elevation	Elevation Gain	Distance
1	Fly to Indonesia				
2	Arrive in Bali				
3	Fly to Timika		103 ft (31 m)		
4	Prepare for climb				
5	Fly to base camp	103 ft (31 m)	12,400 ft (3780 m)	12,297 ft (3749 m)	
6	Acclimatization				
7	Acclimatization				
8	Climb to summit	12,400 ft (3780 m)	16,024 feet (4884 m)	3624 ft (1104 m)	1.5 miles (2.4 km)
	Descend to base camp	16,024 feet (4884 m)	12,400 ft (3780 m)	−3624 ft (−1104 m)	1.5 miles (2.4 km)
9	Contingency				
10	Contingency				
11	Fly to Timika and Bali	12,400 ft (3780 m)	103 ft (31 m)	−12,297 ft (−3749 m)	
12	Fly home				

SAMPLE CLIMBING ITINERARY: CARSTENSZ PYRAMID'S NORMAL ROUTE (TREKKING APPROACH)

Day	Location	Start Elevation	End Elevation	Elevation Gain	Distance
1	Fly to Indonesia				
2	Arrive Jakarta or Bali				
3	Fly to Timika		103 ft (31 m)		
4	Fly to Sugapa	103 ft (31 m)	3431 ft (1046 m)	3328 ft (1014 m)	
5-11	Trek from Sugapa to Carstensz base camp	3431 ft (1046 m)	12,400 ft (3780 m)	8969 ft (2734 m)	50 miles (80 km)
12	Rest at base camp				
13	Climb to summit	12,400 ft (3780 m)	16,024 ft (4884 m)	3624 ft (1104 m)	1.5 miles (2.4 km)
	Descend to base camp	16,024 ft (4884 m)	12,400 ft (3780 m)	−3624 ft (−1104 m)	1.5 miles (2.4 km)
14-18	Trek from base camp to Sugapa	12,400 ft (3780 m)	3431 feet (1046 m)	8969 ft (−2734 m)	50 miles (80 km)
19	Fly to Timika and on to Bali	3431 feet (1046 m)	103 ft (31 m)	−3328 ft (−1014 m)	
20	Fly home				

BASE CAMP TO THE SUMMIT

From base camp, begin by scrambling up steep rock gullies and ramps near camp. The route angles to the right of the north face. An obvious gully system provides a weakness in the mighty north face's defenses. The hardest climbing occurs at the end of the first gully system, climbing out of the notch at 5.8. The rock is generally solid, but be aware of loose debris in the gullies.

Ascend the rock steps angling right for the first 330 feet (100 m). The route then heads straight up and back left for 660 feet (200 m) into the base of an obvious gully. Once at the base of the gully, climb along the base of the steep wall ascending the logical route of lower-angle rock to the summit ridge. The climbing on the face can be fifth class, although most of it is third- and fourth-class scrambling.

Once on the ridge, if the weather is clear you will be rewarded with beautiful views of the Sudirman Range and Ngga Pulu (Sunday Peak), to the northeast. Continue up the ridge heading east over undulating rock, passing four notches. Some of this climbing is technical and exposed. There may be old fixed ropes on the route from previous teams. It's difficult to know the condition of these ropes, so it's always prudent to rely on your own gear.

Partway up the ridge, there is a Tyrolean Traverse across one of the notches. Climbers can choose to use the ropes in place or climb down and back out of the notch. Most teams find it's quicker and easier to use the Tyrolean Traverse. Once past the technical difficulties of this notch, the ridge gives way to easier slopes and the summit. The summit is a small rocky area with room for a few people at a time.

DESCENT

For most of the descent, climbers will be able to scramble down, but several pitches will require a rappel. Bring a figure eight as a rappel device because most of the fixed lines are 11 to 13mm thick. Other devices might not be large enough for the rope. It's important to watch for loose rock above you and not to kick anything down on those below you.

CARSTENSZ PYRAMID GEAR LISTS

As on Vinson Massif, you won't have the opportunity to replace any missing gear on Carstensz. Be extra thorough in checking to make sure you've packed everything you'll need.

TRAVEL AND TREKKING GEAR

- Passport and visa
- Travel wallet
- Money for porters
- 2 large duffels
- Casual clothes for traveling
- Sneakers for travel
- Umbrella and/or poncho
- Rubber boots if approaching via trek

CLIMBING GEAR

- Helmet
- Climbing harness with belay loop
- Rappel device (figure eight often works best on fixed lines)
- 2 locking carabiners
- 4 nonlocking carabiners
- Ascender
- 3 slings
- 2 prusik loops

CLOTHING

Clothing should prepare you for rain and cold conditions on summit day.

FOOTWEAR:

- Lightweight hiking boots
- Gaiters
- 3–4 pairs climbing socks of varying warmth

LOWER-BODY LAYERS:

- Waterproof, breathable rain shell with full zipper
- 2 pairs climbing pants: 1 lightweight, 1 heavyweight
- Insulating pants (synthetic) with full zipper

A local tribesman checking out the action (Photo by Wayne Morris)

- 3 sets underlayers of varying weight (synthetic or merino wool)

UPPER-BODY LAYERS:
- Waterproof, breathable rain shell
- Winter parka with a hood
- 3 pile insulating layers of varying weights and fabrics
- 3 underlayers of varying weights (synthetic or merino wool)

HEADGEAR AND HANDWEAR:
- Warm ski hat
- Buff
- Sun hat or baseball cap
- Heavy climbing gloves
- Leather gloves (3 pairs)
- Lightweight gloves

PERSONAL GEAR
- Ten Essentials
- Backpack (2000 cubic inches, 33 liters)
- Sleeping bag rated to 0°F (-18°C)
- 2 sleeping pads: 1 inflatable, 1 closed-cell foam
- 2 pairs of sunglasses (1 is an extra pair)
- 30-plus SPF sunscreen
- 2 headlamps with spare batteries
- 2 1-quart water bottles
- Water purification (iodine or chlorine)
- Multitool (with pliers)
- Malaria medication
- Insect repellent

- 1-quart pee bottle
- 3 stuff sacks
- 5 garbage bags for waterproofing gear
- Camera

GROUP GEAR
- 4-season tents
- Cooktent for base camp
- Stove and fuel
- Group food
- Ropes for fixing lines or lead climbing
- Carabiners and rock protection for fixing lines or leading
- Satellite phone
- GPS device

SUMMIT CHECKLIST
- Warm clothes
- Buff or balaclava
- Extra leather gloves
- Heavy insulated gloves
- Glacier glasses
- Sunscreen and lip balm
- Headlamp with extra batteries
- Technical climbing gear
- Emergency gear (bivy sack, stove, fuel, cookpot, and sleeping pad)
- Water bottles
- Electrolyte replacement drinks
- Climbing snacks and power gel
- Medical kit

DEBUNKING CARSTENSZ AS THE SEVENTH SUMMIT

FOLLOWING PAT MORROW'S COMPLETION OF HIS
SEVEN SUMMITS WITH CARSTENSZ IN 1986 AND
HIS ASSERTION THAT HE, NOT DICK BASS, WAS THE
TRUE CHAMPION, THE DEBATE WAS KINDLED.

—GLENN PORZAK, FROM *SEVEN SUMMITS* BY STEVE BELL (2000)

This book wouldn't be complete without a discussion about which is the true Seventh Summit: Kosciuszko or Carstensz Pyramid. This ongoing debate has firm adherents on each side of the aisle. There are reasons for including or excluding each mountain. Lately, some have resolved the debate simply by climbing both. People have their own reasons for choosing one peak over the other, but it seems that, more and more, the decision is not based on evidence. After doing my own research on the subject, I have come to the conclusion that there are a lot more reasons to include Kosciuszko on the list than Carstensz. I encourage climbers to challenge themselves to define their Seventh Summit.

WHY USING A GEOLOGIST'S DEFINITION OF A CONTINENT DOESN'T WORK

Morrow's argument rests on the premise that New Guinea is part of the Australian continental shelf and plate. However, New Guinea does not entirely perch atop the Australian continental shelf. The island is a jigsaw of three plates, geologically linking Southeast Asia, the Southern Pacific, and Australia. Only the island's low southern plains are geologically part of the Australian plate. The Java Trench, which cuts through the heart of New Guinea, is the geological border that separates Asia from Australia. Carstensz Pyramid lies to the north of the mountain chain that marks the Java Trench, on the Philippines plate of Asia. Thus it is not on the same tectonic plate as Australia.

—Glenn Porzak, from *Seven Summits: The Quest to Reach the Highest Point on Every Continent* by Steve Bell (2000)

This debate raises basic questions, such as "What are your reasons for climbing the Seven Summits?" and "What are your personal 'rules' for climbing?" An attractive aspect of mountaineering is that we create our own rules, and there's no governing body for the Seven Summits. Climbers don't like to be pigeonholed. We have differing reasons for climbing and differing styles. Why do we want to climb the Seven Summits? Is it to climb only technically challenging routes? Or is it an excuse to travel and climb while experiencing the seven continents and their cultures? Depending on your reasons, you may have a different idea of what the Seventh Summit is.

Dick Bass and Frank Wells, two pioneers of the Seven Summits concept, obviously viewed the Australian landmass, not Australasia, as a continent. They did a lot to popularize the Seven Summits, making the term part of the modern climber's vocabulary, and this initially tied Kosciuszko to the Seven Summits. Since most of us are taught that Australia is one of the seven continents, very few questioned Bass and Wells's assertion that Kosciuszko held the title.

Pat Morrow and Reinhold Messner, two prominent climbers of the day, decided that the definition of a continent should include the continental shelf, an often-submerged piece of the continental mass extending to the edge of the tectonic plate. This definition of a continent means that Australasia's Carstensz Pyramid is the Seventh Summit. If these two vocal and influential climbers hadn't brought Carstensz into consideration, I don't think we'd have the debate that we have today.

At the root of this debate is the definition of what a continent is. In deciding which mountains are part of the Seven Summits, we must first define a continent. For several decades, two definitions have been used: cultural and geologic. I favor the cultural definition as the most appropriate way to define the word.

WHAT IS A CONTINENT?

First, *continent* is a subjective term whose meaning has evolved for as long as the word has been in use. The term was originally introduced in the sixteenth century by those living in that convergence zone at the time to differentiate between Africa, Asia, and Europe. The border between Europe and Asia that includes the Caucasus Mountains is a somewhat arbitrary division point, but it has persisted. This is part of the reason Europe is still considered a continent even though it's on the same continental plate as Asia (the Eurasian Plate) and why

DEBUNKING CARSTENSZ AS THE SEVENTH SUMMIT

the Caucasus Mountains, including Mount Elbrus, are considered part of Europe.

As human influence expanded and we became aware of other large landmasses, the definition of what a continent is beyond just Africa, Asia, and Europe was modified. The Americas were long considered one continent but now are generally accepted as two. Greenland isn't big enough or populated enough to be a continent, but Australia is. Australia wasn't considered a continent at all for a long time. Antarctica was long seen as being included in the Australian continent.

Even today, the number of continents varies, depending on which region of the world you're from. The former states of the Union of Soviet Socialist Republics, including Russia, and Japan teach the six-continent model, with Europe and Asia being combined. Some countries in Latin America teach a six-continent combined-Americas model and sometimes exclude Antarctica since it has no indigenous population, making five continents. If we go by these definitions accepted by a small percentage of people, there is no such thing as the "Seven Summits," only five or six, but certainly not eight.

Despite this confusion, I set out to determine an acceptable definition of the word "continent" as it pertains to us in the modern world. *Encyclopedia Britannica* defines the seven continents as "the larger continuous masses of land, namely Asia, Africa, North America, South America, Antarctica, Europe, and Australia, listed in order of size." Wikipedia defines a continent as "one of several large landmasses on Earth. They are generally identified by convention rather than any strict criteria, with seven regions commonly regarded as continents—they are: Asia, Africa, North America, South America, Antarctica, Europe, and Australia."

Dictionary and encyclopedia definitions reflect what is generally accepted by society at large as the current meaning of the word. Yet some climbers prefer a geologic definition of the earth's continents, and so they change Australia to Australasia. This seemingly arcane disagreement results in two differing lists of the highest peaks on the world's seven continents. If you prefer to consider Australia a continent, your list of the Seven Summits includes Mount Kosciuszko; if you prefer to consider Australasia a continent, your list of the Seven Summits includes Carstensz Pyramid, in Indonesia. That is why this book includes eight peaks: to leave it to readers to decide which is their seventh summit.

For nongeologist laypeople, using a definition based upon plate tectonics and the idea that there are seven major continental plates doesn't make sense. Using plate tectonics to define the seven summits would combine Europe and Asia as one continent, since they share the same lithospheric-tectonic continental plate. This would mean neither Mount Elbrus, nor Mont Blanc as is sometimes argued to be the summit of Europe, would make the list. Also, the Pacific Plate doesn't have enough landmass above sea level to constitute a continent.

Using the plate tectonics definition, Mount Everest is more on the Australian Plate than Carstensz is. Mount Everest sits on the collision zone between the Australian Plate, of which the Indian Plate is a subcontinent, and the Eurasian Plate. As Glenn Porzak points out in *Seven Summits*, Carstensz sits north of this collision zone, making it less a part of the Australian Plate than Mount Everest is. This geological definition would place Carstensz on the Pacific Plate.

The concept of continents is a social construct that we humans define based upon cultural, climatic, social, geophysical, economic, and agricultural identities, so socially accepted ideas are used to define continents rather than geology or plate tectonics. Considering these social constructs, we find that Australia and Irian Jaya are very different in just about every sense. Irian Jaya exemplifies the Pacific islands of Asia. Irian Jaya politically is part of Indonesia, an Asian country.

In addition, their two climates are markedly different. Australia is mainly temperate, whereas Irian Jaya is tropical. People who live in Irian Jaya, whether natives of the island or implanted Indonesians from farther north, are culturally similar to people elsewhere in the Pacific islands and Asia. Australians are overwhelmingly of European descent. Some may argue that people native to

Australia are culturally similar to people on Papua Island, but the cultures are, and have been, quite different.

Irian Jaya is agriculturally different from Australia. It's mostly based around labor-intensive subsistence agriculture, whereas Australia is capital-intensive. Australia has a modern diversification economy with well-established infrastructures, while Irian Jaya largely doesn't. Irian Jaya is also physiographically and geologically very different from Australia. In almost every aspect, Irian Jaya exemplifies the Pacific islands of Asia rather than Australia. This modern cultural argument is used in defining Mount Elbrus as the European high point, as well.

WHY USING A CLIMBER'S DEFINITION OF A CHALLENGING SUMMIT DOESN'T WORK

Keeping in mind this ample definition of what a continent is, consider Morrow and Messner's reasons for choosing Carstensz. Morrow has famously stated in *Seven Summits* by Steve Bell that "being a climber first, and a collector second, I felt strongly that Carstensz Pyramid, the highest mountain in Australasia, was a true mountaineer's objective." But should a desire for technical difficulty on a climb define a continent and its highest peak. If we don't like a climb, it doesn't make sense to throw it out for one that we prefer. Climbing the Seven Summits isn't just about climbing hard routes—indeed, some of the climbs are only moderate—but also about visiting each of the seven continents and experiencing their culture while climbing. If the intent is solely to climb difficult mountains, climbers should not make the Seven Summits their priority. They should stay in the Alaska Range or the Himalayas and climb only hard routes. It seems elitist to say that Kosciuszko can't be included in "the club" because it's not hard enough. If difficulty is the only reason for climbing, then people should climb Mount Kenya instead of Kilimanjaro and K2 instead of Everest.

Although both Morrow and Messner originally climbed Carstensz Pyramid, they later helped legitimize Kosciuszko as the Seventh Summit when they also climbed it in addition to Carstensz. Why would two accomplished climbers reluctantly climb a mountain they didn't feel belonged on the list? Maybe they realized that the climbing community might disagree with their definition of Carstensz as the seventh summit, and they wanted to cover their bases. Significantly Bass and Wells didn't climb Carstensz.

WHERE DO WE GO FROM HERE?

Considering the evidence, I have trouble accepting Carstensz as the Seventh Summit. It's great for climbers to explore different regions and to make difficult climbs there but it seems farfetched to tie such climbs to the Seven Summits. Kosciuszko is undeniably the highest point in Australia and Australia is commonly accepted as one of the seven continents. It follows that Kosciuszko belongs on a list of the Seven Summits while Carstensz, worthy climb though it is, does not.

I'm sure the conversation will continue, and my arguments here may serve only to stoke the debate. If it does, I'm happy. We all stand to benefit from people making up their own minds based upon educated discussions and critical thinking rather than blindly climbing both summits to "cover their bases," as many people freely admit to doing. I include a chapter on Carstensz Pyramid in this book for those who choose to climb both or only Carstensz. One of the beauties of climbing is that there's no one telling us what to think; it's for us to decide.

Peering up at the
Tyrolean Traverse
from below
(Photo by Jason
Edwards)

Denali's
summit ridge

THE "SEVEN SUMMITERS"

COMPLETION OF THIS AMAZING FEAT, KNOWN AS THE
SEVEN SUMMITS, DEMANDS MUCH OF THE CLIMBER—
TO TRAVEL TO THE REMOTE AND EXOTIC CORNERS OF THE
WORLD, SCALE THE HEIGHTS OF MOUNTAIN GIANTS SUCH
AS EVEREST AND McKINLEY, AND FACE EXTREME WEATHER
CONDITIONS AND HOSTILE ENVIRONMENTS FOR LONG
PERIODS OVER MANY YEARS.

— STEVE BELL, *SEVEN SUMMITS* (2000): *THE QUEST TO REACH THE HIGHEST POINT
ON EVERY CONTINENT* BY STEVE BELL

Below is a complete list of everyone who has climbed the Seven Summits (through 2011), including either Mount Kosciuszko or Carstensz Pyramid. For this list I have combined information compiled by Harry Kikstra (7summits.com) and my own database. Information from 7summits.com is used with permission of Harry Kikstra, author and copyright holder. This list may not contain all those who have completed the Seven Summits, however, as some people do not report all their climbs.

LIST OF SEVEN SUMMITERS (COMBINED KOSCIUSZKO AND CARSTENSZ LIST)

Nr	First Name	Surname	Gender	Country	Last Summit	Last Date
1	Richard Daniel	Bass	Male	USA	Everest	1985/04/30
2	Gerry	Roach	Male	USA	Vinson	1985/12/13
3	Patrick	Morrow	Male	Canada	Elbrus	1986/08/05
4	Gerhard	Schmatz	Male	Germany	Vinson	1986/12/02
5	Reinhold	Messner	Male	Italy	Vinson	1986/12/03
6	Oswald	Oelz	Male	Austria	Elbrus	1989/04/20
7	Phil	Ershler	Male	USA	Kosciuszko	1989/12/25
8	Geoffrey C.	Tabin	Male	USA	Elbrus	1990/06/22
9	Rob	Hall	Male	New Zealand	Aconcagua	1990/11/21
10	Gary	Ball	Male	New Zealand	Vinson	1990/12/10
11	Chris	Kopczynski	Male	USA	Kilimanjaro	1991/05/10
12	Jean-Pierre	Frachon	Male	France	Carstensz	1991/11/27
13	Glenn	Porzak	Male	USA	Kosciuszko	1992/03/23
14	Ronald	Naar	Male	the Netherlands	Everest	1992/05/12
15	Skip	Horner	Male	USA	Everest	1992/05/12
16	Vernon	Tejas	Male	USA	Everest	1992/05/12
17	Keith	Kerr	Male	UK	Everest	1992/05/15
18	Ralph	Hoibakk	Male	Norway	Carstensz	1992/05/24
19	Junko	Tabei	Female	Japan	Elbrus	1992/07/28
20	Christine	Janin	Female	France	Aconcagua	1992/12/25
21	Pascal	Tournaire	Male	France	Aconcagua	1992/12/25
22	Mauricio	Purto	Male	Chile	Carstensz	1993/09/15
23	Arne	Naess	Male	Norway	Aconcagua	1994/01/15
24	Todd	Burleson	Male	USA	Carstensz	1994/02/02
25	Doug	Mantle	Male	USA	Kosciuszko	1994/02/16
26	Mary	Lefever	Female	USA	Kosciuszko	1994/03/11
27	Ramon	Portilla	Male	Spain	Elbrus	1994/03/21
28	W. Hall Jr.	Wendel	Male	USA	Everest	1994/05/09
29	Ekkert	Gundelach	Male	Germany	Elbrus	1994/08/05
30	Rebecca	Stephens	Female	UK	Vinson	1994/11/22
31	Jose Ramon	Agirre	Male	Spain	Aconcagua	1994/12/25
32	Mark	Rabold	Male	USA	Kilimanjaro	1995/02/01
33	David	Keaton	Male	USA	Aconcagua	1995/02/05
34	David	Hempleman-Adams	Male	UK	Carstensz	1995/05/07
35	Doug	Scott	Male	UK	Carstensz	1995/05/12
36	Jose Antonio	Pujante	Male	Spain	Denali	1995/06/17
37	John	Dufficy	Male	USA	Kilimanjaro	1995/09/12

Nr	First Name	Surname	Gender	Country	Last Summit	Last Date
38	Gary	Pfisterer	Male	USA	Vinson	1995/12/01
39	Ginette	Harrison	Female	UK	Vinson	1995/12/01
40	Young-Ho	Heo	Male	South Korea	Vinson	1995/12/11
41	Rudy	van Snick	Male	Belgium	Vinson	1995/12/23
42	Vladas	Vitkauskas	Male	Lithuania	Aconcagua	1996/02/25
43	Sandy	Hill Pittman	Female	USA	Everest	1996/05/10
44	Yasuko	Namba	Female	Japan	Everest	1996/05/10
45	Robert	Cedergreen	Male	USA	Denali	1996/07/01
46	Nasuh	Mahruki	Male	Turkey	Kosciuszko	1996/11/08
47	Viktor	Groselj	Male	Slovenia	Vinson	1997/01/05
48	Jeff	Shea	Male	USA	Vinson	1997/01/22
49	Lee	Nobmann	Male	USA	Kilimanjaro	1997/02/14
50	Patrick	Falvey	Male	Ireland	Kosciuszko	1997/02/14
51	Fedor	Konyukhov	Male	Russia	Denali	1997/05/01
52	Brigitte	Muir	Female	Australia	Everest	1997/05/27
53	Steve	Bell	Male	UK	Denali	1997/05/29
54	Thierry	Renard	Male	France	Elbrus	1997/06/07
55	Paul	Morrow	Male	USA	Elbrus	1997/06/16
56	Waldemar	Niclevicz	Male	Brazil	Carstensz	1997/09/21
57	Gerard	Vionnet-Fuasset	Male	France	Vinson	1997/12/13
58	Leszek	Cichy	Male	Poland	Kosciuszko	1998/03/24
59	Bob	Hoffman	Male	USA	Everest	1998/05/20
60	Sundeep	Dhillon	Male	UK	Everest	1998/05/25
61	Louis	Bowen	Male	USA	Kilimanjaro	1998/08/04
62	Neil	Laughton	Male	UK	Carstensz	1999/02/14
63	David	Walsh	Male	UK	Carstensz	1999/02/24
64	Ricardo	Torres	Male	Mexico	Carstensz	1999/02/24
65	Ken	Noguchi	Male	Japan	Everest	1999/05/13
66	Christopher	Brown	Male	UK	Everest	1999/05/13
67	Zhixin	Li	Male	China	Carstensz	1999/06/23
68	Yong-Feng	Wang	Male	China	Carstensz	1999/09/23
69	Ilgvars	Pauls	Male	Latvia	Carstensz	1999/07/14
70	Hugh	Morton	Male	USA	Vinson	1999/12/18
71	Wataru	Atsuta	Male	Japan	Aconcagua	2000/01/17
72	Wally	Berg	Male	USA	Aconcagua	2000/02/20
73	Martin	Adams	Male	USA	Carstensz	2000/02/22
74	Eric	Simonson	Male	USA	Kosciuszko	2000/04/05
75	Anna	Czerwinska	Female	Poland	Everest	2000/05/22
76	Jim	Williams	Male	USA	Everest	2000/05/24
77	Doron	Erel	Male	Israel	Kosciuszko	2000/06/01
78	Geoffrey	Robb	Male	Australia	Denali	2000/06/15

Nr	First Name	Surname	Gender	Country	Last Summit	Last Date
79	Stipe	Bozic	Male	Croatia	Elbrus	2000/07/05
80	Jonathan	Gluckman	Male	New Zealand	Elbrus	2000/08/07
81	Swee-Chow	Khoo	Male	Singapore	Vinson	2000/11/22
82	Joby	Ogwyn	Male	USA	Vinson	2000/12/09
83	Greg	Wilson	Male	USA	Carstensz	2001/02/08
84	Andrew	Salter	Male	UK	Aconcagua	2001/03/09
85	Naoki	Ishikawa	Male	Japan	Everest	2001/05/23
86	Jaime	Vinals	Male	Guatemala	Everest	2001/05/23
87	Sherman	Bull	Male	USA	Everest	2001/05/25
88	John	Waechter	Male	USA	Everest	2001/05/25
89	Lily	Leonard	Female	USA	Denali	2001/06/29
90	Constantin	Lacatusu	Male	Romania	Vinson	2001/12/10
91	Berbard	Voyer	Male	Canada	Vinson	2001/12/10
92	Theodors	Kirsis	Male	Latvia	Vinson	2002/01/10
93	Imants	Zauls	Male	Latvia	Vinson	2002/01/10
94	Eric	Blakeley	Male	UK	Vinson	2002/01/11
95	Jason	Edwards	Male	USA	Kosciuszko	2002/04/01
96	Mikel	Alvarez	Male	Spain	Carstensz	2002/04/13
97	Haraldur	Orn Olafsson	Male	Iceland	Everest	2002/05/16
98	Susan	Ershler	Female	USA	Everest	2002/05/16
99	Diego	Wellig	Male	Switzerland	Everest	2002/05/16
100	Atsushi	Yamada	Male	Japan	Everest	2002/05/17
101	Scott	McIvor	Male	UK	Denali	2002/06/28
102	Francis	Slakey	Male	USA	Carstensz	2002/08/12
103	Erik	Weihenmayer	Male	USA	Kosciuszko	2002/09/05
104	Betrand	Roche	Male	France	Kosciuszko	2002/10/19
105	Claire	Roche Bernier	Female	France	Kosciuszko	2002/10/19
106	Young-Seok	Park	Male	South Korea	Vinson	2002/11/24
107	Benedict	Kashakashvili	Male	Georgia	Vinson	2002/12/25
108	Peter	Hamor	Male	Slovakia	Vinson	2003/01/03
109	Frits	Vrijlandt	Male	the Netherlands	Vinson	2003/01/04
110	Brian	O'Connor	Male	USA	Everest	2003/05/26
111	Robert Mads	Anderson	Male	USA	Everest	2003/05/26
112	Matthew	Holt	Male	UK	Everest	2003/05/30
113	Paul Michael	Obert	Male	USA	Everest	2003/05/30
114	Kin Man	Chung	Male	China	Everest	2003/05/31
115	Alberto	Magliano	Male	Italy	Denali	2003/06/22
116	Stuart	Smith	Male	USA	Vinson	2003/12/15
117	Arnold	Witzig	Male	Switzerland	Kilimanjaro	2003/12/18
118	Ramon	Blanco	Male	Spain	Kosciuszko	2003/12/29
119	Zed	Al-Refai	Male	Kuwait	Aconcagua	2004/02/05

Nr	First Name	Surname	Gender	Country	Last Summit	Last Date
120	Sean	Wisedale	Male	S. Africa	Kilimanjaro	2004/02/19
121	Vicky	Jack	Female	UK	Everest	2004/05/16
122	William	Zachary	Male	USA	Everest	2004/05/17
123	Jeff	Dossett	Male	Canada	Everest	2004/05/24
124	Britton	Keeshan	Male	USA	Everest	2004/05/24
125	Anthony	Baldry	Male	Australia	Everest	2004/05/27
126	Haruhisa	Watanabe	Male	Japan	Denali	2004/06/12
127	Holton	Hunter	Male	Cayman Islands	Denali	2004/06/24
128	Jo	Gambi	Female	UK	Elbrus	2004/07/20
129	Rob	Gambi	Male	Australia	Elbrus	2004/07/20
130	Bruno	Rodi	Male	Canada	Elbrus	2004/09/01
131	Jason	Rodi	Male	Canada	Elbrus	2004/09/01
132	Randall L.	Peeters	Male	USA	Kosciuszko	2004/10/26
133	Craig	Van Hoy	Male	USA	Kosciuszko	2004/11/20
134	John	Rost	Male	USA	Vinson	2004/12/08
135	Eun-Sun	Oh	Female	South Korea	Vinson	2004/12/19
136	James	Clarke	Male	USA	Vinson	2004/12/20
137	Cleve	McDonald	Male	USA	Vinson	2004/12/29
138	Scott	Woolums	Male	USA	Vinson	2005/01/10
139	Miroslav	Caban	Male	Czech	Kosciuszko	2005/02/22
140	Marshall	Ulrich	Male	USA	Kosciuszko	2005/03/10
141	Annabelle	Bond	Female	UK	Denali	2005/05/10
142	Guy	Cotter	Male	USA	Denali	2005/05/10
143	Toshihiko	Tamura	Male	Japan	Denali	2005/05/21
144	Urszula	Tokarska	Female	Canada	Everest	2005/06/02
145	Danielle	Fisher	Female	USA	Everest	2005/06/02
146	Tony	Van Marken	Male	South Africa	Everest	2005/06/02
147	Alexander	Harris	Male	South Africa	Everest	2005/06/03
148	Jake	Meyer	Male	UK	Everest	2005/06/04
149	Robert	Hempstead	Male	USA	Elbrus	2005/07/03
150	Karla	Wheelock	Female	Mexico	Carstensz	2005/10/09
151	Eugene	Rehfeld	Male	USA	Carstensz	2005/09/12
152	Dmitry	Moskalev	Male	Russia	Elbrus	2005/11/13
153	Vladamir	Nosek	Male	Czech	Vinson	2005/12/03
154	Alexander	Abramov	Male	Russia	Vinson	2005/12/14
155	Viktor	Bobok	Male	Russia	Vinson	2005/12/14
156	Srren	Gudmann	Male	Denmark	Vinson	2005/12/14
157	Clare	O'Leary	Female	Ireland	Vinson	2005/12/16
158	Neal	Mueller	Male	USA	Kosciuszko	2005/12/23
159	Brien	Sheedy	Male	USA	Kosciuszko	2005/12/31
160	Boris	Sedusov	Male	Russia	Vinson	2006/01/05

Nr	First Name	Surname	Gender	Country	Last Summit	Last Date
161	Heber	Orona	Male	Argentina	Vinson	2006/01/06
162	Harry	Kikstra	Male	the Netherlands	Vinson	2006/01/06
163	Guiseppe	Pompili	Male	Italy	Kosciuszko	2006/01/10
164	David	Liano	Male	Mexico	Vinson	2006/01/19
165	Daniel Edward	Barter	Male	USA	Kosciuszko	2006/01/22
166	Edward	Diffendal	Male	USA	Kosciuszko	2006/02/09
167	Shokichi	Saito	Male	Japan	Aconcagua	2006/02/13
168	Cecilie	Skog	Female	Norway	Kosciuszko	2006/02/14
169	Chieko	Shimada	Female	Japan	Carstensz	2006/03/26
170	Hiroyuki	Kuraoka	Male	Japan	Carstensz	2006/03/26
171	Maxime	Chaya	Male	Lebanon	Everest	2006/05/15
172	Rhys Miles	Jones	Male	UK	Everest	2006/05/17
173	Jose Ignacio	Jijon	Male	Ecuador	Everest	2006/05/17
174	Walter	Laserer	Male	Austria	Everest	2006/05/18
175	Markus Paul	Buel	Male	Switzerland	Everest	2006/05/18
176	Myung-Joon	Kim	Male	USA	Everest	2006/05/19
177	Suzanne K.	Nance	Female	USA	Everest	2006/05/20
178	Kirk	Wheatley	Male	UK	Everest	2006/05/21
179	Henrik Andre	Olsen	Male	Denmark	Everest	2006/05/21
180	Vaughan	De La Harpe	Male	South Africa	Everest	2006/05/24
181	Sean	Disney	Male	South Africa	Everest	2006/05/24
182	James	Gagne	Male	USA	Everest	2006/05/24
183	Katrina	Sandling	Female	UK	Everest	2006/05/24
184	Robert	Follows	Male	Canada	Everest	2006/05/24
185	Egbert J.	Stam	Male	the Netherlands	Denali	2006/05/29
186	Jorg	Stingl	Male	Germany	Kosciuszko	2006/06/13
187	Charles	Mace	Male	USA	Elbrus	2006/06/13
188	Leonard	Stanmore	Male	Canada	Denali	2006/06/26
189	Esther	Colwill	Female	UK	Denali	2006/07/06
190	Andronico	Luksic	Male	Chile	Kilimanjaro	2006/07/08
191	Mastan Babu	Malli	Male	India	Denali	2006/07/10
192	Monica	Kalozdi	Female	USA	Kosciuszko	2006/08/09
193	Jorge	Egocheaga	Male	Spain	Kosciuszko	2006/08/21
194	Catharine	DesLauriers	Female	USA	Everest	2006/10/18
195	Robert	Huygh	Male	Belgium	Kosciuszko	2006/10/23
196	Kevin	Flynn	Male	USA	Kosciuszko	2006/11/07
197	Dale	Darling	Male	USA	Kosciuszko	2006/11/21
198	Martin	Letzter	Male	Sweden	Vinson	2006/11/26
199	Olof	Sundstrom	Male	Sweden	Vinson	2006/11/26
200	Daniel George	Griffith	Male	Canada	Vinson	2006/11/27
201	Davorin	Karnicar	Male	Slovenia	Vinson	2006/11/28

Nr	First Name	Surname	Gender	Country	Last Summit	Last Date
202	Franc	Oderlap	Male	Slovenia	Vinson	2006/11/28
203	Fredrik	Strang	Male	Sweden	Vinson	2006/12/02
204	Alfonso	Juez	Male	Spain	Kosciuszko	2006/12/12
205	Cliff	Dargonne	Male	UK	Carstensz	2006/12/16
206	Karo	Ovasapyan	Male	Armenia	Vinson	2006/12/18
207	Rex	Pemberton	Male	Australia	Aconcagua	2006/12/20
208	Duncan	Chessell	Male	Australia	Vinson	2007/01/01
209	Rosa Maria	Fernandez	Female	Spain	Kilimanjaro	2007/02/12
210	Koichi	Oyama	Male	Japan	Everest	2007/05/15
211	Samantha	Larson	Female	USA	Everest	2007/05/16
212	David	Larson	Male	USA	Everest	2007/05/16
213	Veronika	Meyer	Female	Switzerland	Everest	2007/05/16
214	Robert	Parfet	Male	USA	Everest	2007/05/17
215	Gian Mario	Trimeri	Male	Italy	Everest	2007/05/18
216	Israfil	Ashurly	Male	Azerbaidjan	Everest	2007/05/20
217	Meagan	McGrath	Female	Canada	Everest	2007/05/21
218	Jeanne	Stawicki	Female	USA	Everest	2007/05/22
219	Werner	Berger	Male	Canada	Everest	2007/05/22
220	Patrick	Hickey	Male	Canada	Everest	2007/05/24
221	Juan Diego	Amador	Male	Spain	Denali	2007/06/11
222	Ian	McKeever	Male	Ireland	Denali	2007/06/30
223	Alistair	Sutcliffe	Male	UK	Carstensz	2007/11/24
224	Jacques	Marmet	Male	France	Vinson	2007/12/01
225	Dirk	Stephan	Male	Germany	Kosciuszko	2007/12/05
226	Christian	Stangl	Male	Austria	Vinson	2007/12/07
227	Jean	Pavillard	Male	Switzerland	Kosciuszko	2007/12/20
228	Fei-Bao	Jin	Male	China	Aconcagua	2007/12/08
229	Dirk	Feige	Male	Germany	Aconcagua	2006/11/19
230	Daniel	Perler	Male	Switzerland	Vinson	2007/12/27
231	Randi	Skaug	Female	Norway	Vinson	2007/12/31
232	Hsiu-Chen	Chiang	Female	Taiwan	Vinson	2008/01/08
233	Tomasz	Koblielski	Male	Poland	Vinson	2008/01/18
234	Tomyasu	Ishikawa	Male	Japan	Vinson	2008/01/21
235	Jesus	Gonzalez Calleja	Male	Spain	Aconcagua	2008/02/15
236	Nikolaos	Magitsis	Male	Greece	Carstensz	2008/03/17
237	Phillipe	Gatta	Male	France	Carstensz	2008/03/30
238	Dianette	Wells	Female	USA	Everest	2008/05/24
239	Mark	Luscher	Male	USA	Everest	2008/05/24
240	Brian	Jones	Male	Canada	Everest	2008/05/25
241	Karl Wolfgang	Flock	Male	Germany	Denali	2008/05/30
242	Henrik	Kristiansen	Male	Denmark	Denali	2008/06/05

Nr	First Name	Surname	Gender	Country	Last Summit	Last Date
243	Peter	Hillary	Male	New Zealand	Denali	2008/06/17
244	Michael	Hsu	Male	USA	Elbrus	2008/06/17
245	Gerhard Alfons	Winkler	Male	Austria	Denali	2008/06/18
246	Igor	Pokhvalin	Male	Ukraine	Denali	2008/07/06
247	Sung-In	Yi	Male	USA	Carstensz	2008/09/25
248	Mike	Hamill	Male	USA	Kilimanjaro	2008/10/08
249	Paul	Taylor	Male	UK	Vinson	2008/11/30
250	Basar	Carovac	Male	Serbia	Carstensz	2008/12/03
251	Sergei	Larin	Male	Russia	Vinson	2008/12/09
252	Sergey	Kofanov	Male	Russia	Vinson	2008/12/12
253	Adolphus G.	Hancock	Male	Canada	Vinson	2008/12/14
254	Tore	Sunde-Rasmussen	Male	Norway	Vinson	2008/12/14
255	Gregory	Konrath	Male	USA	Kosciuszko	2008/12/28
256	Robert	Scull	Male	USA	Kilimanjaro	2009/01/02
257	Lyudmila	Korobeshko	Female	Russia	Vinson	2009/01/02
258	Lorenzo	Gariano	Male	Italy	Vinson	2009/01/02
259	Hong-Bin	Kim	Male	South Korea	Vinson	2009/01/02
260	Francisco	Briongos	Male	Spain	Vinson	2009/01/06
261	Chris D.	Nichols	Male	USA	Kilimanjaro	2009/01/10
262	Robert	Rozmus	Male	Poland	Vinson	2009/01/17
263	Lakpa Rita	Sherpa	Male	Nepal	Kilimanjaro	2009/02/13
264	Douglas	Beal	Male	USA	Carstensz	2009/03/28
265	Richard	Pattison	Male	UK	Everest	2009/05/19
266	Yu-Lung	Wu	Male	Taiwan	Everest	2009/05/19
267	Jyh-How	Huang	Male	Taiwan	Everest	2009/05/19
268	Waymark	Douglas	Male	UK	Everest	2009/05/19
269	Marko Eberhard	Reuss	Male	Germany	Everest	2009/05/20
270	Ramon	Diz	Male	Spain	Everest	2009/05/20
271	Artur	Rudolph	Male	Germany	Everest	2009/05/20
272	Nicholas	Cunningham	Male	USA	Everest	2009/05/21
273	Troy	Aupperle	Male	USA	Everest	2009/05/22
274	Bruce	Parker	Male	USA	Everest	2009/05/23
275	Carolyn (Kay)	LeClaire	Female	USA	Everest	2009/05/23
276	Lori	Scheider	Female	USA	Everest	2009/05/23
277	John Robert	Strange	Male	USA	Kosciuszko	2009/06/09
278	Christopher	Burrows	Male	USA	Elbrus	2009/08/11
279	Theo	Fritsche	Male	Austria	Carstensz	2009/09/04
280	Gernot	Overbeck	Male	Germany	Carstensz	2009/09/04
281	Bill	Tyler	Male	USA	Kilimanjaro	2009/10/08

Nr	First Name	Surname	Gender	Country	Last Summit	Last Date
282	Francois Guy	Thivierge	Male	Canada	Kosciuszko	2009/10/29
283	Jaroslaw	Hawrylewicz	Male	Poland	Kosciuszko	2009/11/02
284	Wolfgang	Fasching	Male	Austria	Carstensz	2009/12/05
285	Noel	Hanna	Male	Ireland	Vinson	2009/12/22
286	John Carl	Collinson	Male	USA	Vinson	2010/01/18
287	Marta Eliza (Martyna)	Wojciechowska	Female	Poland	Carstensz	2010/01/22
288	Rupert Michael	Heider	Male	Switzerland	Aconcagua	2010/01/23
289	Carlos	Soria	Male	Spain	Kilimanjaro	2010/01/23
290	Mike	Boaz	Male	USA	Everest	2010/05/23
291	Jesús (Josu)	Feijoo	Male	Spain	Aconcagua	2010/02/09
292	Jean-Michel	Valette	Male	USA	Kilimanjaro	2010/02/09
293	Takao	Arayama	Male	Japan	Kilimanjaro	2010/02/18
294	Albert	Bosch	Male	Spain	Everest	2010/05/17
295	Amanda (Mandy)	Ramsden	Female	South Africa	Everest	2010/05/22
296	Louis	Carstens	Male	South Africa	Everest	2010/05/23
297	Chien-Min (Davis)	Wang	Male	Taiwan	Everest	2010/05/23
298	Tim	Ralph	Male	UK	Everest	2010/05/23
299	Denise D	Fejtek	Female	USA	Everest	2010/05/23
300	Paul Vladimir	Fejtek	Male	USA	Everest	2010/05/23
301	Sherpa	Ang Chhiring III	Male	Nepal	Everest	2010/05/23
302	Lei	Wang	Female	USA	Everest	2010/05/24
303	Herbert	Blauensteiner	Male	Austria	Everest	2010/05/24
304	Alison	Levine	Female	USA	Everest	2010/05/24
305	Victor Lance	Vescovo	Male	USA	Everest	2010/05/24
306	Darell	Ainscough	Male	Canada	Everest	2010/05/25
307	Richard (Jr)	Birrer	Male	USA	Everest	2010/05/25
308	Richard (Sr)	Birrer	Male	USA	Everest	2010/05/25
309	Elizabeth	Tertil	Female	Canada	Everest	2010/05/25
310	Sissel	Smaller	Female	Norway	Denali	2010/05/25
311	Diahanne (Di)	Gilbert	Female	UK	Elbrus	2010/07/20
312	Elena (Lena)	Gorelik	Female	Russia	Elbrus	2010/07/22
313	James (Dickey)	Wilde	Male	USA	Kosciuszko	2010/10/19
314	Ralf	Dujmovits	Male	Germany	Carstensz	2010/10/28
315	Tony Alan	Hampson-Tindale	Male	New Zealand	Vinson	2010/12/10
316	John Steven	Dahlem	Male	USA	Kosciuszko	2010/12/24
317	Ryan Steven	Dahlem_	Male	USA	Kosciuszko	2010/12/24
318	Sergei	Kovalev	Male	Ukraine	Vinson	2010/12/27
319	Christopher (Chris)	Grubb	Male	USA	Kosciuszko	2010/12/29
320	Vikram (Vik)	Sahney	Male	USA	Vinson	2011/01/06

Nr	First Name	Surname	Gender	Country	Last Summit	Last Date
321	Stephan	Giesecke	Male	USA	Carstensz	2011/01/27
322	Pavel	Bem	Male	Czechia	Aconcagua	2011/02/00
323	Michael Thomas	Kraft	Male	Germany	Carstensz	2011/03/16
324	Frederick	Ziel	Male	USA	Kosciuszko	2011/04/08
325	Marty	Rindahl	Male	USA	Everest	2011/05/13
326	Michael	Matty	Male	USA	Everest	2011/05/13
327	Walter	Elrod	Male	USA	Everest	2011/05/13
328	Robert William	Hart	Male	South Africa	Everest	2011/05/14
329	Yonsuk-Suzanna	Derby	Female	USA	Everest	2011/05/14
330	Michael	Gibbons	Male	USA	Everest	2011/05/19
331	Tatsuo	Matsumoto	Male	Japan	Everest	2011/05/19
332	Broery Andrew	Sihombing	Male	Indonesia	Everest	2011/05/20
333	Janatan	Ginting	Male	Indonesia	Everest	2011/05/20
334	Xaverius	Frans	Male	Indonesia	Everest	2011/05/20
335	Sofyan	Arief-Fesa	Male	Indonesia	Everest	2011/05/20
336	Richard Luke	Millard	Male	USA	Everest	2011/05/21
337	Stephan	Mahlknecht	Male	Italy	Everest	2011/05/21
338	Stefan	Rier	Male	Italy	Everest	2011/05/21
339	Helmut	Kritzinger	Male	Italy	Everest	2011/05/21
340	Maria Gisela	Hoffmann	Female	Germany	Everest	2011/05/21
341	Gerald	Fiala	Male	Austria	Everest	2011/05/21
342	Helga	Hengge	Female	Germany	Denali	2011/05/23
343	George	Atkinson	Male	UK	Everest	2011/05/26
344	Jack	Martin	Male	USA	Denali	2011/05/28
345	Steven R.	Novick	Male	USA	Denali	2011/06/08
346	Lee James	Farmer	Male	UK	Denali	2011/06/23
347	Ahmad Fakhri	Abu Samah	Male	Malaysia	Denali	2011/06/24
348	Richard David (Rich)	Parks	Male	UK	Elbrus	2011/07/12
340	Stina	Peterson	Female	Denmark	Vinson	2011/07/14
350	Jane	Lee	Female	Singapore	Elbrus	2011/08/07
351	Philipp	Schlatter	Male	Switzerland	Carstensz	2011/10/19
352	Megan	Delehanty	Female	USA	Carstensz	2011/11/02
353	Scott	Kress	Male	Canada	Vinson	2011/11/23
354	Stephen	Coney	Male	New Zealand	Kosciuszko	2011/11/23
355	Jordan	Romero	Male	USA	Vinson	2011/12/24
356	Karen	Lundgren	Female	USA	Vinson	2011/12/24
357	Romero	Paul	Male	USA	Vinson	2011/12/24

The last stretch
of trail in to Plaza
Argentina. Aconcagua
and Cerro Ameghino
stand in the distance.

Climbers prepare for
the move to Barafu
Camp, and a summit
of Kilimanjaro
the following day.

RESOURCES

WEBSITES

www.climbingthesevensummits.com: This website includes the most up-to-date information on the Seven Summits, a current list of Seven Summiters; more in-depth information on each mountain, including lodging and dining information; links to gear companies, outfitters, and guide services; links to climbing blogs; information about Seven Summits completion certificates; Seven Summits and other photography; a library; and a Seven Summits store, among other helpful services. For current and continuous stories and information from the Seven Summits and other adventures, visit my personal blog on this site.

www.7summits.com: An information site about the Seven Summits.

BOOKS

Bass, Dick, Rick Ridgeway, and Frank Wells. *Seven Summits*. New York: Grand Central Publishing, 1988.

Bell, Steve. *Seven Summits: The Quest to Reach the Highest Point on Every Continent.* New York: Bulfinch Press, 2000.

Cosley, Kathy, and Mark Houston. *Alpine Climbing: Techniques to Take You Higher.* Seattle: The Mountaineers Books, 2004.

Eng, Ronald C., ed. *Mountaineering: The Freedom of the Hills.* 8th ed. Seattle: The Mountaineers Books, 2010.

Ershler, Phil, and Susan Ershler. *Together on Top of the World.* New York: Grand Central Publishing, 2007.

Random House Australia, *Geographica: The Complete Illustrated Atlas of the World.* Random House Australia, 1999.

Selters, Andy. *Glacier Travel and Crevasse Rescue.* 2nd ed., updated. Seattle: The Mountaineers Books, 2007.

Soles, Clyde, and Phil Powers. *Climbing: Expedition Planning.* Seattle: The Mountaineers Books, 2003.

Wilkerson, James A., Ernest E. Moore, and Ken Zafren. *Medicine for Mountaineering and Other Wilderness Activities.* 6th ed. Seattle: The Mountaineers Books, 2010.

MOUNT EVEREST

PERMITS

Nepal Ministry of Tourism and Civil Aviation: tel +977 1-425-6232; www.tourism.gov.np; info@tourism.gov.np

Chinese Mountaineering Association (CMA): tel +10 67-102787; cmaex@sina.com.cn

DINING

The Rum Doodle Restaurant and Bar: Thamel, Katmandu, Nepal; tel +977 1-424-8692; American and Indian food in a unique climbers' atmosphere; this is where all the Mount Everest summiteers sign their names to the walls and eat for free. You'll see the signatures of Hillary, Norgay, Messner, Bonington, and more. A true Katmandu landmark and a must for climbers.

BOOKS

Bonington, Christopher. *Everest the Hard Way*. New York: Random House, 1977.

Gillman, Peter, and Leni Gillman. *The Wildest Dream: The Biography of George Mallory*. Seattle: The Mountaineers Books, 2000.

Hemmleb, Jochen, and Eric Simonson. *Detectives on Everest: The 2001 Mallory and Irvine Research Expedition*. Seattle: The Mountaineers Books, 2002.

Hemmleb, Jochen, and Eric Simonson, et al. *Ghosts of Everest: The Search for Mallory and Irvine*. Seattle: The Mountaineers Books, 1999.

Krakauer, Jon. *Into Thin Air*. New York: Villard Books, 1997.

McDonald, Bernadette. *I'll Call You in Kathmandu*. Seattle: The Mountaineers Books, 2005.

Noyce, Wilfred. *South Col: One Man's Adventures on the Ascent of Everest 1953*. Portsmouth, NH: Heinnemann, 1986.

WEBSITES

www.everestnews.com

Signing your name on the wall at the Rum Doodle Restaurant in Katmandu is a rite of passage for Everest summiters.

MOUNT KILIMANJARO

ACCOMMODATIONS

Keys Hotel: Moshi, Tanzania; tel +255 27-275-2250 or +255 27-275-1875; www.keys-hotels
.com/moshi.htm; reception@keys-hotels.com

Marangu Hotel: Marangu, Tanzania; tel +255 27-275-6594; www.maranguhotel.com

Mountain Huts: Warden, Kilimanjaro National Park, P.O. Box 96, Marangu, Tanzania

AIR TRANSPORTATION

Air Tanzania: www.airtanzania.com

Kenya Airways: www.kenya-airways.com

GROUND TRANSPORTATION

East Africa Shuttles: www.eastafricashuttles.com

Impala Shuttles: Impala Hotel; tel +255 275-1786; impala@kilinet.co.tz

Riverside Shuttles: tel +255 572-2639; www.riverside-shuttle.com

MAPS

Adventurous Traveler Bookstore: http://atb.away.com/index.html; books@atbook.com

Nature Discovery: info@naturediscovery.com

SAFARI

Wildersun Safaris Tanzania: tel +255 27-254-8847 or +255 27-254-8849;
reservations@wildersunsafaristanzania.com; wildersun@cybernet.co.tz

BOOKS

Allan, Iain. *The Mountain Club of Kenya Guide to Mount Kenya and Kilimanjaro.* 4th ed. Nairobi,
Kenya: The Mountain Club of Kenya, 1998.

Burns, Cameron M. *Kilimanjaro and East Africa: A Climbing and Trekking Guide.* 2nd ed. Seattle:
The Mountaineers Books, 2006.

Dorr, Daniel. *Kissing Kilimanjaro: Leaving It All on the Top of Africa.* Seattle: The Mountaineers
Books, 2010.

Ridgeway, Rick. *The Shadow of Kilimanjaro: On Foot Across East Africa.* New York: Henry Holt and
Company, Inc., 1999.

Salkeld, Audrey. *Kilimanjaro: To the Roof of Africa.* New York: National Geographic, 2002.

An exotic lobelia
plant encountered
en route to Barranco
Camp, Mount
Kilimanjaro

DENALI

CLIMBER REGISTRATION

Talkeetna Ranger Station: P.O. Box 588, Talkeetna, AK 99676; tel +1 (907) 733-2231;
  dena_talkeetna_office@nps.gov

WEATHER SERVICES

National Weather Service: Fairbanks, Alaska; tel +1 (907) 456-0372

GROUND TRANSPORTATION

Alaska Railroad: tel +1 (907) 265-2494; reservations@akrr.com

Denali Overland Transportation: tel +1 (907) 733-2385; info@denalioverland.com

Go Purple: tel +1 (907) 644-8090; information@gopurpleshuttle.com

AIR TRANSPORTATION

Doug Geeting Aviation: tel +1 (907) 733-2366; www.talkeetnaalaska.com

K2 Aviation: tel +1 (907) 733-2291; info@flyk2.com

Talkeetna Air Taxi: tel +1 (907) 733-2218

DINING

Talkeetna Roadhouse: Talkeetna, Alaska; tel +1 (907) 733-1351; the spot for breakfast.
  Grab a cinnamon roll, or two, for the mountain.

West Rib Pub and Grill: Talkeetna, Alaska; tel +1 (907) 733-3354; quality burgers and
  seafood with generous portions. Try the 9 percent Ice Axe Ale!

MAPS

Alaska Mountaineering School Pro Shop: tel +1 (907) 354-1233; info@climbalaska.org

United States Geological Survey: tel +1 (907) 786-7000

GEAR SHOPS

Alaska Mountaineering and Hiking: Anchorage, Alaska; tel +1 (907) 272-1811; amh@ak.net

Alaska Mountaineering School Pro Shop: Talkeetna, Alaska; tel +1 (907) 354-1233;
  info@climbalaska.org

REI: Anchorage, Alaska; tel: +1 (907) 272-4565

BOOKS

Coombs, Colby. *Denali's West Buttress: A Climber's Guide to Mount McKinley's Classic Route*. Seattle: The Mountaineers Books, 1997.

Davidson, Art. *Minus 148˚*. Seattle: The Mountaineers Books, 1999.

Freedman, Lewis. *Dangerous Steps: Vernon Tejas and the Solo Winter Ascent of Mount McKinley*. Mechanicsburg, PA: Stackpole Books, 1990.

Haston, Dougal. *In High Places*. Seattle: The Mountaineers Books, 1997.

Kikstra, Harry. *Denali–Mt. McKinley: Summit of North America*. Dunblane, Scotland: Rucksack Readers, 2006.

Moore, Terris. *Mount McKinley, The Pioneer Climbs*. Seattle: The Mountaineers Books, 1981.

Stuck, Hudson. *The Ascent of Denali*. Torrington, WY: The Narrative Press, 2004.

Washburn, Bradford, and David Roberts. *Mount McKinley, Conquest of Denali*. New York: Harry N. Abrams, 1991.

Waterman, Jonathan. *High Alaska: A Historical Guide to Denali, Mount Foraker, and Mount Hunter*. Golden, CO: American Alpine Club, 1991.

———. *Surviving Denali: A Study of Accidents on Mount McKinley, 1903–1990*. 2nd ed. Golden, CO: American Alpine Club, 1991.

Wood, Michael, and Colby Coombs. *Alaska: A Climbing Guide*. Seattle: The Mountaineers Books, 2002.

ACONCAGUA

CONTACTS

Aconcagua Provincial Park frequency: 142.800 MHZ FM

Club Andinista Mendoza: tel +54 261-4319870; info@clubandinista.com.ar

PERMITS

Dirección de Recursos Naturales Renovables: Avenida San Martin, Mendoza, Argentina; tel +54 425-2031; aconcagua@mendoza.gov.ar; weekdays 8:00 AM–6:00 PM, weekends 9:00 AM–1:00 PM

Climbers take in
the views from
Camp 2 on Denali.

GEAR SHOPS

Jose Orviz: Juan B Justo 536, Mendoza, Argentina; tel +54 261-4251281; orviz@lanet.losandes.com.ar

Pire: Avenida Las Heras 615, Mendoza, Argentina; tel +54 261-4257699; info@piremont.com.ar

GROUND TRANSPORTATION

Grupo Sur: tel +54 437-5511; reservas@grpsur.com

MULE SERVICES

Aconcagua Express: tel +56 22-179101; info@aconcagua-express.com

Fernando Grajales Expeditions: tel (800) 516-6962; www.expediciones@grajales.net

Rudy Parra: tel +54 261-429-2650; info@aconcaguatrek.com

ACCOMMODATIONS

Hotel Refugio Plaza de Mulas: tel +54 2642 490422; www.refugioplazademulas.com.ar

WINE TOURS

Caminos de Perdriel: Mendoza, Argentina; tel +54 15-517-2761; www.caminodeperdriel.com

BOOKS

FitzGerald, Edward Arthur, T. G. Bonney, and George Charles Crick. *The Highest Andes: A Record of the First Ascent of Aconcagua and Tupungato in Argentina, and the Exploration of the Surrounding Valleys.* Charleston, SC: Nabu Press, 2010.

Secor, R. J. *Aconcagua: A Climbing Guide.* 2nd ed. Seattle: The Mountaineers Books, 1999.

Taplin, Thomas E. *Aconcagua—The Stone Sentinel; Perspectives of an Expedition.* Santa Monica, CA: Eli Ely, 1992.

WEBSITES

www.aconcaguaexpeditions.com

VINSON MASSIF

AIR TRANSPORTATION AND GUIDE SERVICES

Antarctic Logistics and Expeditions (ALE): US tel +1 (801) 266-4876;
www.antarctic-logistics.com; info@antarctic-logistics.com

ALE in Punta Arenas, Chile: tel +56 61-247735; manager.punta@antarctic-logistics.com

ALE frequencies at Vinson Base Camp: VHF simplex (line of sight) 145.100MHZ; VHF
repeater—transmit 144.025MHZ, receive 148.975MHZ

Transporte Privado de Turismo: Rolando Torres Fuentes, tel +56 98-859556;
transtourchile@yahoo.es

BOOKS

Anderson, Robert Mads. *To Everest Via Antarctica*. Mechanicsburg, PA: Stackpole Books, 1996.

Gildea, Damien. *Antarctic Mountaineering Chronology*. Wellington, New Zealand:
New Zealand Mountain Safety Council, 1998.

———. *Mountaineering in Antarctica: Climbing in the Frozen South*. Brussels, Belgium:
Editions Nevicata, 2010.

Lansing, Alfred. *Endurance: Shackleton's Incredible Journey*. New York: Basic Books, 1999.

Lewis-Jones, Huy, and Martin Hartley. *Face to Face: Portraits of Polar Explorers*. Cornwall,
England: Polarworld, 2008.

MOUNT ELBRUS

ACCOMMODATIONS

Hotel Chyran-Azau: Azau, Russia

Hotel Moscow: 2 Alexander Nevsky Square, St. Petersburg, Russia 193317;
tel +7 (812) 274-3001; www.servis@hotel-moscow.ru

Hotel Volfram: Terskol Village, Elbrus Region, Russia, 361605

Metropol Hotel: 1/4 Teatralny Proezd, Moscow, Russia 103012

GEAR SHOPS

Alpindustria: Viktoria Voroshilova, general director; Terskol Village, Elbrus Region,
Russia, 361605; tel +7 (866) 387-1330, fax +7 (866) 387-1300; www.voroshilova@
alpindustria.ru, www.elbrus-team.com

BOOKS

Literature on Mount Elbrus is limited. Short stories of climbing on Mount Elbrus can be found in the two Seven Summits titles listed at the start of Resources.

Various. *Climbing in the Caucasus: A Collection of Historical Mountaineering Articles on the Caucasus Mountain Range*. Read Books, 2011.

MOUNT KOSCIUSZKO

GUIDE SERVICES

High & Wild Mountain Adventures: tel +61 0247-829-075; www.peakachievements.com.au

K7-Kosciuszko Adventures: tel +61 0421-862-354; www.k7adventures.com

BOOKS

Costin, A.B., M. Gray, C.J. Totterdell, and D.J. Wimbush. *Kosciuszko Alpine Flora*, 2nd ed. Collingwood, Victoria, Australia: CSIRO, 2000.

Paterson, Andrew Barton. *The Man from Snowy River and Other Verses*. New South Wales, Australia: University of Sydney Press, 2009.

Storyozynski, Alex. *The Peasant Prince: Thaddeus Kosciuszko and the Age of Revolution*. New York: St. Martins, 2010.

CARSTENSZ PYRAMID

INDONESIAN EMERGENCY NUMBERS

Ambulance: 118.

Police: 110

BOOKS

Boardman, Peter. *Sacred Summits*. London, England: Hodder & Stoughton, 1982.

Harrer, Heinrich. *I Come from the Stone Age*. Boston: E. P. Dutton, 1965.

Matthiessen, Peter. *Under the Mountain Wall: A Chronicle of Two Seasons in Stone-Age New Guinea*. New York: Penguin, 1987.

INDEX

Descending the fixed
lines on Denali

ABOUT THE AUTHOR

Mike Hamill is a professional mountain guide, writer, and photographer. He regularly leads expeditions to the mountains of the Seven Summits, among others, and has climbed all of the original Seven Summits at least four times, some as many as twenty. He has climbed them all in the course of one year several times, finishing them in 2008 in 220 days, the tenth fastest time to date. Mike was featured in the Discovery Channel's television production entitled *Everest: Beyond the Limits*. Mike has been guiding for more than a decade and calls Seattle home when not on the road. He began his climbing career on the steep rock and ice of New England and New York State while obtaining a bachelor of science from St. Lawrence University in Canton, New York. He hails originally from Hanover, New Hampshire, and Bridgton, Maine. Please visit his website at www.climbingthesevensummits.com.

OTHER TITLES YOU MIGHT ENJOY FROM THE MOUNTAINEERS BOOKS

MOUNTAINEERING: THE FREEDOM OF THE HILLS, 8TH EDITION
The Mountaineers
The climbers' bible: comprehensive, authoritative instruction on all things mountaineering

STAYING ALIVE IN AVALANCHE TERRAIN, 2ND EDITION
Bruce Tremper
A practical guide for analyzing risks and avoiding avalanche danger

MEDICINE FOR MOUNTAINEERING & OTHER WILDERNESS ACTIVITIES, 6TH EDITION
James A. Wilkerson, M.D.; Earnest E. Moore, M.D.; and Ken Zafren, M.D.
Comprehensive reference and guide for emergency medical care in the backcountry

MINUS 148°
Art Davidson
The gripping first-person account of the first winter ascent on Denali

EVEREST: THE WEST RIDGE
Thomas Hornbein
A legendary book about a legendary climb: the first ascent of Mount Everest's West Ridge

50 FAVORITE CLIMBS
Mark Kroese
Favorite climbs in North America—rock, alpine, and ice—picked by fifty of America's greatest climbers

The Mountaineers Books has more than 500 outdoor recreation titles in print.
For details visit www.mountaineersbooks.org

ABOUT THE MOUNTAINEERS

THE MOUNTAINEERS, founded in 1906, is a nonprofit outdoor activity and conservation organization whose mission is "to explore, study, preserve, and enjoy the natural beauty of the outdoors…" Based in Seattle, Washington, it is now one of the largest such organizations in the United States, with seven branches throughout Washington State.

The Mountaineers sponsors both classes and year-round outdoor activities in the Pacific Northwest, which include hiking, mountain climbing, ski-touring, snowshoeing, bicycling, camping, canoeing and kayaking, nature study, sailing, and adventure travel. The Mountaineers' conservation division supports environmental causes through educational activities, sponsoring legislation, and presenting informational programs.

All activities are led by skilled, experienced volunteers, who are dedicated to promoting safe and responsible enjoyment and preservation of the outdoors.

If you would like to participate in these organized outdoor activities or programs, consider a membership in The Mountaineers. For information and an application, write or call The Mountaineers Program Center, 7700 Sand Point Way NE, Seattle, WA 98115-3996; phone 206-521-6001; visit www.mountaineers.org; or email info@mountaineers.org.

THE MOUNTAINEERS BOOKS, an active, nonprofit publishing program of The Mountaineers, produces guidebooks, instructional texts, historical works, natural history guides, and works on environmental conservation. All books produced by The Mountaineers Books fulfill the mission of The Mountaineers. Visit www.mountaineersbooks.org to find details about all our titles and the latest author events, as well as videos, web clips, links, and more!

The Mountaineers Books
1001 SW Klickitat Way, Suite 201
Seattle, WA 98134
800-553-4453
mbooks@mountaineersbooks.org

The Mountaineers Books is proud to be a corporate sponsor of The Leave No Trace Center for Outdoor Ethics, whose mission is to promote and inspire responsible outdoor recreation through education, research, and partnerships. The Leave No Trace program is focused specifically on human-powered (nonmotorized) recreation.

Leave No Trace strives to educate visitors about the nature of their recreational impacts and offers techniques to prevent and minimize such impacts. Leave No Trace is best understood as an educational and ethical program, not as a set of rules and regulations. For more information, visit www.lnt.org, or call 800-332-4100.